Displacing Desire

Displacing Desire

Travel and Popular Culture in China

Beth E. Notar

University of Hawai'i Press
Honolulu

11 10 09 08   6 5 4 3 2

Library of Congress Cataloging-in-Publicaton Data

Notar, Beth E.

Displacing desire : travel and popular culture in China /

Beth E. Notar.

p.   cm.

Includes bibliographical references and index.

ISBN-13: 978-0-8248-2980-3 (hardcover : alk. paper)

ISBN-13: 978-0-8248-3071-7 (pbk : alk. paper)

1. Dali Shi (China)—Description and travel.   2. Dali Shi (China)—Ethnic

relations.   I. Title.   II. Title: Travel and popular culture in China.

DS797.86.D37N67 2006

306.4'819095135222

2006018803

University of Hawai'i Press books are printed on acid-free

paper and meet the guidelines for permanence and durability

of the Council on Library Resources.

Printed by The Maple-Vail Book Manufacturing Group

Contents

Acknowledgments · vii

Abbreviations · ix

A Note on Transcription · xii

Measure Conversions · xiv

Chapter 1

With the Sign Begins the Search · 1

Chapter 2

Lonely Planeteers and a Transnational Authentic · 20

Chapter 3

Five Golden Flowers: Utopian Nostalgia and
Local Longing · 47

Chapter 4

Heavenly Dragons: Commodifying a Fantastic Past · 80

Chapter 5

Earthly Demons: Displacing the Present · 111

Chapter 6

Off and On the Road to Reform · 137

Notes · 141

Bibliography · 151

Index · 187

Acknowledgments

In conducting research on the relationship between popular culture, travel, and transformations of place, I have ventured into many fields of learning and have incurred untold debts. My most heartfelt thanks go to the people of Dali, Yunnan, who have offered me their hospitality for years. I would especially like to thank my host families, my research assistant, and my friends, who have graciously endured my seemingly countless questions. To protect their privacy, I have used pseudonyms to refer to people unless they are well-known figures or published authors.

Financial support for research was provided by the Committee for Scholarly Communication with China, a Fulbright Hays Fellowship, and a National Science Foundation summer research grant. Institutional support came from the Yunnan Nationalities Institute and the Dali Cultural Bureau. Lin Yuehua of the Central Nationalities Institute and Lin Chaomin of Yunnan University were instrumental in helping me to establish the project. In addition, I was privileged to have received guidance and instruction from Wang Shuwu, He Shaoying, Yang Guocai, and Zhao Xiaoniu in Kunming, and Yang Zhengye, Shi Lizhuo, Shi Zhenhua, and Zhang Xilu in Dali. Huan Youming, Yang Zhaoyun, and Yingyue Li Boretz exhibited great patience in teaching me Bai. Through his zest for Bai and English idioms, He Liyi motivated me to keep learning. Over the course of my research, I had the good fortune to meet more seasoned researchers of Yunnan who offered advice and encouragement: Jackie Armijo-Hussein, Susan Blum, Laurel Bossen, Charles McKhann, Lucien Miller, Jeffrey Schmitt, Peggy Swain, Grace Wiersma, and Yokoyama Hiroko.

Many librarians have assisted me in finding textual, visual, and online materials. Special thanks go to Chen Xiaofei and the staff of the University of Michigan Asia Library, Charles d'Orban and the staffs of the Wason and Rare Book collections at Cornell University, Jean Hung and the staff of the University Services Centre, Chinese University of Hong Kong, Jane Ting of the Mount Holyoke College Library, and the staff of the University of Washington Asia Library.

The seeds of this book first germinated at the University of Michigan. I am extremely grateful to Norma Diamond, Jennifer Robertson, and Erik Mueggler for their inspiration and in-depth comments on early drafts and to Yi-tse Feuerwerker and Tom Fricke for their literary and analytic insights, respectively. During the process of transforming the manuscript into a book, I have greatly benefitted from a writer's group composed of Michelle Bigenho, Julie Hemment, Joshua Roth, and Barbara Yngvesson, as well as the keen eye of Kathleen Zane. King-Fai Tam and Chris Hamm offered aid in approaching Jin Yong Studies. Rob Culp, Hue-Tam Ho Tai, and Jeffrey Wasserstrom provided helpful suggestions for thinking about nostalgia. Two anonymous reviewers for the University of Hawai'i Press (who subsequently identified themselves as Susan Blum and Charles McKhann) offered excellent suggestions for revision.

Colleagues and students at Trinity have created a lively atmosphere in which to think and teach. I am particularly grateful to Frederick Errington, Jane Nadel-Klein, King-Fai Tam, Thomas Thornton, and Jim Trostle for feedback on work in progress. Presentations of portions of this research at Bard College, Dartmouth College, Harvard University, MIT, the University of Illinois, University of Washington, Whitman College, and meetings of the Association for American Anthropology and the Association for Asian Studies have led to stimulating discussion. Todd Thomas and the folks at the Thirsty Mind have comforted me with many warm cups of coffee and tea.

Special thanks go to Patricia Crosby, Cheri Dunn, and Susan Stone for their editorial expertise as well as to the production staff at the University of Hawai'i Press. Most of all, I would like to thank my family. My parents, Ellen and Russell, and my sister, Susan, have been a sustaining source of love and creativity. Joshua Roth has been both my harshest critic and my strongest supporter, debating with me late at night and reading numerous drafts. He, Isaac, and Emile continually teach me the power of laughter and curiosity.

Abbreviations

BJS Baizu jianshi bianxie zu (A Concise History of the Bai Nationality Editorial Group), ed. 1988. *Baizu jianshi* (A Concise History of the Bai Nationality). Guojia minwei minzu wenti wuzhong congshu (part of the National Minority Commission's collected series on nationality issues). Kunming: Yunnan renmin chubanshe.

BSLD Yunnan sheng bianjizu (Yunnan Province Editorial Group). 1987–1991. *Baizu shehui lishi diaocha* (Investigations into Bai Nationality Social History). Vols. 2–4. Kunming: Yunnan renmin chubanshe.

BSLD1 "Minzu wenti wuzhong congshu" Yunnan sheng bianji weiyuanhui (Yunnan Province Editorial Committee of the "Five Types of Collected Books on Nationality Problems"), ed. 1981. *Baizu shehui lishi diaocha* (Investigations into Bai Nationality Social History). Vol. 1. Kunming: Yunnan renmin chubanshe.

BZSH Yunnan sheng minjian wenxue jicheng bangongshi (Yunnan Province Folk Literature Collection Office), ed. 1986. *Baizu shenhua chuanshuo jicheng* (Collection of Bai Nationality Myths and Legends). Beijing: Zhongguo minjian wenyi chubanshe.

CCSZ Changchun Shi difangzhi bianzuan weiyuanhui (Changchun Municipal Gazetteer Editorial Committee), ed. 1992. *Changchun shi zhi: Dianying zhi* (Changchun Municipal Gazetteer: Film Gazetteer). Changchun: Dongbei shifan daxue chubanshe.

CYWN Changchun dianying zhipianchang (Changchun Film Studio), ed. 1996. *Changying wushi nian, 1945–1995* (English title: Fifty Years of Chang Chun Film Studio). Changchun: Jilin sheying chubanshe.

DSLY Yunnan sheng Dali shi linyeju (Yunnan Province, Dali Municipal Forestry Bureau), ed. 1993. *Dali shi linyezhi* (Gazetteer of Dali Municipal Forestry). Dali: Dali Baizu zizhizhou wenhuaju.

DSZ   Dali shi zhi bianzuan weiyuanhui (Annal of Dali Municipal-
            ity Editorial and Compilation Committee), ed. 1998. *Dali shi zhi*
            (Annal of Dali Municipality). Dali: Zhonghua shuju.
DXSZ   Zhong gong Shenzhen shiwei xuanchuanbu (Propaganda De-
            partment of the Shenzhen Municipal Committee of the Chi-
            nese Communist [Party]), ed. 1992. *Deng Xiaoping yu Shenzhen*
            (Deng Xiaoping and Shenzhen). Shenzhen: Haitian chubanshe.
DZNJ 1990   Dali Baizu zizhizhou difangzhi bianzuan weiyuanhui (The Al-
            manac of Dali Prefecture Editorial and Compilation Commit-
            tee), ed. 1990. *Dali Baizu zizhizhou nianjian* (Almanac of Dali
            Prefecture). Kunming: Yunnan minzu chubanshe.
DZNJ 1993   Dali Baizu zizhizhou difang bianzuan weiyuanhui (Dali Bai
            Nationality Autonomous Prefecture Editorial and Compilation
            Committee), ed. 1993. *Dali zhou nianjian* (Almanac of Dali Pre-
            fecture). Kunming: Yunnan minzu chubanshe.
DZNJ 1995   Dali Baizu zizhizhou difangzhi bianzuan weiyuanhui (Dali Bai
            Nationality Autonomous Prefecture Gazetteer Editorial Com-
            mittee), ed. 1995. *Dali zhou nianjian* (Almanac of Dali Prefec-
            ture). Kunming: Yunnan minzu chubanshe.
DZNJ 2004   Dali Baizu zizhizhou difangzhi bianzuan weiyuanhui (Dali Bai
            Nationality Autonomous Prefecture Gazetteer Editorial Com-
            mittee), ed. 2004. *Dali zhou nianjian* (Yearbook of Dali Prefec-
            ture). Kunming: Yunnan minzu chubanshe.
DZZ   Dali Baizu zizhizhou difangzhi bianzuan weiyuanhui (Dali Bai
            Nationality Autonomous Prefecture Gazetteer Editorial Com-
            mittee), ed. 1999. *Dali Baizu zizhizhou zhi* (Gazetteer of Dali
            Prefecture). Vol. 3. Kunming: Yunnan minzu chubanshe.
PDDY   *Pipan ducao dianying ji* (A Collection of Criticisms of Poisonous
            Weed Films). 1971. Shanghai: Renmin chubanshe.
PRCY   Editorial Department of the PRC Year Book, Beijing. 1996. *PRC
            Year Book 1995/96*. Vol. 15. English edition. Hong Kong and Bei-
            jing: N.C.N. Limited and PRC Year Book Ltd.
RMRB   *Renmin ribao* (People's Daily).
YDY   Yunnan Sheng ditu yuan, ed. 2004–2005. *Dali-Lijiang daoyou tu*
            (English title: The Tourist Map of Dali). Hunan ditu chubanshe.
YHSLD   Yunnan sheng bianjizu (Yunnan Province Editorial Commit-
            tee), ed. 1985. *Yunnan Huizu shehui lishi diaocha* (Investigations
            of Yunnan Hui Nationality Social History). 2 vols. Kunming:
            Yunnan renmin chubanshe.

YNRB   *Yunnan ribao* (Yunnan Daily News).
YNRK   Yunnan sheng renkou pucha bangongshi (Population Census
           of Yunnan Office), ed. 2002. *Yunnan Sheng 2000 nian renkou pu-*
           cha ziliao (English title: The Reference of Population Census of
           Yunnan in 2000). 4 vols. Kunming: Yunnan keji chubanshe.
YSYZ   Yunnan sheng shaoshu minzu yuwen zhidao gongzuo weiyuan-
           hui (Committee for the Guidance Work of Yunnan Province's
           Minority Nationality Languages). 1992. "Baizu wenzi fang'an
           (caogao)" (Orthographic Scheme for the Bai Nationality, Draft).
ZTNJ   Zhonghua renmin gongheguo guojia tongjiju (National Bureau
           of Statistics of China). 2001. *Zhongguo tongji nianjian* (China
           Statistical Yearbook). Beijing: Zhonguo tongji chubanshe.

A Note on Transcription

Mandarin Chinese Orthography

In this book all transcriptions of Mandarin Chinese, including the Yunnan and Dali dialects, follow the standard pinyin romanization system. I have made exceptions for commonly used place names such as Hong Kong and Taipei, and personal names that have been published elsewhere using Wade-Giles or other romanization systems. I have designated Mandarin transcriptions with the abbreviation "M."

Bai Orthography

Most villagers in Dali, Yunnan, whether Bai or Hui (Muslim), speak Bai, of which there are three main dialects: southern (Dali), central (Jianchuan), and northern (Bijiang) (Xu and Zhao 1984, 4). Within these dialects there are additional village variations. Bai has been included in the Sino-Tibetan language family. However there has been much debate over whether it should be further classified as part of Loloish, Lolo-Burmese, Tibeto-Burman, or Sinitic (see Wiersma 1990, 2003). There has also been debate over whether the Bai had their own writing system that was subsequently destroyed during the fourteenth-century Ming dynasty conquest (Wiersma 1990, 15–16; Yang Yingxin 1992). Bai speakers have long used Chinese characters to designate Bai sounds, a practice still used among Bai who are literate in Chinese (Wiersma 1990, 28–32). In 1958 a Bai orthography based on the Dali dialect was developed using the pinyin romanization system for Chinese, but owing to national political upheavals and local debates, it was never officially approved. In 1982 this orthography was revised based on the Jianchuan dialect, because of the density of Bai speakers in the Jianchuan area, and officially approved in 1984 (Wiersma 2003, 654; YSYZ 1992, 1). In 1993 a symposium that incorporated community consultation attempted to devise a new orthographic scheme that could represent both the Dali and Jianchuan dialects, particularly with regard to alphabetic tone markers. For example, while the 1984 scheme transcribed the word for "to study" as *hhert,* using the tone markers *rt* at the end, the 1993 scheme represented it as *hhep,* using the tone marker *p* at the end. While this new scheme was approved at the national level, it has not been promulgated at the local level (Wiersma 2003, 654). For ease of reading, I have not included alphabetic tone markers here.

Bai has eight tones: tone 1 is high, level, tense (55); tone 2 is mid, level, tense (44); tone 3 is low, falling, breathy (31); tone 4 (Jianchuan) is mid, falling, tense (42); tone 4a (Dali) is mid, falling, modal (32); tone 5 is low, falling, harsh (21); tone 6 is high, level, modal (55); tone 7 is mid, level, modal (33); tone 8 is high, rising, modal (35) (see Wiersma 2003).

Where the Dali Bai dialect resembles the Jianchuan dialect, I have based my transcriptions on Zhao and Xu 1996, the *Bai-Han cidian* (Bai-Han Dictionary). Where the Dali dialect differs markedly from the Jianchuan dialect, I have used the glossary at the end of Wang Fu 2003 as my guide. I have distinguished transcriptions of Bai from transcriptions of Mandarin Chinese by using the abbreviation "B."

Measure Conversions from Chinese to American and Metric

fen   unit of land area; 0.10 *mu*, 0.607 acres, 0.00667 hectares, or 66.66 square meters

mu   unit of land area; 6.07 acres, 0.0667 hectares, or 667 square meters

jin   unit of weight; 1.1 pounds or 0.5 kilograms

li   unit of distance; 0.31 miles or 0.5 kilometers

yuan   unit of currency; the official exchange rate was set at 8.28 yuan =US$1.00 between January 1, 1994, and July 21, 2005, when it was revalued at 8.11 yuan=US$1.00 (for large sums I have rounded to the nearest dollar)

CHAPTER 1

With the Sign Begins the Search

It was gone. The old No. 2, the center of backpacker culture in Dali for two decades, where I had first stayed as a student traveler, had been reduced to rubble. In its place stood a wall of billboards advertising that this would be the future site of "Foreigner Street Plaza," an open-air mini-mall of elegant shops and boutiques. On "Foreigner Street" the few foreign backpackers wandered a bit forlornly. Whereas they had once congregated in this borderland town in the Himalayan foothills of southwest China to get off the beaten track and view exotic minority peoples, *they* were now the objects of exotic interest for crowds of cosmopolitan Chinese tourists. The Bai minority market women who had occupied the steps of the No. 2 Guesthouse for years selling souvenirs to backpackers had scattered and staked out spaces in side alleyways.

The story of the No. 2 Guesthouse in Dali encapsulates China's dramatic cultural, economic, and political changes over the past half century. The No. 2 had begun its life as a landlord's villa—a flagstone courtyard and garden surrounded on three sides by carved wooden doors and balconies. In the 1950s, shortly after the Communist revolution in 1949, the new government had criticized the landlords, appropriated their villa, added a cement-block building, and turned it into a state guesthouse. With China's "reform and opening" to the outside world in the mid-1980s, the government had designated the No. 2 as the only place in town that officially allowed foreigners to stay overnight. Tens of thousands of "lonely planeteers," drawn to Dali as I was because of the Lonely Planet guidebook they carried, stayed there, leading to the formation of "Foreigner Street"—several blocks of banana pancake cafés, beer joints, and sukiyaki shops. Most Dali townspeople tried to avoid this place, considering it dirty and somewhat dangerous because of the grungy travelers and some of their illicit dealings in money and drugs. But minorities in Dali—Muslims, Tibetans, and Yi—opened cafés there, and entrepreneurial Bai market women gathered there to sell souvenirs and change money with the travelers. The next change came in 1995, when, to make room for the millions of well-heeled Chinese tourists who were prospering with the economic reforms and who were drawn to Dali because of a popular movie musical and a martial arts novel, the town government tore down the landlords's villa and constructed a glass hotel in its place. A decade later, as the market reforms in China intensified, the government sold the No. 2 to a private company. The company demolished the glass hotel and started construction of a mini-mall, which was to be built in the style of an old landlord's villa. From a landlord's villa to a re-created landlord's villa, with a revolution in between, things had seemingly come full cycle.

The metamorphosis of the No. 2 Guesthouse and the transformation of Dali serve as a microcosm of the tremendous changes that have occurred across China. In the current reform-era shift from a socialist to a capitalist system, China is the world's fastest growing economy and the largest potential consumer culture in the world.[1] While the hallmarks of China's revolutionary era were class struggle, collectivization, and nationalization, the hallmarks of the reform era have become competition, decollectivization, and globalization. Instead of a communal culture, China is rapidly developing a consumer culture (see D. Davis 2000a; Gillette 2000; J. Watson 1997a). People have been encouraged not only to consume material goods, but to consume leisure experiences. As in other "postrevolutionary" places, Chinese officials and developers are seeking to tap into this consumer desire and collect the vast potential profits that tourism offers (Babb 2004, 2005; Bissell 2005; Kennedy and Williams 2001; Schensul 2005). In less than a decade, the Chinese tourism industry, catering to both national and transnational tourists, grew from 163.8 billion yuan (US$19.78 billion) in 1996 to 496.7 billion yuan (nearly US$60 billion) in 2004.[2]

To provide the electricity, infrastructure, and services for national and transnational consumers, existing structures have been razed, and new dams, airports, railways, highways, hotels, condominiums, shopping plazas, golf courses, and amusement parks have been constructed in their place. Not only have structures such as the No. 2 Guesthouse been demolished, homes have also been removed. Farmland has been bulldozed and built over. In this massive destruction and construction process, it is estimated that between 40 and 70 million Chinese farmers have been displaced in only ten years of development from 1995 to 2005 ("China's Land" 2005, 40; Ramirez 2005).

The transformation of Chinese urban spaces and the emergence of China's so-called floating population have been well documented (e.g., Gaubatz [1995] 1999; Pun 2005; Solinger [1995] 1999; Yan Hairong 2003; L. Zhang 2001). Rural migrants have been drawn to cities owing in part to a growing income gap between urban and rural areas, global manufacturing demands for cheap labor, as well as the consumer desires of younger villagers. Relatively neglected, however, has been the increasingly significant reverse movement of urbanites to rural areas as part of China's emerging leisure culture and the transformations of place that this movement has wrought.[3] To understand reform-era China, this book argues, it is imperative to understand the relationship between socioeconomic change, transformations of place, and displacement.

More specifically, this book explores the relationship between cultural representations and material transformations of place. Although Dali is located in Yunnan province, part of the margins, the borderlands of China—that 60 percent of China's territory that is home to 100 million minority peoples—it has figured centrally in national and transnational popular culture. In fact, it is because of its borderland location near Tibet and Myanmar (Burma), its vibrant minority culture, as well as its stunning scenery of snow-capped peaks surrounding fertile valleys that Dali has been popularly represented as an exotic place apart from dominant Han Chinese culture.[4]

In China's reform era, millions of people have been drawn to Dali because of three popular representations in particular—a guidebook, a movie musical, and a martial arts novel. Each representation in turn has had different material after-effects on the people and the place. By material after-effects I mean social and economic consequences that arise following an interval of time, often decades after the production of the representation itself. The Lonely Planet guidebook of China, first published in 1984, represents Dali as a place "off the beaten track"; yet in so doing, it has encouraged tens of thousands of transnational travelers to trek to the town over two decades. When it was made in 1959, the movie musical *Five Golden Flowers (Wuduo Jinhua)* illustrated Dali as a model socialist utopia just as utopian policies were in the process of failing and creating a nightmarish place. Yet surprisingly, the movie now draws millions of nostalgic national tourists to Dali to reenact scenes from the film. Jin Yong's enormously popular 1963 Hong Kong martial arts novel *Heavenly Dragons (Tianlong babu)* describes Dali as a fantastic place of the past, a Buddhist "wild, wild West."[5] Four decades after publication hundreds of thousands of fans travel to Dali to view and perform their favorite parts from it at a martial arts "film city" theme park, dubbed "Daliwood" in English. Almost six million people visited Dali in 2004.[6] This is nearly the same number who visited the Eiffel Tower that year and double the number who visited the Taj Mahal, one of the world's wonders, the previous year.[7]

Not only do these popular representations entice millions to travel there, they portray Dali in different ways, as do officials, tourists, townspeople, and villagers. Since narratives and representations of place are produced and interpreted by different social actors, they may overlap, compete, and be contested, thereby reflecting power and income inequalities (Rodman 1992, 652; Shields 1991, 18; Urry [1995] 1997, 2). For example, as I will show in chapter 3, well-off national tourists view the film *Five Golden Flowers* with utopian nostalgia amidst prosperity and uncertainty, while older villagers view it as a historical document of the destruction of their place.

Because different groups use the place of Dali in different ways, it also comes to have different meanings for them (see Rodman 1992, 646–647). For example, in chapter 5 I will show differences in the ways in which tourists, townspeople, and older villagers view a newly constructed highway—as a convenient means of transport, as leading to a modern future, or as creating wandering spirits. These divergences highlight the argument that places are culturally constructed and may be more or less meaningful depending on our experience there and the cultural narratives we attach to them.[8]

This book emphasizes the need to analyze place as well as social relations of space. In recent years, the field of anthropology has been influenced by writings in cultural geography that have favored discussions of space over place, where space represents mobility and possibility, and place represents fixity, rigidity, and control (Certeau [1974] 1988; Harvey [1989] 1990; Lefebvre [1974] 1996). However, we do not live in abstract "space." At any given time we are always somewhere, in some place (Casey 1996). Space and place are complementary: if "space [is] that which allows movement," notes Yi-fu Tuan, "then place is pause; each pause in movement makes it possible for location to be transformed into place" ([1977] 1997, 6). Anthropologists of China's reform era have only begun to research corresponding transformations of place and social space (Flower 2004; J. Jing 1996; Makley 2003; Mueggler 2001; M. Yang 2004).

By examining different representations of place, the material after-effects of these representations, and contestations over the uses and meanings of place, we can learn much about the ways in which different groups of people experience socioeconomic change. The transformations and struggles over place have been particularly intense in China, influenced by political upheavals, the rapidity of recent socioeconomic change, and population pressures— China has the largest population in the world, over 1.3 billion persons by 2005 ("China Population" 2005). This makes it a particularly compelling context for exploring popular culture and transformation of place through travel at the nation's borderlands.

With the Sign Begins the Search

Representations of borderland peoples and places have had the power to in-spire consumers to journey far afield to view for themselves what they had seen in print or on screen; in other words, "with the sign begins the search" (Lyotard [1989] 1998, 3). Journeys are increasingly prompted by and medi-ated by previously consumed images. As anthropologist Arjun Appadurai has observed: "More persons throughout the world see their lives through the prisms of the possible lives offered by mass media in all their forms. That is, fantasy is now a social practice" (1991, 198).

Although it has been suggested that "fantasy has no fixed geographic lo-cation" (Kirshenblatt-Gimblett 1998, 147), the case of Dali illustrates that travelers and tourists willingly journey thousands of miles to a place that in-spires their fantasies. And while it has been observed that "myth and fantasy play an unusually large role in the social construction of *all* travel and tourist sites" (Rojek 1997, 53; emphasis in original), some sites such as Dali already have a heightened mythic status because of preexisting narratives that have circulated in the popular realm for decades. In Dali we will observe tensions between nostalgia for a fantasized place and the lived experience of that place, a place that is in turn shaped by nostalgic fantasies.

Both growth and uncertainty in a global market economy, I argue, lead to quests for an imagined place of the past where tourists can perform their fan-tasies, nostalgia, and status for themselves and others.[9] This performative as-pect of travel highlights that tourism is not only about seeing, not only about gaze and spectacle (cf. Schwartz 1998; Urry 1991). Tourism also means ex-periencing for oneself—smelling, listening, trying, wearing—as well as per-forming for others one's status, one's style, one's fantasies (see Veijola and Jokinen 1994). These experiential and performative aspects of travel con-sumption help to explain the growth of tourism despite the possibility of vir-tual travel through computers, film, television, and travel narratives. Instead, popular media enhance the desire to travel. Motivated by representations in popular culture, millions of tourists journey to Dali to consume a place of an imagined exotic past where they can perform their nostalgia for previously consumed narratives as well as enact a new social status. Dali has become a "site of desire" (Swain 2005).

In being fantasized as an exotic place in the past, Dali shares a connec-tion with other borderland peoples and places around the world that have been represented in guidebooks, films, and novels. These borderland places and peoples may have been marginalized, impoverished, and discriminated against, yet they will be appropriated for symbolic, economic, and political purposes. In national and transnational projects, the socially and politically peripheral often become symbolically central (Babcock 1978, 32; Shields 1991, 5; Stallybrass and White 1986, 5). This is a familiar scenario in the North American context, where images and narratives of Native American Indians and First Nations peoples have been used in advertising, popular films, novels, and children's story books to formulate a national identity (Bird 1996; Deloria 1998; DeLyser 2003; Root 1996). Similarly, in China, minority peoples, officially referred to as "minority nationalities" (M. *shaoshu minzu*), have figured prominently in constructions of the national self (Gladney 1994; Schein 2002, 29).

Fantasies of other places are not only envisioned at home, they are projected onto the places that engendered them (see Urry [1990] 1994, 3). Enraptured by images of tartan-clad men of the Highlands, tourists search Scotland for the setting of *Braveheart* (filmed in Ireland) or *Brigadoon* (filmed in Hollywood) (Nadel-Klein 2003, 180). Mainland U.S. tourists, inspired by such films as *From Here to Eternity* (1953) and *South Pacific* (1958), fly to the islands of Hawai'i to see and learn the hula (Desmond 1999, 133). Prompted by guidebooks, brochures, and films like *The King and I*, Europeans and Americans travel to Thailand envisioning a land of Peter Pan–like "eternal children" (Selwyn 1993, 123). In Germany fans of the novels of Karl May and the films based on them form "Indian" hobby clubs and travel to the American Southwest (Calloway, Gemünden, and Zantop 2002; Frayling 1995).

Sometimes the people of the place are not the draw, but the place itself. Film fans of the *Lord of the Rings* and the *Last Samurai* travel to scenic set sites in New Zealand, where in this case the indigenous Maori people simply become part of the backdrop (Olson 2004). Tourists from around the world, especially Japanese, go to Prince Edward Island to experience the place of the novel *Anne of Green Gables* (Fawcett and Cormack 2001; Hendry 2000). In the late nineteenth century Americans journeyed to California to find the imagined home of the heroine of the novel *Ramona*, a woman of mixed Native American–Scottish ancestry adopted by a wealthy Hispanic family (DeLyser 2003).

Literary fans have long journeyed to their favorite authors' haunts: Dickens' London, Joyce's Dublin, Scott's Scotland, Twain's Hartford or Missouri. (DeLyser 2003, 902; Nadel-Klein 2003, 180; "Mark Twain House" 2005; "Welcome to" 2001–2005). In *Life on the Mississippi* (1883), Mark Twain describes his own journey as a nostalgic tourist to his childhood home (Melton 2002, 123), and in *Innocents Abroad* (1869) he describes his experiences as a tourist in Europe, alternately thrilled and dispirited at sights that did or did not measure up to the ways in which he had imagined them from literary and visual depictions (Twain [1869] 1984; see Melton 2002; Wasserstrom 2004). Because narratives engender fantasy and anticipation (see Urry [1995] 1997, 132), there is potential for both delight and disappointment in the actual place visited, as we will see in later chapters.

In examining popular culture, travel, and transformations in place, this book builds on burgeoning anthropological scholarship of the Chinese borderlands.[10] Anthropologists of China have drawn on the insights of Edward Said's *Orientalism* (1978), which highlighted the connection between exoticized "Western" literary representations of the "East" and colonial power, to examine both European colonial representations of Chinese borderland peoples and places (Harrell 1995c; Swain 1995b) and Chinese imperial and national representations of them.[11] Harrell's work (1995c) has been particularly important in identifying similarities in representations between the three "civilizing projects" of Chinese empire, European colonialism, and Chinese nation-building. However, scholars have focused primarily on representations of the Chinese borderlands intended for elite consumption—histories, natural and social science publications, museums, and art-house films.[12] Only recently have some anthropologists begun to turn to representations in popular culture in the form of postcards (Schein 2002), theme parks (Anagnost 1997; Oakes 1998, 2006), children's books (Bulag 2002; Khan 1996), and a movie musical (Swain 1994, 2001, 2005).

The three representations of Dali that this book examines—the Lonely Planet guidebook *China—a Travel Survival Kit,* the Chinese movie musical *Five Golden Flowers,* and Jin Yong's martial arts novel *Heavenly Dragons*—have been "popular" in the sense that they have circulated widely. In Chinese, one would say they had been "welcomed by the people" (M. *shou huanying*). My use of "popular culture" thereby differs from some scholarly examinations of popular culture in China where popular has been equated with the unofficial and as a site of social resistance to the state (Link, Madsen, and Pickowicz 1989, 10) or as a site of globalizing consumer culture outside of state control (Link, Madsen, and Pickowicz 2002, 3). I draw on other discussions that see popular culture as a contested site of meaning between different social actors (Baranovitch 2003; Hall 1981; Litzinger 2001; Wang 2001a, 2001b), where the boundaries between "mass culture" produced for the people and "popular culture" favored and/or produced by the people are often blurred (Chu 1978; Keane 2002; Mukerji and Schudson 1991, 3; Robertson 1998, 34).

Rather than reading popular culture as "text," I analyze popular representations in practice: looking at the meaning, use, and material after-effects of representations both for the people of the place who are purportedly represented and for the consumers of this place. Thus, this book is based not only on my interpretation of representations, but on what Michel de Certeau has called the "secondary production" process of a representation (1988, xiii). What do people do with a guidebook, film, or novel once it is in circulation? How do people "talk back" (hooks 1989) to these representations? How do they interpret the after-effects of these representations?[13]

In this secondary-production process, borderland peoples are not passive objects of outside tourist gazes but are themselves cultural producers and consumers who are actively negotiating political and economic change. While officials and entrepreneurs have aggressively shaped Dali to mirror its image in popular culture, townspeople and villagers have ambivalently both rejected and embraced popular images in attempting to gain wealth and status, represent their own historical identity, and define the future of their place.

A Place at the Borderlands

Focusing on one particular place, the people who live there, and the people who pass through, this book investigates processes of representation, interaction, and transformation. Dali is a dynamic place, a place shaped but not wholly defined by outside forces, a place where people attempt to define themselves and their futures within waves of local, national, and global changes. We may think of Dali as a "cultural nexus" (Duara [1988] 1991), where economic, political, and religious forces converge to shape a place. Like light through a prism (Robertson 1991), outside forces pass through Dali, altering it, but in doing so they are themselves refracted. National and transnational projects are altered, if only slightly, as they alter local ones.

Eric Wolf (1982) long encouraged anthropologists to consider places not as isolated communities but as tied in crucial ways to larger national and global processes, a point that has been reemphasized recently (Gupta and Ferguson 1997b, 1997d). Cultural geographer Doreen Massey has urged us to develop a "global sense of place," which recognizes the multiple identities and varied connections of any one place. She proposes that we consider places as "articulated moments in networks of social relations," where each place is a "unique point of . . . intersection" (1993, 66). This view leads us to visualize each place on the planet as connected to many other places through people, supplies, products, money, and technology. These points of intersection may continually shift.

The name of the place, Dali, comes from a Buddhist kingdom that once ruled over parts of Myanmar, Laos and Vietnam, and most of what is present-day Yunnan province. Yunnan is China's eighth largest province, about the same size as California and the most multicultural—or, in Chinese terms, most "multinational" (M. *duominzuhua*)—inhabited by twenty-five of China's fifty-five officially recognized "minority nationalities" (M. *shaoshu minzu*).[14] These minority nationality groups live spread across a landscape that ranges from nearly 7,000-meter Himalayan peaks in the north to tropical rainforests in the south. Mountains rise up from the land like the ridges on so many dragon tails, while silver snakes of rivers—the upper Yangtze, Mekong, and Salween—wind between them. One finds lonely villages perched precariously on the sides of gorges and densely populated villages and towns clustered in river valleys and lake basins (see maps).

"Dali" refers to an administrative region, an alpine basin, and a town (just as "New York" refers to a state, a metropolitan area, and a city). Since 1956 the administrative region has officially been called the Dali Bai Nationality Autonomous Prefecture (M. Dali Baizu zizhizhou) (*DZNJ* 1990, 26), after the predominant minority group who live there. The Bai nationality (M. Baizu) had a population of 1,081,167 according to the 2000 census and 1,121,700 by 2003 (*DZNJ* 2004, 31; *YNRK*, 1:105), making them the fourteenth largest minority group in China and the second largest in Yunnan, after the Yi. Bai refer to themselves as "speakers of Bair" (B. *sua Bair yin gain; sua Bair ni ge*). They have been classified as speakers of a Sino-Tibetan language (see Dell 1981; Wiersma 1990), although there has been much academic debate as to further classification (Wiersma 1990, 2003; Zhao 1982) and the origins of the Bai people—whether they are descendants of the Shan/Tai, the Burmese, the Yi, or Han Chinese, and whether or not the ancestors of the Bai ruled the Nanzhao and Dali kingdoms.[15] These debates, in Dali as elsewhere, often assume "purity" of groups over time and overlook the possibilities of intermarriage and cultural diffusion (Litzinger 2000a; Notar 1992).

What is clear is that the Dali region has long been a crossroads between what is now China, Tibet, Myanmar, and Vietnam, and religious, cultural, and material influences have traveled these roads. In its conquest of regions to the north and south, Nanzhao generals brought back diverse prisoners to the Dali basin (see Fan [864] 1962). When Dali was conquered by Kublai Khan in the thirteenth century, by Ming troops in the seventeenth century, and again by Qing troops in the late nineteenth century, soldiers settled in the region and took local women as their wives (Armijo-Hussein 1997; Lighte 1981; *YHSLD*; Yokoyama 1994). At present Dali is still a diverse area of over

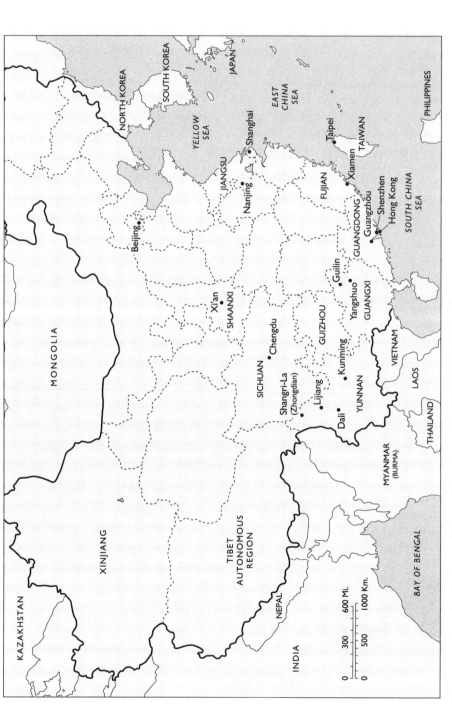

Yunnan province in relation to China and Southeast Asia. (Map by Bill Nelson)

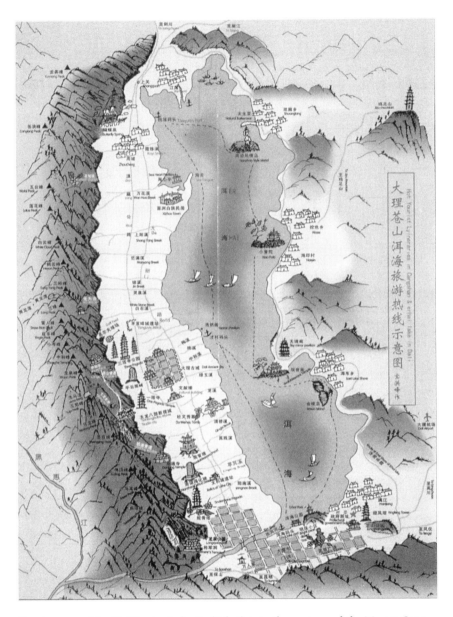

Tourist map of the Dali basin. Lake Er (Erhai) is in the center and the Mount Cang range to the west (left). Butterfly Spring is at the upper left, the old town of Dali near the Three Pagodas, and the martial arts "movie city" is just southwest of town. (*YDY*, detail)

three million persons.[16] Many of Dali prefecture's Muslims, who had a population of 66,085 in 2000 and 67,500 by 2003 (*YNRK*, 1:105; *DZNJ* 2004, 31),
are speakers of Bai, yet as practitioners of Islam, they are officially called the
"Hui nationality" (Huizu) (see Yokoyama 1987). Other officially recognized
groups in the region include Han Chinese (1,659,730), currently outnumber-
ing all other groups, as well as Yi (426,634), Lisu (31,972), Miao (10,967), Naxi
(4,302), Achang (3,330), Dai (3,047), Zhuang (1,955), Hani (1,585), Tibetans
(1,424), Mongolians (367), and 31 others (*YNRK*, 1:85–161).

The Dali basin centers on a large alpine lake, Erhai (Lake Er). Mountains
rise up on either side of the basin: low mountains to the east and high mountains to the west, the Mount Cang range, which rise up to 4,000 meters. During the dry season (December to April) the snow-capped mountains shine as
they tower over people working in fields of broad beans and winter wheat.
During the rainy season (May to November) the low clouds obscure all but
the mountains' feet, and farmers tend their corn and plant, transplant, and
harvest rice amidst a chorus of invisible frogs.

"Dali" is also the name of an old town located in the basin that long
served as the administrative, economic, and cultural center of this region.
Between the seventh and thirteenth centuries, the town (or a site near the
present-day town) was the capital of several Buddhist kingdoms, the Nanzhao, Houli, and Dali. After the defeat of the Dali Kingdom by the armies
of Kublai Khan in 1253, Dali lost political primacy of place to what is now
the provincial capital of Kunming (then called Yunnan Fu) (Armijo-Hussein
1997). Despite its political fall Dali remained the economic center of the province owing to its long-standing trade location as the place "where all important roads from mainland Southeast Asia met" (Prasertkul 1989, 72). From
1856 to 1873 Dali competed with Kunming again politically when it became
the capital of a Muslim-led independent state, the Pingnan Kingdom, until
it was brutally suppressed by Qing imperial troops in 1873.[17] After this suppression, a large earthquake in 1925, and the construction of the Burma Road
(Bradley 1945; Fitzgerald 1941; Smith 1940), a city at the southern end of Lake
Er, Xiaguan ("southern gate pass" in Mandarin), surpassed Dali as the administrative and trade center. Xiaguan, now called "new Dali," is the official administrative, economic, and cultural center of the region, but "old Dali" remains its true cultural heart.

Because Yunnan province was not occupied by Japanese troops during
the Sino-Japanese War (1937–1945), Dali became a haven for merchants (who
traded primarily in cotton, medicine, opium, tea, silver, and sulfur), missionaries, and coastal intellectuals (*BSLD1*, 1–78; Fitzgerald 1941). At this time

Charles Patrick Fitzgerald and Francis L. K. Hsu conducted ethnographic research in Dali (Fitzgerald 1941; Hsu 1967 [1948]). Their monographs serve
as important, and contradictory, sources of information on prerevolutionary Dali, Fitzgerald describing the Bai (then called Minjia in Mandarin) as a
"tribal people" and Hsu referring to them as "typically Chinese."

Reform Era Research

In the spring of 1988, when I was studying Chinese language, history, and
economics in Nanjing, like many other foreign students, I was drawn to Dali
because of the Lonely Planet guidebook *China—a Travel Survival Kit*. Since
1985 I had studied in or visited other major east coast cities—Beijing, Guangdong, Shanghai, Shenzhen—and was intrigued by the initial rumblings of
China's reform era: the construction of business hotels and discos for foreigners, and the proliferation of small-scale street entrepreneurs who would repair
a bicycle tire, fix an umbrella, or sell warm roasted chestnuts. Yet I wondered
how China's reforms were being experienced in other parts of the country.
Armed with the Lonely Planet guide, the "green bible" as we foreign students
called it, because the cover showed a woman working in a bright green rice
field and because we considered it the key text for accessing a "real" China beyond the gated universities and guarded dormitories where we lived, I set off
during spring break to see some of the rest of the country.

In Shanghai I hopped a train to the city of Kunming, provincial capital of Yunnan province, which the guidebook told me had "remained an isolated frontier region" and was inhabited by a "veritable constellation of ethnic minorities: the Zhuang, Hui, Yi, Miao, Tibetans, Mongols, Yao, Bai, Hani,
Dai, Lisu, Lahu, Va, Naxi, Jingpo, Bulang, Pumi, Nu, Achang, Benglong, Jinuo
and Drung" (Samagalski 1984, 725). On the three-day train journey in my
"hard sleeper" bunk-bed class, I chatted with an older couple going to visit
their grandchild and with a woman surgeon going to a conference. I watched
the scenery change from flat lands, to rainy red clay hills, to steeply terraced
mountainsides. From Kunming I rode a rickety bus twelve hours over serpen-
tine mountain roads to the town of Dali, which the guidebook told me was
"just off the Burma road," the former "centre of the Bai Nanzhao kingdom"
and "a town of little significance" (ibid., 747).

For a town of "little significance," Dali captivated me. As chance would
have it, I had arrived right before the famous millennia-old "Third Month
Fair" (B. *sawa zi;* M. *sanyue jie*). Tibetan medicine merchants selling bears'
paws and tigers' tails, Burmese jade dealers delicately setting up stalls, Shang-

hai clothiers carrying the latest coastal fashions, Yi minority women wearing umbrella-sized black hats and long pleated skirts, and Bai minority men bearing bamboo water pipes were descending on the town along with Han Chinese bureaucrats from Beijing. I had expected a sleepy borderland town but instead found myself amidst a bustling, unconventional crowd.

Near the cement-block No. 2 Guesthouse where I stayed, I discovered that, in order to cater to other transnational travelers who were also using the Lonely Planet as their guide, a "Coca Cola Café" had opened in Dali.[18] The menu included "Western" food: rice noodles with tomato sauce, goat cheese on toast, yak steaks with potatoes. A Tibetan-Muslim man who called himself "Bill" had started renting bicycles and hiring a fisherman to take travelers out on Lake Er.

I could only spend a few days in Dali before I had to take the bus and train back to classes in Nanjing but decided that I wanted to return to understand China's reform-era transformations in this place. After four years of graduate school in anthropology, I returned to Dali in 1993 to conduct research. By the time I got there, however, much had changed.

The year 1988, the year I had first gone to Dali as a "lonely planeteer," had been a year of great hope in China. After the death of Chairman Mao in 1976 and the ascendancy of Deng Xiaoping in 1978, the country had proceeded with a decade of economic reforms like a locomotive, starting out slowly and gradually picking up steam until it was zooming along. Although people were not sure exactly how the tracks were laid out or if the train might derail, they were jumping on board. In 1989 this hopefulness crescendoed into student democracy demonstrations in Beijing and other cities. The demonstrations grew as workers and professionals joined the students and as the international media stimulated worldwide attention. A violent state suppression on June 4, 1989, however, derailed the movement. Foreign researchers, students, and journalists fled China, as did some Chinese students who had been connected with the demonstrations. They didn't know what direction the country would take and whether they would be able to return to China.

Events in China appeared in contradistinction to events in the former Soviet Union and Eastern Europe. In Berlin demonstrations led to the fall of the Berlin wall and the reunification of Germany. Almost overnight, it seemed, the Soviet Union broke apart into Russia and newly independent states. The cold war melted. "Why couldn't China have taken the same road to democracy?" people in the United States asked.

Yet, by 1993, when I returned to China to conduct research, things were once again looking hopeful. In the spring of 1992, Deng Xiaoping had taken an imperial style "southern tour." His speeches encouraged "gutsier reform and opening" (M. *gaige kaifang de danzi zaida yidian; DXSZ* 1992, 42–44). This encouragement opened the gates to the faster development of markets, private businesses, and increased Sino-foreign joint ventures. The trickle of returning foreign business people, teachers, and students became a steady flood. However, the country could not turn the clock back to 1988, and a different mood prevailed. Economic, not political, reform was primary. No one talked explicitly about the "June 4" (M. *liu si*) demonstrations and suppression of 1989, but people would often comment: "Look at Russia. They have their democracy now but no food or money. At least we have some of both."

When I arrived in Yunnan's provincial capital of Kunming in the fall of 1993, markets were thriving, tourists were arriving, and talk of money was on everyone's tongue. Yet not everyone had equal amounts of money: millionaires (M. *baiwan fuweng*) in Mitsubishi sport utility vehicles were driving past street beggars. Instead of quiet avenues where people dressed in shades of blue and gray cycled slowly to and from work, the streets sizzled with mini-skirts and mini-vans, high heels and private sedans. Vendors hawked cigarettes and souvenirs on the sidewalks, while young women in tight, high-necked, thigh-slit red sequined *qipao* dresses beckoned customers into posh shops. I spent four months in Kunming at the Yunnan Nationalities Institute (now University) studying Yunnan history and Bai language while I waited for the Ministry of Education to approve my research visa. I was worried, since one of the researchers who had applied before me had been denied permission.

Fortunately, my research visa was approved. One of my professors at the institute who had grown up in Dali arranged for me to live with two families, one in the old town of Dali and one in a village north of town. This was no small feat. While Dali was "open" to foreigners, most of the foreign researchers who had preceded me in Yunnan had been required to stay in specially designated guesthouses or official government buildings. My teacher managed to convince officials that, as a single woman, I would be much safer living with families than living by myself. She further vouched to be my official research assistant (M. *peitong*) although she stayed in Kunming and I stayed in Dali. Previous foreign researchers had had difficulties with their officially assigned assistants. In at least two cases of which I knew, these assistants were not from the research area, could not speak the local language, were miserable away from Kunming, and acted more as supervisors than as assistants.

In early February 1994 my teacher accompanied me to Dali, introduced me to my two Bai host families, and negotiated what I would pay them for room and board. Teacher Zhang and Teacher Duan, a middle-aged couple, lived in an apartment in town. Their children, who were about my age, lived away, so it was a small household of two. They had both grown up in villages but had attended college, so everyone referred to them as "teachers," although only one of them worked formally as such. On weekend nights I ate dinner with them, and we talked about local history and current events. They introduced me to other townspeople, and from them I learned more about how people viewed the transformation of Dali through tourism. During the weekend days I would walk around the town of Dali, observing the activities of townspeople and tourists. I spent many afternoons chatting with Muslim, Tibetan, and Yi café owners, transnational travelers, and Bai women who sold souvenirs on "Foreigner Street."

The second family, the Yaos, a father, mother, three daughters, a married-in son-in-law, and one grandchild, lived in a relatively new village home behind a centuries-old courtyard house shared by six families, a family being defined as those who ate together (A. Wolf 1974b, 176). The courtyard was a lively place: someone was always coming or going, and something was always going on. Their village had served as the setting for many of the film scenes in the movie *Five Golden Flowers,* which I will discuss in detail in chapter 3.

While living in the village, I conducted participant observation, joining in and observing events such as baby naming parties, weddings, funerals, house birthday parties, and temple festivals. I assisted the family during the intensive planting and harvesting times by providing child care or shucking corn (something familiar to me from a childhood in Wisconsin; however, I discovered I was inept at threshing beans and wheat). During the busy winter wedding season, I would spend days helping with food preparation, peeling such quantities of garlic and ginger with other women that our fingers remained fragrant for days. However, I did not participate in farm or fishing work. Schistosomiasis—an eventually fatal disease carried by a snail-borne parasite—was a village health concern, and Mr. Yao, feeling responsible for my well-being, did not want me working in the fields or marshes.

I lived in the Yaos' village home on weekdays for over a year. Subsequently, I arranged to stay with a third family in another village located on the Yunnan-Tibet highway. This village was famous for its weekly market, which had become a tourist site for lonely planeteers. Living there allowed me to conduct interviews with many market women who sold souvenirs to tourists. Transformation through tourism was also a particularly pressing topic in this village because the construction of a new tourist highway was going to displace several village households, as I discuss more in chapter 5.

While I was initially overjoyed at not having an officially assigned re-search assistant, after three months I came to wish that I had some kind of assistant. Although I was fluent in Mandarin, I was still learning Bai, and many older Bai did not speak Mandarin. It was difficult for me, as a woman, to speak with village men between the ages of twenty and sixty on my own, since women's and men's social and work spheres were largely separate.

Finding someone with the time, energy, and patience to be my research assistant was not an easy matter. Initially, Mr. Yao volunteered his third daughter, but she was shy and not keen on tramping around the village with me. Most of the younger people were too busy doing their own work to take on any additional activities. Elderly people had the time but not the energy. Finally, I was introduced to a recently retired middle school teacher, Teacher Du. As an active man who suddenly had too much time on his hands, Teacher Du was the perfect person.

To my great good fortune, Teacher Du had patience, a sense of humor, and a worldly perspective. To offset his family's "landlord" assigned class status, he had volunteered to join the People's Liberation Army in the early 1950s. The army sent him to Korea, where he fought in the "American War" (what people in the United States call the Korean War). Through this experience he had seen other parts of China and the world, and had developed a deep sense of compassion for human suffering. Later we reflected on the twists and turns of history: as a younger man he had fought against Americans; as an older man he was helping an American woman understand his home.

Together Teacher Du and I conducted random sample surveys of 113 households in three villages. These surveys gave me a broader understanding of village household economies and villager perspectives on transformations in Dali. Teacher Du would knock on a courtyard door and call out in Bai, "Is anyone home?" (B. *ni ge ze hodv nimu?*). If someone answered the door, Teacher Du would assure him or her that we were not with the tax bureau or the health department, and in all cases except two the person invited us in. Teacher Du would then explain what we were doing. If men or older women (younger village women did not smoke) were present, Teacher Du would pass around cigarettes (which he told me to purchase), as was the usual way for men to start a reciprocal social relationship (see Wank 2000). Teacher Du would then ask the survey questions (on family size, education levels, land use, supplemental income, consumption, and views on socioeconomic change) in Bai and translate the answers back to me in Mandarin. As my Bai improved, I was able to ask questions and understand responses. However, we continued to follow the original format, for it allowed me time to write and observe. Our survey would last anywhere from thirty minutes to five hours, depending on how many people were at home, how much they wanted to talk, and whether or not they invited us to join them for a snack (for example, homemade rice flour dumplings with brown sugar filling).

Many times after we had asked people questions, they would ask me about life in the United States—family, food, crime, and American views of China. They were as curious about me as I was about them. Especially for older villagers, my identity was not at all clear. Since I spoke Mandarin (what Dali Bai speakers called *Ha hua*), people wondered whether or not I was a strange-looking urban Chinese. However, since I did not eat pork—I had once eaten one too many pig's feet at a Chinese luncheon and was thereafter hampered from enjoying future pork delights—almost a travesty among Bai in Dali, where the local specialty was a kind of *porc tatare*, ground raw pork with chili sauce (B. *he gai, he xiu;* M. *shengrou*), and since I had brownish curly hair and hazel eyes like some of Dali's Muslims, people asked me if I was Muslim (Huizu). Others knew that I was a "foreigner" but couldn't quite place me: was I American or Japanese? I looked like some of the Americans on television, but I could use chopsticks and liked to drink tea like Japanese. People had heard rumors that perhaps I was one of the new transnational investors or missionaries in the area. I heard my favorite of the rumors circulating about me when my Asian American fiancé came to visit. From a distance, villagers thought that he looked Bai (which indeed he did). "Now we know why you have come here!" several villagers said to me. "Your father was one of the American army men stationed here during World War II, when supplies were flown from India over the mountains or trucked along the Burma Road just south of Dali. He arranged a marriage for you, and you have returned to get married." I was sorry to tell them that this was not the case.

In the town of Dali, people initially assumed that I was a "lonely planeteer," simply one of the thousands of transnational travelers who passed through town. However, as I spent more time there and as I got to know shopkeepers, restaurant owners, and souvenir sellers, I became not just an "outsider" (M. *laowai*) or a "foreign ghost" (M. *yang guizi*) but a person with a name, Na Peisi.

Four years later, in 1999, I returned to Dali for three months to conduct follow-up research. I visited my former teachers, host families, and friends, eager to discuss with them the astonishing changes that had taken place since I had been away. I conducted formal interviews with local officials, transnational tourism developers, and ritual specialists, and joined tourists on their rounds of Dali.

That spring the United States had bombed the Chinese Embassy in Budapest. Teachers, friends, and strangers all asked me: "How could your country do that! For what reason?" No one believed that it was a mistake. "How can your government say that it was a mistake when they have such advanced military technology and can do 'surgical strikes'"? I deeply regretted that I did not have an answer for them. "I cannot explain it to you," I said. "It makes no sense to me. I am sorry that Chinese people were killed there."

In the spring of 2005, as I was completing this book, I returned again to Dali to conduct follow-up research on the recently opened "Daliwood" martial arts theme park, where much of a forty-part *Heavenly Dragons* television series had been filmed. Everyone with whom I spoke asked me about the U.S. war in Iraq, and again I could not explain why, given U.S. satellite technology, my government had not known that there were ultimately no "weapons of mass destruction" there, the justification for the war. It seemed to me more important than ever for there to be attempts at cross-cultural understanding. I hope that this book will contribute to that goal.

CHAPTER 2

Lonely Planeteers and a Transnational Authentic

What is universal is the drama itself, not the outcome.
(Wilk 1999, 248)

"They are trying to turn all of China into America and all of America into New York," Frank sighed. Frank was a twenty-something Muslim who, with his family, ran one of the most successful transnational backpackers' cafés in Dali. Like the other café owners in town, he had given himself an English name for the convenience of his customers. Frank had slept in the back of his café in a turquoise vinyl booth—it had been a late night of serving beer and playing tunes for the backpackers in town—and had just awakened. He did not seem embarrassed to appear in his boxer shorts in front of foreigners who were eating lunch—most likely he had seen them do stranger things. He pulled on his faded jeans, and he and his brother, Sam, came over to join me in a booth where I was eating an "Indonesian" item—chicken satay over egg noodles—from the cosmopolitan menu. While Frank and Sam looked like brothers, they exuded completely different styles. Frank's hair was almost to his shoulders, whereas Sam had a short trim. Sam had been going to a technical school and had just finished an apprenticeship in a factory. This was in 1999, and Frank was hoping that he might take a break from late nights, go back to school or travel, and turn the café over to Sam for a while.

I had asked Frank what he thought China's reform era was bringing to Dali, and while his words themselves could be interpreted either positively or negatively, it was clear from his tone that Frank meant them negatively. Frank was pessimistic, even though the new house recently constructed down the street indicated that he and his family had been profiting from China's "opening to the outside" (M. *duiwai kaifang*) that had let in thousands of transnational tourists. He had never been to America, but he imagined that China in the future would be turned into an America of the present, and he did not look forward to that future.

How do people experience intensifying transnational connections, the phenomenon that has come to be called "globalization"? In investigating this question, a key issue has been whether globalization leads to increased cultural homogenization or increased heterogenization (Appadurai [1990] 1994, 328). Contrary to those who have suggested that globalization creates a culturally homogenized "McWorld" of indistinguishable fast food restaurants and shopping malls (Barber 1995), many anthropologists have illustrated that people are not passive in the face of global processes and institutions but will "localize" them (e.g., Friedman [1990] 1997; Hannerz 1989, [1990] 1997; Hendry 2000; J. Watson 1997b). For example, urban residents in Beijing, Taipei, or Hong Kong will use the space of a McDonald's differently than do people in New York or Chicago. In turn the McDonald's corporation will alter its practices to cater to local demands (J. Watson 1997b, 1997c; Wu 1997; Yan 1997).

While I agree with other anthropologists who have argued against the blanket homogenization of globalization and have illustrated the creative processes of localization, I discovered during the course of my research that Frank, other café owners, and transnational travelers all seemed convinced that Dali was destined to become "just like" other places. They predicted that Dali's future was going to be like the present of other places. It is this perception of homogenization that I will explore here in the context of the formation of a transnational place in Dali called "Foreigner Street" (M. *yangren jie*) as stimulated by the Lonely Planet's *China—a Travel Survival Kit*.

For over a decade and a half, tens of thousands of transnational travelers have followed the Lonely Planet's written road into Dali. This steady stream of transnational bodies has shaped a section of Dali into a distinctly different kind of place. Foreigner Street—several blocks of cafés serving banana pancakes, cold beer, spaghetti, teriyaki, and other foods catering to foreign palates—has been an interstitial space between the local, the national, and the global, where "new signs of cultural difference and innovative sites of collaboration and contestation" (Bhabha 1994, 269) have been generated. In this chapter I am particularly interested in the kinds of transnational travelers who have passed through Dali and their interactions with café owners, themselves minorities within Dali. I suggest that the interstitial space, the "globality" (Rees and Smart 2001, 1), they have formed is not a completely homogenized place, yet it is one that is more familiar to transnational travelers than it is to Dali townspeople or Chinese nationals.

I also challenge the long held premise of travel theory that "Western" (assumed Euro-American) travelers primarily seek a cultural authentic in an exotic elsewhere to counter their alienation from modernity (MacCannell 1976;

for a review see N. Wang 1999). According to Dean MacCannell's classic formulation: "Pretension and tackiness generate the belief that somewhere, only not right here, not right now, perhaps just over there someplace, in another country, in another life-style, in another social class, perhaps, there is genuine society. The United States makes the rest of the world seem authentic; California makes the rest of the United States seem authentic" (MacCannell 1976, 155). In this chapter I show that travel is more complex than a dichotomy between a tacky, inauthentic Us and a genuine, authentic Other. Recently, analysts of tourism and globalization have argued that tourists want to either consume that which is different (Urry [1990] 1994) or consume that which is familiar (Hannerz [1990] 1997, 241; Ritzer and Liska 1997, 99). These are not necessarily mutually exclusive. Transnational travelers have hoped to discover Dali as both a culturally authentic place of the past and a trendy cosmopolitan place of the present, a place that they and café owners like Frank have recognized as sharing similarities with other transnational places. In particular, I suggest that transnational travelers in Dali have wanted to consume both a visual cultural authentic of borderland sights and a visceral transnational authentic of familiar food and music from home, which they have done in cafés such as Frank's. In this context the "authentic" can mean both that which is familiar and that which is unfamiliar. It is the availability of the visceral transnational authentic that has made Dali especially appealing to transnational travelers, primarily backpackers.[1] While visual consumption in the form of the "tourist gaze" (Hutnyk 1996; Rojek and Urry 1997a; Schwartz 1998; Urry [1990] 1994) and "bodily display" (Desmond 1999) have been powerfully theorized, other forms of bodily consumption have only begun to be analyzed (Veijola and Jokinen 1994; Wilk 1993, 1999).

Opening to the Outside

As part of China's national "opening" to the outside world, Dali officially "opened" to transnational tourists in February 1984 (*DSZ* 1998, 38). This was the second "opening" of Dali to Europeans. The first had been over a century earlier, in 1874, when the British official Augustus Raymond Margary journeyed to Dali, only two years after the bloody imperial suppression of the Panthay Rebellion and the massacre of most of the town's Muslim population. Margary secretly sought to establish a trade route between British-occupied Burma and the coastal Chinese city of Shanghai and saw Dali as a key town with which to build relations. He congratulated himself at the time: "I have established the very best relations with both officials and people, opened Ta

Li Fu [Dali], and vanquished the dragons which guarded its gates! More than one foreigner has been driven away in attempting to gain admissions" (Margary 1876, 278–279).[2] While Margary's nineteenth-century "opening" of Dali constituted part of a larger colonial effort to force China open to trade, the "opening" over a century later in 1984 formed part of a national Chinese shift in political and economic policy to bring in transnational capital.

Between Communist victory in 1949 and Chairman Mao's death in 1976, the few foreigners to travel to Dali were primarily visiting Soviet bloc or Southeast Asian dignitaries who were welcomed with choreographed celebrations and state banquets. When Burmese Prime Minister U Nu and his family visited Dali in 1961, for example, "several thousand singing and dancing celebrants thronged the streets as the honoured guests drove through the city."[3] Such state visits were a far cry from what would become the backpacker's more informal style.

People in Dali recalled that the first two independent travelers who arrived in the mid-1980s were "a rather plump white woman" and her young child. Crowds gathered to watch them, and the police followed them around, asking anyone who spoke with them: "What did she say to you? What did she want? What did you say to her?" At that time people were suspicious of all foreigners and thought they were spies. For Dali townspeople the apparition of the foreign woman and her child walking down the street marked the beginning of China's reform era and the start of a steady stream of transnational travelers that would soon become a flood. By the mid-1990s at least ten thousand transnationals walked through town each year.[4]

The Lonely Planet Empire

After the 1984 opening to the outside world, most transnational travelers were drawn to Dali because of a single book, the Lonely Planet's *China—a Travel Survival Kit*.[5] The first edition of the guidebook was published in October 1984, nine months after Dali's opening. By that time, the Lonely Planet guidebook phenomenon had been in existence for over a decade and was on its way to becoming "a $15 million-a-year publishing empire, the largest independent travel book company in the English-speaking world" (Shenon 1996, 35).

The Lonely Planet publishing empire had started out modestly as the brainchild of a young British couple, Tony and Maureen Wheeler. Following others on the overland "hippie trail" from Europe to Asia, they had arrived in Australia in 1972 broke but inspired. To earn money, they typed out a ninety-four-page travel guide, *Across Asia on the Cheap,* which they sold door-to-door in Sydney. In only ten days they sold out all of their 1,500 hand-stapled copies (Schwarz 2001, 69; Shenon 1996, 35–36). In 1975, after traveling for eighteen months, they wrote their second guidebook, *South-East Asia on a Shoestring*. It sold over half a million copies (Wheeler 1996, 15).

Recognizing the untapped potential of their off-the-beaten-track guides, the Wheelers set out to write a low budget guidebook for every country in the world. The name of their publishing company, Lonely Planet, had come from the Joe Cocker song, "Space Captain," from the rock 'n roll road movie *Mad Dogs and Englishmen*: "Once while traveling across the sky, this lonely planet caught my eye . . ." (Schwarz 2001, 69; Shenon, 1996, 36). This panoptic vision of the earth from outer space, a kind of "planetary consciousness" (Pratt 1992, 29–30), became ironically appropriate for a publishing team that aimed to write about every inch of the planet. In an interview with a reporter, Tony Wheeler once commented: "At Lonely Planet, we like to say that our writers go to the end of the road . . . and they had damn well better. Because I go to the end of the road." (Shenon 1996, 37). By the end of the twentieth century, in addition to over 150 city, country, and walking guides, Lonely Planet produced language phrasebooks, "audio packs," videos, and a popular television program (*Planet Talk* 1996). They had a staff of over two hundred employees in offices located in Melbourne, London, Paris, and Oakland, California (Wheeler 1996, 15).

By 1998 the Lonely Planet's *China—a Travel Survival Kit* included ten pages on Dali in the Yunnan province section and highlighted Dali several times in the opening chapters of the volume. Out of seven suggested China travel itineraries, the guide included Dali on two, the "Beijing to Hong Kong via the Southwest" and the "Hong Kong to Kunming via Guilin," the latter described as "the most favoured backpacker trail" (Storey et al. 1998, 102–103). In a special "Highlights in China" section, the guide featured Dali twice, as a "backpacker getaway" that has "achieved legendary status on the travel circuit" and as part of the "minority regions," where "many travellers make a beeline directly" and where minorities "still dress in traditional costumes and regularly hold colourful festivals and markets" (ibid., 112–113). It would have been difficult for a traveler reading the guide to ignore Dali.

In the Footsteps of Marco Polo

The Lonely Planet guides were marketed to backpackers who wanted to "get off the beaten track," yet ironically most backpackers whom I met in Dali fervently followed the guidebook's track. The guide provided the dots on the map that backpackers would then connect with their bodies. Rarely did backpackers venture between dots, even though there were other places and people to see between them. Around Dali there were famous Buddhist and Daoist mountains with hundreds of temples, Muslim communities with active mosques and schools, and log cabin Yi villages where men wore long capes and women donned umbrella-sized embroidered hats. Yet because these places were not listed in the Lonely Planet guide, most backpackers never saw them.[6]

Narratives of risk and adventure are important to backpacker identity, as researcher Torun Elsrud has shown through her interviews with Swedish and other backpackers. One traveler told Elsrud of the "risk zone" she enters as soon as she leaves home, and another told her of the "tyranny of the familiar" back home that he had to escape (Elsrud 2001, 605). I observed, however, that most backpackers took few risks and followed familiar routes.

I found this phenomenon surprising for self-proclaimed adventurers and asked backpackers about it. "It is easier for you," one person told me. "You speak Mandarin and some Bai too and can ask your way around. You can read signs. We can't do any of that." I agreed. Still, backpackers might have asked any of the multilingual speakers in Dali to write out simple questions and directions for them, yet I only encountered one backpacker who took this initiative.

The backpackers practiced what Jean-François Lyotard has called "the tourism of the return, retourism, a succession of explorations that always follow the same outline" (Lyotard [1989] 1998, 4). This "retourism" operated in two ways. First, backpackers followed the Lonely Planet guide almost to the letter, retracing the footsteps of the guide's writers and other lonely planeteers who had come before them. Second, they followed in the footsteps of foreigners who had passed through Dali before them.

Dali had long been a place of interest for European, Australian, and American explorers. *The Travels of Marco Polo* describes the land of the Dali Kingdom, focusing on the cities of Yachi (present-day Kunming) and Carajan (present-day Dali), which had been conquered by Kublai Khan in the mid-thirteenth century.[7] Marco Polo's text describes these places as two great cities, situated on large lakes, inhabited by Saracens (Muslims), "Idolaters" (Buddhists), and Nestorian Christians who ate rice (but also raw meat), drank wine, and used white porcelain shells as currency. As Marco Polo described it, the Dali Kingdom was a land of plenty, containing abundant fish and excellent horses. Yet it was also a land of danger: terrible serpents lurked there, and inhabitants carried a special poison to use on visitors, purportedly to keep auspicious visiting souls within the kingdom (Yule 1929, 66–80).

British and French colonial officials and explorers who passed through Dali in the late nineteenth and early twentieth centuries searching for a trade link between India and the Yangtze or a river route between French Indochina and southwest China (hoping that Yunnan might become an eastern extension of British colonial Burma or a part of "l'Indochine du Nord")[8] expressed intense interest in trying to retrace the footsteps of Marco Polo. They spent much energy trying to verify his route and sometimes remarked on reaching sites where they thought Marco Polo must have stood. Marco Polo became the apical ancestor of colonial travelers, and it was as if, by following in his presumed footsteps, these "explorers" could claim greatness themselves.

E. Colborne Baber, who traveled through Dali with the British Grosvenor Mission of 1876, "compared," as Hugh Fraser wrote in a letter to the Earl of Derby, "Marco Polo's relation with his own experiences, and verifies in many respects the accuracy of the Venetian's information."[9] Alexander Hosie, of Her Majesty's Consular Service, described seeing the mountains and town of Dali for the first time and immediately thinks of Marco Polo: "As we approached Ta-wang-miao [Dawang Temple], our eyes were gladdened . . . by the first glimpse, through the white-hot haze of the afternoon sun, of the summits of the Tsang-shan [Cang Shan] range capped with snow, at the base of which lies Ta-li Fu [Dali], the capital of Marco Polo's Western Carajan" (Hosie 1897, 128–129).

Even twentieth-century travelers framed their narratives through the lens of Marco Polo's text. British consular official Michael Gillet, who went to Yunnan in 1934, traveled through Zhaotong, Dongchuan, Kunming, and on to Dali. "This is the route, as I afterwards satisfied myself," he narrated years later, "by which Marco Polo returned from his trip to Burma" (Gillet 1969, 5). American travel writer Henry Franck, who traveled via the recently constructed French railroad from Hanoi to Yunnan in 1922, introduced his book *Roving through Southern China* by stating: "This volume is concerned with my almost random roving through what Marco Polo called 'Manji'" (Franck 1925, vii). While he acknowledged that he was following in the footsteps of the Venetian, he saw himself as getting off the beaten track:

> In any country one must get off the "beaten track" to see the real life of the people, and must pick up at least a smattering of their language in order to make even that much worth while. This is double true in China because of the peculiar situation of foreigners in that land. No doubt it is more to the discredit of the foreigner than to the Chinese themselves that we are to a certain degree despised, sometimes hated, in the treaty-ports where

we live in numbers and beyond which nine out of ten travelers never get. (ibid., ix)

Franck's statements highlight the paradoxical nature of retourism, where one could follow in the footsteps of other Europeans and simultaneously "get off the beaten track." It was possible to say "I was where he was before me, I saw that too," as well as to "go where no man (assumed European, Australian, American) had gone before."

In the late twentieth century this paradoxical discourse was structured into the Lonely Planet phenomenon. The guide appealed to travelers in search of remote, little-known places, but the existence of the guidebook insured that thousands would be following in the footsteps of those who came before them. What Marco Polo's text was for the colonial travelers, the Lonely Planet text was for the backpackers.

Some of the lonely planeteers expressed an explicit colonial nostalgia for the Europeans who had come to Yunnan before them. In their backpacks they carried recent reprints of colonial travel narratives—some of which enterprising café owners asked to photocopy and then sold reprints to subsequent travelers. This formed part of a larger late-twentieth-century Euro-American commodification of colonial nostalgia in film and clothing (see Enloe 1990, 51–52; Rosaldo 1989, 70). Back home, companies such as Alfred P. Harriman, Isabella Bird (named after an actual British woman traveler), Anthropologie, and Banana Republic marketed imagined "safari" and "exploration" style attire to middle- and upper-middle-class consumers.

Only the Old . . .

In the early years of China's reform era, transnational backpackers in Dali were required to stay at the No. 2 Guesthouse. When I interviewed the manager in 1995, Ms. Zhang, a youthful woman in her forties who wore her hair in a single thick, short braid, she told me proudly that "only after the No. 2 opened to foreigners was there the creation of Foreigner Street." She shared with me statistics that she had compiled on the tourists who stayed there: "In 1994 tourists came from over thirty countries. Starting in 1994, the number of individual tourists decreased and the number of tour groups increased. In 1994 there were 19,885 persons, 12,103 international and 7,600 national; 1,237 were from Hong Kong and Macao, 565 from Taiwan, and 10,301 foreign. Our 1994 gross income was 2.13 million yuan (US$257,246.00) and net profit was 710,000 yuan (US$85,749.00). This was up 40 percent from 1993."

A few transnational trav-
elers on Foreigner Street.
(Photo by B. Notar, 2005)

"Foreigner Street," the English translation of *yangren jie* (literally "ocean people street"; people in Dali usually pronounced the Mandarin *jie* as *gai*), was what townspeople called the street that became the center of backpacker culture in Dali. Cafés catering to backpackers started to spring up near the entrance to the No. 2 Guesthouse along Protect-the-Nation (Huguo) Road. From a solitary café in 1985 there grew over twenty cafés by 1999.[10] Eventually, foreigners were allowed to stay not only at the No. 2, but also at small guesthouses along the street. These guesthouses were privately managed, but the *zhuguan bumen*, the "upstairs boss," as one guesthouse manager put it, was the Public Security Bureau, which required a so-called management fee of 40,000 yuan (US$4,831.00) per year (roughly one-third of a guesthouse's annual income) per guesthouse. These small guesthouses offered more atmosphere—a flower-filled courtyard, a gazebo, a "Thai" style bar—than the concrete No. 2.

By the mid-1990s, three main types of transnationals came to Dali and congregated on Foreigner Street. The majority were self-declared "lonely planeteers": European, North American, and Australian backpackers on the Lonely Planet trail. (Japanese backpackers began to follow a Japanese guidebook—Chikyū no arukikata [How to Walk the World]—in a similar phenomenon.) The second type of transnationals were expatriates who lived and worked elsewhere in Asia (as executives, teachers, entrepreneurs, or students), and who came to vacation in Dali, using the Lonely Planet as their guide. The third group were "long timers," those who came to Dali to live and work for several years, either as researchers, like myself, or as foreign investors, teachers, writers, or missionaries.[11]

Most of the first group of transnationals, the backpackers, traveled in pairs or small groups—college students on summer vacation, physical therapists from Germany, teachers from the Netherlands—and usually sought temporary escape from their regular routines. They rented bikes to ride out to the villages to see and photograph the "real" Bai people (many village women wore colorful headdresses, while women in town did not). Café owners on Foreigner Street started to recognize this quest for a visual cultural authentic and to cater to it. One day while I was having a cup of coffee at Shirley's, a café run by a Muslim family, Shirley was preparing to take a group of Dutch travelers out across the lake "to a small, poor village where no one speaks Chinese and where 'no foreigners go.'" She smiled knowingly at this last phrase, since she took a group of foreigners there at least once a week.

During the day the lonely planeteers would sightsee, and in the mornings and at night they would gather at the cluster of backpacker cafés on Foreigner Street that had arisen to accommodate them. At the cafés they shared stories of adventure and complained about the "backwardness" of the country. With their adventure stories they distanced themselves from the staid lives of their parents and others "back home," but with their complaints about Dali's underdevelopment, they reaffirmed their "superior modern" status (see Errington and Gewertz 1989). The transnational backpackers expected a visually authentic place in the past where, in fact, modern minority peoples would seem a contradiction in terms.[12] However, they simultaneously expected Dali to be a cosmopolitan modern place harboring a visceral transnational authentic of backpacker cafés . The backpackers did not completely reject their homelands and modernity but engaged in a narrative double movement, at the same time distancing themselves from and reclaiming their home away from home.

One day at the Shaping village market, I met a British couple, both dressed in pale blue and aqua. "We have been to Asia many times!" they said. "We are disappointed in this trip: the culture has disappeared. They have built new ugly buildings. It is a shame really."

In their "tourist gaze" (Urry [1990] 1994), the British couple expected to see what they imagined to be an authentic culture through its architecture, not the "new" and "ugly" architecture that had replaced the "true culture." In his analysis of tourism, Kevin Meethan has suggested that comments like these represent a form of "implicit moralizing" where "we can see a form of cultural imperialism at work." He continues: "Other more exotic societies need to preserve their culture, not perhaps for their own benefit, but to cater for the demands for the authentic from the tourists of the developed economies, or to satisfy the moral preoccupations of the analysts" (Meethan 2001, 110; see also Nash 1993). The travelers expressed a kind of colonial nostalgia through a narrative of complaint where they bemoaned the disappearance of a visual cultural authentic. As Renato Rosaldo has remarked (in what he calls "imperial nostalgia"): "When the so-called civilizing process destabilizes forms of life, the agents of change experience transformations of other cultures as if they were personal losses" (Rosaldo 1989, 70).

In August 1994 I spoke with Duan Mo, a thirty-something Bai-Han man who had grown up in Dali and had once worked as a tour guide. I asked him why he had quit working as a guide and started working for an international NGO (nongovernmental organization) instead. In response he asked me if I had seen the documentary film *Cannibal Tours*.[13] I shook my head, "Not yet."

"You really should see it. A foreign teacher in Kunming lent me a copy of it. It's about a group of German, Dutch, English, and American tourists who go to Papua New Guinea. The film shows this American couple walking along a path in the woods. The path is used by the local people every day, and there is nothing special about it, but the husband turns to his wife and says, 'This is an adventure, isn't it?'

"After I saw this film I was so embarrassed to be a tour guide that I swore that I would never do that work again. I saw myself and my tourists clearly in the film. Before, I'd been dissatisfied with being a guide, but I couldn't say why. After I saw the film, it became clear to me. I used to take these American and European tourists to places in Yunnan. There would be these women who couldn't walk up hills and would be complaining. They would be complaining about everything, and I would think, 'Can nothing be right?' And then they would see an old building torn down and say, 'What a pity! What a pity!' It seemed to me that only the old was good, only the traditional was valued, only poverty was beautiful. We saw people in poor living conditions and shabby clothes. 'This isn't right,' I thought. 'These foreigners come all this way, and they want to see what is different, but if the old has been torn down and replaced by the new, they are not satisfied, and if conditions are not good, or modern, they are not satisfied either. I couldn't stand it. They didn't want people to change."

Duan Mo's comments highlight the narrative double movement of the transnationals, who wanted to see what they expected to be the "authentic" indigenous culture, the authentic nonmodern, but then complained of inefficient, nonmodern systems of transportation or infrastructure. In other words, the travelers could critique other places on all fronts inconsistently: they are too backward/they are too modern; they are uncivilized/they have destroyed their culture. These criticisms reveal more about the tourists than the toured (see also Errington and Gewertz 1989; Gewertz and Errington [1991] 1994).

Yet many backpackers recognized the irony of what van den Berghe and Keyes have called the "Heisenberg effect," where a "search for the exotic is self-defeating because of the overwhelming influence of the observer on the observed" (1984, 345–346; see also E. Cohen 1996, 81; van den Berghe 1994). While recognizing this process, backpackers also distanced themselves from it (see Hutnyk 1996).

One afternoon in 1994 I sat with a sandy-haired American backpacker, Karen, in Frank's Café. She was on her second glass of warm beer. "I really hate tourists," she lamented. "They destroy a country. Thailand has been destroyed by tourism. . . . I worry that the same thing will happen in China and in Dali." Karen's comments were typical of the comments made by transnational backpackers in Dali in their attempt to distinguish themselves from the older, mass "tourists." MacCannell has written that "tourists dislike tourists" (1976, 10), but it is really that self-proclaimed "travelers" dislike "tourists" (Errington and Gewertz 1989; see also Desforges 1998; Welk 2004). If mass "tourists" are there, then the place is clearly no longer "off the beaten track" (E. Cohen 1996, 73, 195).

In their comments to me, many travelers recognized that they were part of a larger process of commodification that held destructive potential. One afternoon I was sitting at the La Dee Da Café looking at some photographs I had taken. A man with chestnut hair down to his shoulders and a large turquoise earring who was sitting at the next table asked if he could see them. Luc was from Montreal. He had come to Dali from Vietnam and was heading northwest toward Tibet. He financed his travels by buying crafts along the way and then selling them at a Sunday market back home. He asked what I was doing in Dali. I told him that I was studying popular culture, travel, and socioeconomic change.

In response Luc reflected: "I was talking to a guy in Kathmandu who had been there years ago. He said that there just used to be one street with a few shops on it. Now there's a whole section of town dedicated to tourists. They paved the roads, built lots of shops and restaurants. When I came to Dali I thought 'little Kathmandu.' Of course, it's cleaner here, not so dusty, and not as poor, but I would love to come back to this place in ten years. Will it be like Kathmandu?" Luc continued: "Sometimes I think tourism is like an invasion. Of course, I don't want people's lives to stay exactly the same. Things have changed from a hundred years ago in the United States and Canada, and tourism does bring in money and jobs. But what happens if people leave their lives of cultivating the land and then something happens to the tourist industry and the tourists stop coming? Could they go back to their old lives? It would be very difficult. What would they do? I think about these things sometimes. Of course, the invasion isn't like one of soldiers, but once foreigners start coming, who can stop them? The local people don't really have a say in the matter. I have a funny feeling being part of this. Like maybe I shouldn't go up to see those hill tribes sometimes."

Although Luc did not expect people's lives to remain unchanged, he expressed ambivalence about his participation in a process for which he did not imagine a positive outcome. Luc also recognized an important problem in tourism development: most locals did not have a say in the process of development and what forms it might take. Like the American traveler Karen above, Luc thought that Dali's future was presaged in what had already happened in other touristed places. Dali's future was predicted in the present of other places.

Out of twenty-three travelers from Australia, Belgium, Canada, Denmark, Japan, Poland, Spain, Sweden, and the United States who responded to a survey I distributed at the Lhasa Café one morning in the spring of 1995, all were pessimistic about what Dali would be like in a decade. Like Luc and Karen above, some of the survey respondents predicted that Dali's future would be specifically like that of other places: "Greenwich Village or Haight-Ashbury of the sixties—scary thought," suggested a North Carolina woman, age forty-seven. "Go to Poland and see Zakopane," a twenty-three-year-old man from Warsaw wrote. "That look[ed] like Dali not ten years before. Really bad place."

Two of the respondents answered metaphorically: "Have you seen The Lorax [a Dr. Seuss cartoon]? All these Once-lers came and totally ruined the area because they didn't have a real connection to it. I wonder if the Westerners will do that here—use it until it is 'wasted' and leave it without afterthought (leave it and find another place to abuse)," a twenty-three-year-old Minnesota woman worried. A twenty-four-year-old woman from Virginia (who had perhaps been smoking too much weed) wrote: "I think little green [picture of man] will invade and turn it into a filling station for intergalactic vessels."

Other survey respondents answered more generally: "Dali I think will be a big Hugholu" [Huguolu, i.e., Foreigner Street], a twenty-six-year-old woman from Quebec wrote. "I hope it will not be too commercialized, but I fear it will be. It'll lose its charm fast," a twenty-eight-year-old woman from Halifax responded. "At this point, I feel the city will be enveloped by the drive to cater to the tourist, thus overly commercializing the people's city," a twenty-three-year-old man from Wisconsin noted. It will be "a Western-oriented town," a twenty-five-year-old Swede predicted. "One big hippie commune," wrote a Belgian woman, age twenty-four. "Nothing like it is today. SPOILED. (It is getting too touristy)," answered a man from Melbourne, age twenty-three. A thirty-two-year-old man from Vancouver envisioned Dali as "another stressful place on the tourist trail." Dali will be "one big tourist trap," concluded a Dane, age twenty-two. The travelers saw the transformation of Dali as part of a process of transformation that had already happened elsewhere. The transnational travelers expressed a kind of "nostalgia for the present" (Jameson 1989; see also Errington and Gewertz 1989). They expected that they were among the last to experience an "unspoiled" Dali before the mass tourists arrived.

A Visceral Transnational Authentic

While backpackers wanted to see and photograph the "nonmodern" before it disappeared, for the most part they did not want to eat local food or listen to local music.[14] In other words they did not want to consume the indigenous cultural authentic all the time. Backpacker cafés on Foreigner Street prospered because they served food that catered to traveler palates: coffee with cream and sugar, cucumber sandwiches, potato salad, pizza, pork tonkatsu. The cafés played retro European and American pop music from pirated cassette tapes or from tapes that travelers left behind: Bob Marley, Prince, Abba.

The search for a visceral transnational authentic of food was not new in Yunnan. Late-nineteenth-century colonial explorers not only wanted the visceral authenticity of home, but often brought it with them. Their official reports, letters home, and published travel narratives provide multiple references to food and drink. Some of the most vivid descriptions are provided by Augustus Raymond Margary, who traveled through Dali in 1874. In a letter to his parents on November 29, he describes breaking the cups and spirits he brought with him: "All my glass, and the cups were smashed a few days before getting here, and five precious bottles of wine; however . . . brandy goes a long way to guard against the effects of bad water" (Margary 1876, 238). Along with wine and brandy Margary also brought a more stimulating beverage, which a servant prepared for him: "In a few minutes I shall have a good hot cup of coffee, which my boy is getting ready in an Etna. The thermometer marks 45° and it is 7am. At ten I shall start in my chair for Ta-Li Fu [Dali]" (ibid., 275–276). From Yongchang (now Baoshan, west of Dali) Margary wrote to his parents of a Christmas feast he ordered prepared: "I ordered my cook to make the biggest dinner he could command, and invited my three gentlemen and the two civil and military mandarins to try an Englished spread. It was amusing, to see the difficulties they suffered under in trying to use a knife and fork. We had mock turtle and veal from Crosse and Blackwell, roast duck and boiled fish from the market, curry and two puddings, besides fish, which I had forgotten in its proper place" (ibid., 290–291). Margary's description reveals a sense of the extent and expense to which he was willing to go in order to travel with familiar food.

Mr. F. S. A. Bourne, who traveled through Yunnan a decade after Margary on a British mission "'to inquire into the commercial condition and communications' of that little-known region" (Bourne [1888] 1915, 20), details the size of the retinue necessary to carry his baggage and escort him: "On the morning of the 26th October we started from Ch'ung-ch'ing [Chongqing], the party consisting of thirty persons, namely: nineteen porters, whose function was to carry men and baggage; their leader, who was responsible for property, for the due carriage thereof, and for the conduct of the gang; a Chinese clerk and his servant, a lieutenant, with his son, and two men forming an escort kindly provided by the local authorities; an official messenger and myself, and two servants" (ibid., 20).

Bourne and other colonial explorers describe ordering familiar food to be prepared for them. Bourne notes that at "Pei-yin-shan we had to stop a day to make bread, &c." (Bourne [1988] 1915, 21).[15] Australian George Ernest Morrison, who traveled from Shanghai to Burma in 1894, was willing to "cross-ethnick" (Robertson 1995, 1998) by dressing in Chinese clothes but was not willing to eat local food: "I travelled as a Chinese, dressed in warm Chinese winter clothing, with a pigtail attached to the inside of my hat. I could not have been more comfortable. I had a small cabin [on a riverboat from Shanghai to Hankou] to myself. . . . By paying a Mexican dollar a day to the Chinese steward, 'foreign chow' was brought me from the saloon" (Morrison 1902, 2).

Lonely planeteers did not travel in the grand caravan style of the nineteenth- and early-twentieth-century colonial officials who came before them, nor did they bring foodstuffs from home, but while in Dali they continued the colonial culinary tradition of demanding familiar food.[16] This food could be cosmopolitan (such as a variation on Indonesian chicken satay) but usually not local (such as lake fish stewed in chili sauce with dried green papaya). Lonely planeteers ate most of their meals on Foreigner Street and over time taught the café owners and their staffs to prepare familiar food for them: chocolate cake or hash browns. The Japanese backpackers taught some café staffs to prepare tonkatsu, rice omelettes (omuraisu), and donburi. Only rarely did I see a transnational traveler try out one of the small local restaurants just around the corner from Foreigner Street. I knew that when I went one block over to eat spicy noodle soup or fried erkuai (rice cakes), I would be the only foreigner there. The travelers' sense of adventure usually did not extend to their stomachs.

Some of the lonely planeteers seemed to fit MacCannell's classic description of "alienated moderns" (MacCannell 1976; see also Selwyn 1993) who longed to escape the problems of their home countries, their old routines, and themselves. They were like those described in Joni Mitchell's words "traveling, traveling, traveling; looking for something, what can it be?"[17] However, contrary to MacCannell's influential idea that alienated moderns search for another cultural authentic to ameliorate their condition, the alienated lonely planeteers did not seem interested in looking for a cultural authentic but spent their time hanging out on Foreigner Street. Most of these lonely planeteers were men who either had felt dissatisfied at work or had never "found themselves."[18] John, a former stockbroker, had quit his job to see the world. He sat in the backpacker cafés, drank coffee, and mused. Hiroshi had quit his corporate sarariman (salaryman) job in Tokyo and spent his afternoons getting high. (Dali villagers grew hemp for rope and used the seeds for snacks. Enterprising travelers soon learned to pilfer leaves from hemp fields to make their own pot. Even more enterprising souvenir sellers observed this phenomenon and some of them began to sell small bags of dried leaves to travelers.) "Crazy" Mark, an Australian, whom souvenir seller women nicknamed Zhubajie (Pigsy), the humorous, gluttonous, and lecherous character of the classic Chinese novel Xiyouji (Journey to the West), moved from café to café getting drunk on sorghum liquor and trying to propose marriage to local women. A Welshman named Davydd told me that he did not want to live in either Wales or England, where he could not be himself: "The English think all Welsh work in coal mines and shag sheep." He showed me a photo album he carried with him. Each photo showed him (and only him) in different scenic sites in the world. He exemplified the idea that "travel is a strategy for the accumulation of photographs" (Urry [1990] 1994, 139), where his photo album was his document of a lonely life on the road.

Other transnationals, mostly expatriates, gathered in Dali primarily because they knew it had a laid-back atmosphere where they could enjoy a "home away from home." They were attracted to Dali by the Lonely Planet's description of it as "one of the few places in China where you can well and truly forget about China" (Storey et al. 1994, 872). European, North and South American, Australian, and Israeli expatriates who worked and studied in China and other parts of Asia came to Dali because they knew that they could drink "real" coffee, eat "real" pizza, and listen to "real" tunes while sitting on comfy old couches. They could read foreign-language books and magazines left behind by backpackers, speak their own languages, and catch up on foreign news. This group included travelers such as Sherry, an acupuncturist from Chicago who studied traditional Chinese medicine in Kunming; Søren, a tall Dane with long blond hair who studied Mandarin in Sichuan province; two Anns from Cincinnati who worked for banks in Hong Kong; Carlos from São Paulo, who was doing an undergraduate degree in Minnesota and had come to China on a semester study abroad program. Two Israelis, Daniel and Abraham, who, after completing their mandatory military service made their living selling Thai jewelry on the streets of Japan, came through Dali on their way to Thailand. They spent most of their time in Dali playing video games. Two Americans, Burt and Martha, taught English in Hubei at different institutions and had come to Dali for rest and relaxation. Burt told me that one day, when it was very cold in his unheated classroom back in Hubei, he was writing on the blackboard—the chalk was breaking and going under his fingernails—and he felt like falling down on the floor. "I was losing the will to go on," he said. Burt had a difficult time convincing his institution's foreign affairs office to let him travel during Chinese New Year, but finally they agreed to let him go. He had come to Dali to "recuperate." Martha said similarly that her classroom was freezing cold, to the extent that she had to pace back and forth to keep warm. "The thought of coming to Dali kept me going the last week of the semester," she smiled.

A third group of transnationals in the Dali basin were either those like myself, long-term researchers (another anthropologist, an ethnomusicologist, a folklorist); foreign language teachers, missionaries, and foreign investors; or, in one case, a Japanese writer who stayed in Dali several months while work-ing on his new novel. Like the expatriates from elsewhere who came through Dali, we also gathered on Foreigner Street because of its visceral transnational appeal. Each weekend I came into Dali from the village where I lived during the week. I would take a shower, get a cup of coffee, catch up on foreign news. I sometimes arranged to meet another researcher to compare notes and share stories. Although my participation in Foreigner Street was similar to that of other transnationals, for me it was not only a place of relaxation, but a place of work, as I tried to analyze the interactions that were taking place there.

A Transnational Place

While Foreigner Street may not have been a homogenized place, it became a globalized place that was more familiar to transnational travelers than it was to Dali locals or to Chinese nationals. Foreigner Street became a cosmopolitan space of interaction, but the space was limited to transnational tourists and a certain group of local actors, such as guesthouse workers, café owners and their staffs, souvenir sellers, and shoe repairmen. Unless they worked there, I noticed that most townspeople avoided walking down Foreigner Street. When I took an after-dinner stroll with my town host family, Teacher Zhang and Teacher Duan, they would never walk down that street. When I asked Teacher Duan about this, he laughed and said: "All those strange-looking and smelly people! It makes me uncomfortable to go there."

Foreigner Street was similarly unfamiliar to Chinese nationals from the coastal cities. In mid-February 1995 two Han Chinese women reporters heard that I was living in Dali and wanted to do a series of interviews about For-eigner Street with me as their guide. One of them was a friend of one of my teachers back in Kunming, so I felt I should try my best to assist them.

The women reporters met me at Teacher Zhang and Teacher Duan's apart-ment. They were stylishly dressed in tight raspberry and blackberry colored sweaters and exuded a professional manner. Before we went to Foreigner Street, they asked me a number of questions about Dali and Bai women. It felt strange to be on the other side of an interview. I found myself answering in ways I thought they might want to hear, editing the words as they emerged from my mouth. I thought of the Bai cautionary proverb "before you speak, your upper lip and lower lip should have a discussion" (B. *sua do ca, niu do jui-bei ni er juibei ga saye*).

After a brief interview, I walked them to Foreigner Street. Our first stop was Bill's Café. Bill's was empty except for Bill's twenty-something wife Lili, a

teenage waitress, and a twenty-something man who sat playing with his cigarette lighter—draining fluid on his fingers and then setting them on fire for
a few seconds. I asked Lili if the two reporters could interview Bill about his
café and Foreigner Street. Lili said that Bill was out, but she would be happy to
talk with the reporters. We all sat down in comfortable wicker chairs around
low wooden tables.

Lili wore a large purple acrylic fur coat and red lycra stretch pants that
had the English word "Love" stamped on them in black letters. Gold and jade
bracelets adorned her wrists. She asked us what we wanted to drink and had
the waitress make the reporters two cups of instant Nescafé and me a cup of
brewed Yunnan coffee. Lili told us that she had graduated from a performing
arts institute in piano and voice and had originally hoped to be a teacher of
both. As a child performer growing up during the Cultural Revolution, she
had sung the glories of Madame Mao and the Gang of Four. However, she did
not go on to be a performer or a teacher because she had met Bill and got-
ten married. "It was love at first sight." She didn't mention that she was Bill's
second wife, and I didn't mention that I had heard stories of his temper and
abuse.

Just then Bill sauntered in, wearing cowboy boots and a suede coat. He
poured himself a brandy snifter full of "white lightning" rice liquor and sat
down. I introduced him to the two reporters.

Bill came from a Tibetan-Muslim family who had suffered greatly during the Cultural Revolution. In Dali those households that had been the most
marginalized during the Maoist years were the first to take entrepreneurial
risks in the early years of reform. Those who first opened cafés were minorities within Dali: Muslim or Yi families, or former landlord families who had
been persecuted as members of the "bad classes" between 1949 and 1979.[19]
Although they had suffered for three decades, these families often still had a
knowledge of past commercial practices, and some had connections to overseas relatives who could provide startup capital.[20]

Bill told us that he had begun in the mid-1980s by renting bicycles to for-
eigners. Back then he made only a few yuan a day. He switched from renting
bikes because "my bikes were stolen, all seventeen of them" and subsequently
opened the first restaurant for transnationals in Dali, the Shed. He rented the
Shed space from landlords and made good money. "But the landlords saw that
I was making money and decided to have a go at it themselves," Bill scowled.
"They saw that there was money in my pocket, and they wanted that money.
They thought that if I could do it, they could do it. But it wasn't like that. They

didn't know English, and they didn't understand foreigners," he noted, shaking his head. Once the landlords took over, the Shed lost business.

Bill now owned the building his café was in, but business was not as good as it had been. "Now there are so many restaurants for foreigners, nearly twenty: the Dian, Mia's, Egret, Red Flag, Lucky, Lhasa, Hard Luck, La Dee Da, the Shed, Shirley's, Mountain Goat, JP, Welcome, Frank's, Sunny, Sally's, Why?, Mister Dali, and Aladdin's [pseudonyms].[21] There is too much competition; it is keeping the prices down. This is especially bad during this time of inflation."

Bill continued: "I hope to open my own guesthouse, but the Public Security Bureau does not want competition. Now they subcontract out the small foreign guesthouses. They say they will subcontract out to others, but who gets those contracts? Only those with good connections (*guanxi*) to them. The leaders sit pretty. There are private guesthouses in other places like Lijiang, but here the local bureaucratism (M. *tudi guanli*) is too strong." The reporters did not write down this comment on local corruption.

One of the reporters changed the subject to foreigner interest in Bai culture. "Oh yes, they are very interested. They often ask about marriage customs," Lili said. I asked Bill if foreigners also ask about Hui (Muslim) customs because I wanted the reporters to recognize that Bill was not Bai. "Sometimes," Bill said. "Actually, I am Muslim-Tibetan. My mother is from Qinghai." The reporters looked surprised but nodded.

"Foreigners are very interested in Tibetan culture," Lili added. "It is more mysterious. They are more interested in minority nationalities in general. They sometimes have a reaction against Han culture (M. *dui Han wenhua you yige fan'gan*)." Somehow I didn't think this was going to make it into the newspaper report either, although one of the reporters acknowledged that "it seems like in Dali, Western and Bai cultures have formed a bridge, crossing over Han culture."

"Yes," said Lili. "Here in Dali, Westerners and locals are like equals. We come together as friends. They do not look down on us. This is important for a minority person to feel equal."

I was surprised that Lili was speaking so openly to the Chinese reporters. Was she a bit drunk? She suddenly stood up and with a strong, sweet voice sang the song about Dali's Third Month Fair from the popular 1959 film *Five Golden Flowers* (*Wuduo Jinhua;* see chapter 3). Bill sat back in his chair, took a drink, closed his eyes, and looked like he might cry. After Lili finished singing, I thanked them and ushered the reporters out to the next café, Frank's.

Frank and his family were practicing Muslims, actively involved in the life of the nearby mosque, and their family-run café was one of the most popular in Dali. Frank, his parents, brother, and later his wife put in long hours at the café from ten in the morning until the wee hours of the following day. Despite his intensive work, Frank had an easygoing style. Over the years he had learned excellent colloquial English and would joke and chat with his customers. Frank once told me: "Some foreigners will talk to you even if you don't understand them. Usually if a Chinese person thinks a foreigner doesn't understand, they will stop talking. But some foreigners talk and talk, they don't care whether you understand or not. It is a good way to learn English."

Moreover, Frank was a savvy businessman, constantly updating the music he played in the café to match European and American trends. The last time I visited, Frank and his brother Sam had added an Internet room with three computers so that tourists could check their email while on the road.

When the two reporters and I entered, Frank's Café was packed with backpackers who were drinking beer, laughing, and listening to old Abba tunes. Frank wasn't there, but I recognized a Canadian traveler, Adam, who had been hanging out in Dali for several weeks. I asked if the reporters might interview him. "How long will it take?" Adam asked. He agreed when assured that it would not take long, and the four of us went to sit at a separate table.

Adam had come to Dali from India, through Nepal, Tibet, and Sichuan. The reporters asked him (and I translated) what he thought about Foreigner Street and Dali. "Well, you know, it is difficult to be a tourist in China. It is difficult to buy tickets, and when you buy things you always have to bargain. Dali is not like the rest of China. One can rest here and play. I think most of the travelers who come to Dali also feel this way."

"Let's go," said the reporter in the red sweater. I was surprised, for they had only talked with Adam for a few minutes. The two reporters nearly ran out of the café: "That place is too noisy! The air is not good in there!" Whereas I had thought that Frank's was warm and lively, the reporters thought the atmosphere was unbearable. I realized that the two Chinese women had probably never been around so many foreigners before, nor had they been in an environment that was so unfamiliar to them This evening was not going well.

I thought of Hua's sophisticated Dian Café. "Let me take you to another place," I said. We walked the few blocks down the street in silence to Hua's place.

Hua's parents were of the Yi minority nationality from Chuxiong, east of Dali, and had opened one of the first cafés in Dali in 1985. For years, Hua had helped her parents by keeping accounts. She had graduated from a prestigious

Dali high school but had not gone on to college. In 1994 Hua decided to start her own place and opened the Dian Café. She had to pay a rent of 1,000 yuan (US$120.77) per month a full year in advance, but she was able to get a six-year contract at a fixed rate.

Hua had decorated the café so that it looked like a trendy American bistro. Across the ceiling ran a trellis from which hung dried flowers. Woven bamboo fish baskets served as lamp shades, producing wavy shadow nets on the walls. Wicker chairs encircled marble-topped tables. Indigo-dyed cloth was wrapped around menus written in both Chinese and English on parchmentlike paper. Hua had invested in a small electric oven and learned to make excellent pizza and chocolate cake.

As compared with Frank's place, the Dian was quiet. The foreigners inside drank tea or perused the large collection of English books that Hua had collected. When we walked in, Hua was playing chess with an Englishman. I introduced the two reporters to her, but she flatly refused to talk with them. I apologized for interrupting the chess game and turned to go. But the reporter in the raspberrry sweater persisted: "Why don't you want to be interviewed by us?" she sounded insulted and shocked.

"I just do not want to be interviewed right now," Hua replied firmly.

"What is the reason? There must be a reason!" the reporter nearly shouted. I almost had to push the reporters out the door. I felt bad for having created an uncomfortable situation. Outside, I told the reporters that Hua was a very capable businesswoman, but she was busy, and since it was late, she must be tired. In addition, she had already been interviewed by other newspapers, so perhaps she was tired of being interviewed. The reporters could not believe that she had refused to talk with them.

I apologized to the reporters and, thinking of my obligation to my teacher in Kunming, promised to take them to the Lhasa Café the next morning. I walked them to their hotel and then walked home to the teachers' apartment. Walking home, I realized that the two reporters were experiencing a form of culture shock. They had never been in strange-smelling and sounding cafés filled only with foreigners before. Nor were they used to interacting with minority women who openly complained of Han Chinese prejudice or flatly refused to speak with them. Their universe of knowable spaces and cultural hierarchies had been challenged.

Fortunately the following morning made up for the discomfort of the night before, and I was able to save face on behalf of myself and my teacher. I took the reporters to the Lhasa Café, and Simon, the owner, was there to talk with us in a separate side office, set apart from the grungy lonely planeteers drinking coffee and eating toast in the next room. Like Bill, Simon was Muslim-Tibetan, but instead of Bill's rakish, "bad boy" style, Simon had a smooth, professional persona. He appeared relaxed but crisp in New England style khakis, a blue cotton button-down shirt, and leather boat shoes. An expert public relations man, he moderated his style from a low, soft, fast, Yunnan dialect—to give the women a taste of the local—to a slower, perfectly toned Beijing dialect—to show them he could converse skillfully on their terms. He placed the women at ease.

Simon said that he had opened his café in 1986 and his art gallery in 1989. The reporters asked him to tell them about his past, but he evaded them: "The past is past. It is time to start a New Year. Let's look to the future." He told them about his plans to build a mini "Pompidou" art center that would include a private museum, artist's colony, and cultural exchange center. Almost conspiratorially, he revealed his idea to create an "Upper Mekong Regional Arts Association" that would include artists from Yunnan, Myanmar, Laos, Cambodia, and Vietnam. He showed them paintings that his Bai wife, Qinglan, had done in imitation of the Yunnan School's "primitivist" style. With the help of a French traveler, Simon had arranged for Qinglan to have an art exhibit in Paris earlier that year. Some of her paintings had sold for over a thousand U.S. dollars.

The two reporters were clearly impressed with Simon's style, business acumen, and inspired ideas. They were able to leave Dali and publish an article about a Muslim-Tibetan and Bai couple who were grasping the opportunities of China's reform era and who were creating ethnic and transnational bridges into the future. They could leave out their shock and discomfort in Foreigner Street the night before.

Touring the Travelers

By the late 1990s, Dali's Foreigner Street had itself become a tourist attraction for well-heeled Chinese tourists. Chinese tour guides carrying lemon-colored pennants would usher groups of twenty to thirty tourists down the street while shouting through their megaphones: "Foreigner Street is Dali's foreigner district and represents true global culture. You can see uniquely clad foreigners from all around the world eating pizza and drinking beer" (see illustration).

The Chinese tourists would raise their expensive Nikon cameras with telephoto lenses to take close-up photographs of the tie-dyed lonely planeteers drinking beer outside the backpacker cafés. The transnational travelers

Touring the travelers on Foreigner Street. (Photo by B. Notar, 2005)

squirmed and often fled inside. The tourist gaze that they had focused on the Chinese and the Bai had now been turned on them. Once they themselves became objects of tourist interest, the backpackers started to seek out what they considered to be more "off the beaten track" destinations farther north, such as the Tibetan town of "Shangri-La," formerly Zhongdian.

In 1997 the town of Zhongdian declared itself the real "Shangri-La," after the supposed site of James Hilton's 1933 romantic novel *Lost Horizon* about Europeans and Americans stranded in a remote Tibetan valley. Zhongdian was not the only town to claim it was the real Shangri-La but competed with other towns in the area such as Lijiang. But by 2002 Zhongdian was officially allowed to change its name to Shangri-La and receive national funding for tourism development. The number of tourists jumped from 170,000 in 1996, two years after the town was first "opened" to foreign tourists, to one million in 2001 (Goodman 2002, A20). Clearly, linking itself to a preexisting narrative of the place was an effective official strategy for generating tourist interest and profits.

In 1995 I had visited Zhongdian before it had changed its name and found one café catering to backpackers. A Tibetan woman, who called herself

"Mary" in English, sat down at the table to chat with me. Mary was dressed in bell bottom jeans, a jean jacket, and leather work shoes. She was waiting for a group of transnational travelers to arrive from Lijiang. I asked her what she thought of tourism in general.

"First Dali will be overrun and ruined," Mary replied. "Then people will go to Lijiang and do the same and finally come up here to Zhongdian and do the same. I like Dali. In Dali one can still find quiet places, but it is rapidly changing. Those quiet places won't last for long."

Like Frank in Dali, Mary was profiting from transnational travelers, and like Frank she pessimistically described the tourism process as a homogenizing one, where each place in succession would become like those transformed before it. While Frank had described this in global terms—"they are trying to turn all of China into America"—Mary described this in more localized terms: "people" would "do the same" to Zhongdian as they are doing to Dali.

Mary told me that she had studied English at the teacher's college in Dali. She knew Frank and often went to his café to practice her English there with the transnational travelers. One night Mary, Frank, and some friends had been talking and one of them asked the question: "Which would a beggar choose, a book or a bowl of noodles?" "A bowl of noodles, of course," Mary had replied. "But Frank said, 'Not if he had just eaten.' And then he added, 'Do you know who is more pitiful than the beggars? Those who dress in fancy clothes but have nothing in their minds. They are more beggarly than the beggars (M. *bi qigai haiyao qigai*).'" Both Frank's comment and Mary's narration of his comment expressed their ambivalence over their quest for profit and the process in which they were engaged. While Mary and Frank both sought after and profited from tourist dollars, they realized that these dollars could not walk into town by themselves: they had to be carried in by the transnational travelers. Both saw themselves as part of a process of negative transformation.

By 1999 Dali tourism officials had made a conscious decision not to direct their marketing attention to low-budget transnational travelers but to wealthier national tourists as well as Hong Kong and Taiwan "compatriots" and Overseas Chinese from Southeast Asia.[22] When I returned to visit Dali in May 2005, the No. 2 Guesthouse was gone. In its place was being built "Foreigner Street Plaza," a mini-mall of high-end boutiques that would sell "foreignness" to Chinese consumers.

Not surprisingly, there were few foreigners on Foreigner Street in 2005. As one souvenir seller put it, they had "dispersed" (M. *fensan le*) to smaller guesthouses around Dali and to other towns in Yunnan. The Dian, La Dee Da, and Mr. Dali cafés had closed. Frank had left Dali to run a café in another backpacker enclave, Yangshuo, in Guangxi province, and had left his brother Sam to run Frank's. Other cafés remained in the same location but had changed names and owners. The owners of the well-known Lhasa Café had relocated the café to another road and changed its name. Yet, the cafés and shops on Foreigner Street were still doing a thriving business, no longer to transnational travelers but to Chinese tourists, come to consume the authentic, exotic "foreign."

Conclusion

Both café owners and travelers have *perceived* changes in Dali to be part of a homogenizing process where Dali was destined to become "just like" other backpacker places. While transnational travelers purchased the Lonely Planet guidebook as a way to distance themselves from mass tourists and "get off the beaten track," their purchase of the book placed them within a circuit of re-tourism that led them to follow in the footsteps of colonial explorers before them. In fact the concept of getting "off the beaten track" in China had been used by colonial travelers since at least the 1920s.

While the lonely planeteers sought visually to consume "authentic" (i.e., culturally different) sights, they sought viscerally to consume "authentic" (i.e., familiar) foods and music from back home. This led to the formation of cafés in Dali that catered to the travelers' demands for a visceral transnational authentic. In this context, that which was "authentic" could mean either that which was culturally familiar or that which was unfamiliar.

"Foreigner Street" in Dali was not necessarily just like other backpacker enclaves, but it was a familiar-feeling place for transnational travelers and a surprisingly unfamiliar one for both the majority of Dali townspeople and the Chinese nationals who experienced it. Dali's Foreigner Street had more in common with other globalized spaces shaped by the Lonely Planet guide-books and travelers who follow the suggested routes—Khatmandu's Thamel, Bangkok's Kao San Road, Jakarta's Jalan Jaksa, and the town of Yangshuo in Guangxi province—than it did with the streets of other Bai towns close by.

The development of backpacker tourism in Dali seems especially similar to the development of backpacker tourism in Thailand, which began in the 1970s. Erik Cohen has described the "low-cost guest houses, eating places, and coffee shops" that sprung up in the northern border towns of Chiang Mai and Chiang Rai, Thailand, close to the "hill tribes" (Cohen 1996, 37), or on the island of Phuket (Cohen 1996), where travelers "sought out the company of other travelers" (ibid., 198–199). As places like Phuket developed for mass tourism, the low-budget travelers moved on to other less "touristy" places (ibid., 195–197), as travelers have begun to move from Dali to "less touristy" towns like Shangri-La to the north. In Vietnam in recent years, there has been a similar development of colonial nostalgia tourism and the opening of bars and cafés that cater particularly to transnational travelers (Kennedy and Williams 2001).

Richard Wilk has offered insight into the seeming contradiction between anthropologists' observations of the creative localization of global processes and local perceptions of global homogenization. Wilk argues that globalization has created "structures of common difference" that "are built through processes of commoditisation and objectification" (1995, 118). In this process, globalization "creates larger relations of uniformity, casting local differences in ways that, on a global scale, are predictable and surprisingly uniform" (ibid., 110). In other words, local differences may proliferate in the process of globalization, but these differences are shaped in ways that are increasingly familiar within a global framework. A café catering to transnational travelers in Dali is not the same as a café in Chiang Mai or Hanoi, but all three would be recognizable to transnational travelers. Moreover, these cafés will be more familiar to travelers than to locals. While the particular contents may vary widely, the structures are similar. As Wilk has highlighted: "If we think of the global culture as constituted by drama, we can perhaps locate the homogeneity in a common dramatic structure of encounter, while the local actors, symbols, and performances of the drama proliferate in splendid diversity. In this way, the global ecumene becomes a unifying drama, rather than a uniform culture, a constant array of goods or a constellation of meanings" (1999, 248).

Dali officials did not actively promote Dali based on *The Travels of Marco Polo*, as "Shangri-La" (Zhongdian) officials have done with the novel *Lost Horizon*. They did not need to promote Dali to transnational travelers; the Lonely Planet travel guide already did that for them. However, Dali officials *have* used one of China's most enduring movie musicals, *Five Golden Flowers*, to market Dali to national Chinese tourists and have employed one of the world's most popular martial arts novels, *Heavenly Dragons*, to draw in Overseas Chinese tourists and a younger generation of mainland Chinese. Whereas this chapter has examined the transnational travelers' ironic search for a place that is "authentic," both visually different and viscerally like home, the following chapter investigates national tourist quests for the mimetic, where they hope to discover Dali as a place that mirrors its representation in a movie musical.

CHAPTER 3

Five Golden Flowers
Utopian Nostalgia and Local Longing

*The twentieth century began with a futuristic utopia and
ended with nostalgia.*

(Boym 2001, xiv)

As usual, the television set was on in the Yao family living room. Every night after dinner, Mr. Yao, two of his daughters, some neighbor children, and I would sit on bamboo settees in the living room and gaze at the screen. The television had been placed in a position of honor against the west wall, atop a wooden rice chest, next to where the family genealogical scroll was hung during the seventh lunar month, when the ancestral spirits returned to visit.

This evening, however, the living room was crowded with other villagers, and we were not watching a Hong Kong martial arts series, a Singaporean family drama, or an old James Bond adventure—the usual television fare. Instead, someone in the village had brought over a video cassette player so that I could watch *Five Golden Flowers (Wuduo Jinhua)*, a Chinese movie musical set in the village almost four decades earlier. I had purchased a copy in the provincial capital, and Mr. Yao had invited people over so that I could hear their reflections on it.

When it was first released in 1959 for the tenth anniversary of the founding of the People's Republic, *Five Golden Flowers* celebrated Chinese socialist modernization, agricultural collectivization, and women's liberation through a boy-meets-girl(s) love story amongst the Bai people. The beautiful scenery, romantic songs, and buoyant mood captured the hearts of audiences nationwide. In addition to being projected throughout mainland China, *Five Golden Flowers* played to sold-out crowds in Hong Kong and was released in forty-six countries throughout the Soviet bloc, a veritable "bloc buster" (Su Yun 1985, 38; *CCSZ*, 64–65). It went on to win Silver Eagle awards for best director (Wang Jiayi) and best actress (Yang Likun) at the Second Asia-Africa Film Festival in Cairo in 1960 (Su Yun 1985, 38; *CYWN*, 113). During the Cultural Revolution, along with most other films, it was banned as an "antisocialist poisonous weed" (M. *ducao pian*) for its romanticism and even criticized by

Chairman Mao's wife, Jiang Qing; but in 1978, at the start of China's reform era, it had been "rehabilitated" and re-released.[1]

While my initial interest in showing the film to Dali villagers was to listen to their comments on representations of gender and culture in the film—how did they think the film depicted Bai minority women? Bai customs?—the villagers were not as interested in talking about these subjects. Instead they directed my attention to something else. "Look *behind* the characters," they said. "What do you see?"

What did the villagers want me to see? It was not at all apparent. In our discussion that day and in subsequent conversations, I began to see the film from their perspective.

Although the film was produced as a fictional, symbolic account of life in Dali during the Great Leap Forward (1957–1961), I learned that older Dali villagers viewed it as a historical account of their place. By the late 1990s they came to view the fictional film as a documentary of the changes in their village between 1959 and the present.

As I spent more time conducting research on reform era changes, I discovered that, in contrast to the older Bai villagers, others had differing views on and interpretations of the film. In the revolutionary era, the film was originally used by national officials to exemplify Dali as a model socialist utopia. Now, in the reform era, local officials use the film to market Dali as an ideal vacation destination.

How is it that a film intended as political propaganda to glorify the Great Leap Forward, an experiment in agricultural collectivization that led to one of the largest famines in modern history, came to be used to promote tourism? I suggest in this chapter that the current journey of millions of tourists to Dali is motivated not only by exotic fantasies, but also by a utopian nostalgia for "a return to something . . . never had" (Harper [1955] 1966, 26), a reflection on a dream of socialist utopia during the current time of intensified cynicism.

In chapter 2 we saw that transnational travelers to Dali, who followed in the footsteps of colonial explorers before them, expressed a colonial nostalgia that was shaped by the Lonely Planet travel guide. For transnational travelers, Dali represented an "authentic" place supposedly "off-the-beaten-track," yet one that they feared was destined to become like other globalized places. The nostalgia of Chinese tourists I will discuss in this chapter is similarly shaped by a popular representation. However, the national tourists do not expect Dali to be a culturally "authentic" place per se but a place that mimics its filmic representation.

Both representations—the Lonely Planet guide and the film—have had

Revolutionary romanticism revisited: *Five Golden Flowers* on video compact disk. (Hubei yinxiang yishu chubanshe, [1959])

material after-effects on Dali as a place, the former leading to the creation of Foreigner Street, and the latter, as we will see, leading to the reshaping of a place called Butterfly Spring. Travelers and tourists are drawn to Dali through popular narratives that depict an exotic place, yet in coming to Dali, they reshape the place itself. As anthropologist Margaret Rodman has highlighted, "Places come into being through praxis, not just through narratives" (1992, 642). The millions of tourist bodies transform the place they expect to find.

Bringing in the Borderlands

Five Golden Flowers vividly promoted the successes of China's first decade of socialist modernization. Collectivization, massive labor projects, and agricultural mechanization provide the backdrop for a romance between a Bai minority maiden, Jinhua (Golden Flower), and a Bai youth, Ah Peng. In the film, socialist modernity celebrates, and does not erase, borderland difference. Along with images of modernization, the film also shows images of more "traditional" life in Dali, in particular, fairs and weddings. For example, the film opens with vivid scenes of Dali's famous Third Month Fair—young Bai women in headdresses gaily shop for herbal medicines and young men in turbans race horses. This contradistinction between the "traditional" and the "modern" has been a key formula of nation-building (Hobsbawm 1983), particularly for colonial states and national empires. As Robert Foster has observed in the process of colonial modernization in Papua New Guinea, "what takes the place of assimilation—the replacement of the primitive with the modern—is juxtaposition, a complementarity of differences made viable by a new structural equation: modernity is to tradition as economy is to culture" (2002, 47). This juxtaposition plays out clearly in the film. While the film extols socialist modernity through the productive lives of the commune members, it also pokes fun at modern technology: at the moment when Ah Peng and Golden Flower need the telephone the most, the line goes dead. Despite the fact that the film was intended as a political tool to celebrate the tenth anniversary of the People's Republic, it is an exuberant comedy of errors.

When it was produced in 1959, the film *Five Golden Flowers* was not an anomaly but appeared within a context of broader symbolic and political interest in the borderlands. Between 1959 and 1960, the years marking the tenth anniversary of the People's Republic, films about borderland minority peoples became one of the most significant film genres, accounting for 15 percent of all films made.[2] Between 1950 and 1959, in addition to *Five Golden Flowers*, the Changchun Film Studio alone made seven other feature-length films about minorities: four about Mongolians, one about a Korean woman soldier, and one each about two other Yunnan nationalities, the Lahu and the Wa.[3] Between 1960 and 1964 the studio made an additional five films on minority nationalities: the popular *Third Sister Liu (Liu Sanjie,* 1960), based on a Zhuang nationality folktale; *Glacier Guests (Bingshan shang de laike,* 1963), about the Tajik; as well as three others about the Jingpo (Kachin), Qiang, and Yi.[4] There was also a series of state documentary films made about the borderland peoples, produced by the Beijing Scientific and Educational Film studio, the Chinese Academy of Sciences, and the Institute of Nationality Studies.[5]

Many of the feature films and the documentaries showed the suffering of and class conflict among minorities in the "old society" (pre-1949) under evil landlords, headmen, and chieftains. If the feature films were based on folk legends, they sometimes ended tragically, as when the heroine Ashima (of the film by the same name) dies trying to escape a lecherous headman. If they were set in the revolutionary era, they would often show the ways in which the People's Liberation Army or the Communist Party made life better than before. Although clearly propaganda films, most are not dull, for they portray exotic settings and costumes, and involve intrigue or romance (see Clark 1987a, 1987b; Loh 1984; Marion 1997; Yau 1989). The minority film genre overall represents "traditional exoticization in service of the state" (Gladney 1995, 165) and confirms "Han cultural hegemony" over the borderlands (Yingjing Zhang 2002, 165). Similar to other projects, for example in Vietnam, where minority identity has been appropriated and "nationalized" (Taylor and Jonsson 2003), representing the Chinese borderlands through film was one of the ways to control and neutralize borderland difference (Mueggler 1991, 207–208).

However, *Five Golden Flowers* differs from many of the other minority films in that it does not show suffering in the past, class conflict, or the Communist Party as a savior in the present. It simply portrays Bai minority people working hard and living romantically during the Great Leap Forward (a time of great suffering for people in Dali, as we will see below). This romantic exuberance would later cause problems for the film's crew and cast, particularly for its female star Yang Likun, when the film was criticized during the Cultural Revolution (see Notar, n.d. b).

In using film as a means to spread revolutionary ideology, the Chinese Communist Party had grasped well the political possibilities of "art in the age of mechanical reproduction" (Benjamin [1936] 1969). Film offered the potential to be produced in one place but to be reproduced and sent to many places for viewing. It further offered standardization of language, culture, and ideology—although in the borderlands and in other non-Mandarin-speaking areas, interpreters had to translate standard Mandarin into other languages. Still, if the Party could control production and distribution, it could better control those representations to which the population had access.

Unlike pre-1949 China, where films were seen only by urban audiences, after 1949 rural audiences became film spectators as well (Clark 1987a). The Party used mobile projectionists to show films even in remote villages at the borderlands, bringing the nation together through film (T. Chen 2003). In 1951 only one in ten persons in Yunnan province viewed one film per year, but by 1959, owing to nearly four hundred mobile projection teams, every person in the province saw at least three to four films per year. Film had become the "most popular of the arts."[6] We might describe this as a form of celluloid socialism, which helped to create the "imagined community" (Anderson [1983] 1991) of the nation.

It is not surprising that a film genre featuring China's borderland peoples developed in the first decade of the People's Republic. Since the new Chinese nation was built on the body of the former Qing empire (1636–1911) (Hostetler 2001), the borderland peoples had to be incorporated politically if the borders of the national empire were to be retained. Symbolic representation of this incorporation further reinforced political incorporation. In this process, the Chinese Communists drew on national-imperial imagery that had been created during the Republic of China (1911–1949), which the Communists had overthrown in 1949.

That the film was called *Five Golden Flowers* and not three or four golden flowers was significant. In classical Chinese cosmography, the number five was key to a conceptualization of the natural and cultural universe: the five basic elements (wood, fire, earth, metal, water), five directions (east, south, center, west, north), five colors (green, red, yellow, white, black), five smells (goatish, burning, fragrant, rank, rotten), and five flavors (sour, bitter, sweet, acrid, salty) were all considered to correspond. This system of correspondences located human bodies within the cosmos and was used in guiding everything from medicinal prescription to imperial sacrifice to the heavens (de Bary, Chan, and Watson [1960] 1969, 198–199). In this cosmography, a Han Chinese center (yellow) was imagined to be encircled by the so-called barbarians of the four directions, which were symbolically associated with different colors, the eastern Yi (green), the Western Rong (white), the southern Man (red), and the northern Di (black).[7] While these names for "barbarians" may have at one point referred to specific groups, they later came to represent symbolically the four divisions of the world outside of a fifth imagined Han Chinese geocosmic center (Notar 1992, 19–20; Prusek 1971, 66–67).

After the collapse of the Qing dynasty in 1911, national founding father Sun Zhongshan (Sun Yat-sen) and his Nationalist Party established the Republic of China, also called the "Republic of Five Nationalities" (Harrell 2001b, 29). The term "nationality" (M. *minzu*) was borrowed from the Japanese term *minzoku*, for "nation," "race," and "people" (ibid., 29; L. Liu 1995, 292, 345; Mackerras 1994, 53–55). Use of the term distanced the new Chinese nation-state from the former empire by imagining a nation to be a group of people distinguished by heredity rather than by culture. Yet at the same time the use of "five nationalities" continued the imperial cosmographic conception of a five-part division of human geography. The first flag of the Republic of China illustrated this national-imperial cosmography by showing five horizontal bars, each bar representing one of China's "peoples"—Manchus, Han, Mongolians, Tibetans, and Hui Muslims.[8]

Once the Chinese Communists defeated the Nationalists and declared the establishment of the People's Republic of China in 1949, they sought to maintain the bounds of national empire. In their consolidation of the borderlands, the Communists continued the use of the term *minzu* for "nationality" but labeled the new nation a *duo minzu*, "multinationality," nation (Harrell 2001b, 31), which in the United States might be translated as a "multiethnic" nation. Even though the new nation was now considered a multinationality nation and no longer one of just five nationalities, the title of the film *Five Golden Flowers*, each "flower" representing one of five Bai women in the film, would recall the earlier five-part symbolic national-imperial imagery of the borderlands among urban audiences. If the number five recalled the symbolism of the "five peoples" of the borderlands, the rest of the film's title, "golden flowers," would conjure a long-standing stereotype of the people of the borderlands as closer to nature, even raw in their supposed lack of civilization (see Diamond 1995; Schein 2002).

The film *Five Golden Flowers* appeared at a time not only of symbolic, but also of ethnographic interest in the borderlands. In 1956 the Nationalities Affairs Commission of the State Council (M. *guowu yuan minzu shiwu weiyuanhui*) and the Nationalities Committee of the National People's Congress (M. *renda minzu weiyuanhui*) had organized research teams to classify the borderland peoples. Although this vast ethnographic project was "presented as primarily a scholarly undertaking," there was "little doubt that a major purpose of the study would be to provide information necessary for the further implementation of socialist reforms" (Dreyer 1976, 142). Using Stalin's criteria for determining a nationality as their guide—common language, territory, economy, and psychology—hundreds of anthropologists, archaeologists, economists, historians, linguists, and experts in art, music, and literature were sent to nationality areas to investigate.[9]

The Chinese Communist effort to classify and control the borderland peoples resembled previous "civilizing projects," namely, the Confucian imperial and Christian colonial ones.[10] As a national empire, the new socialist state was similar to a colonial state in its desire to classify the population, for classification "shaped the way in which the colonial state imagined its dominion—the nature of the human beings it ruled, the geography of its domain, and the legitimacy of its ancestry" (Anderson [1983] 1991, 164). Yet the project, like other projects in Thailand and Vietnam, was particular to the nation-state in its scope and claims to "scientific" classification (Keyes 2002; see also Taylor and Jonsson 2002).

In 1956 Dali was recognized to be the heartland of the Bai nationality (Baizu) and was officially designated as the "Dali Bai Nationality Autonomous Prefecture" (Dali Baizu Zizhi Zhou) (DZNJ 1990, 26). Most of the in-depth research in the Dali area was conducted a few years later, in 1959, the same year that Five Golden Flowers was produced and released.[11] Two of the researchers appear as characters in the film: an artist and an ethnomusicologist come to collect the sights and sounds of Dali. These two characters serve as a vehicle of "touristic gazes" (Yau 1989, 120; see also Urry [1990] 1994) through which the urban Chinese film-viewing audience could vicariously travel to Dali and see the Bai people. Like Dorothy in The Wizard of Oz (MGM, 1939), the Chinese characters wandering in a strange land allow the urban audience to see what they see and hear what they hear. The presence of the ethnomusicologist adds incentive for the characters to sing "folk songs" (in Mandarin Chinese, not Bai), which he records. The artist brings the long, familiar tradition of painting to the new medium of film, creating representations within representations.

Five Golden Flowers is a feel-good film that celebrates work, love, and communalism. It captures "revolutionary realism" in its depiction of the work of the time: hundreds of laborers cart dirt to build a reservoir, women gather seaweed for fertilizer, men and women smelt metal at a "backyard furnace." It celebrates "revolutionary romanticism" through the relationship between Assistant Commune Head Golden Flower and Ah Peng.[12] It salutes cooperative spirit through these two new-day folk heroes who help their comrades out in any way they can. It is this revolutionary romanticism and cooperative spirit that I suggest evoke nostalgia for contemporary national tourists in the cynical and competitive context of the reform era. Between 1984 and 1990 over half a million national tourists traveled to Dali (DSZ, 908). By 1992 national tourist visits for that year alone had risen to 592,905 (DZNJ 1993, 157). By 1995 this number had jumped to 2.3 million, in 1998 to nearly 4.3 million, in 1999 to 5.4 million, and by 2004, including transnational tourists, a record 5.95 million traveled to Dali.[13]

Utopian Nostalgia and the One-Day Tour

It was a clear, calm day in May 1995. The snow-capped peaks of Mount Cang shone and large Lake Er glistened in the early light. I walked through the cobblestone streets of Dali to the history museum, where I was to meet the tour bus. Shop owners were starting to take down the wooden shutters on the old shop fronts and open the metal grates on the new ones. At the museum I waited with two middle-aged women from Sichuan. They were quiet, their body posture turned inward. After having lived in Dali for over a year, I had become used to the expressive body language and boisterous joking style of most older and middle-aged Bai women.

A few more tourists joined us. A tour director with two leather cases slung over his arm and a sport shirt unzipped to expose his bare chest appeared and told us to get on a waiting bus. There was no one on the bus to welcome us—we were to meet up with the other tourists at the southern end of Lake Er in the larger administrative town of Xiaguan.

The bus driver sounded the horn repeatedly the entire twenty-five kilometers from Dali to Xiaguan, not only to warn villagers on foot, bicycle, horse cart, and tractor to get out of his way, it seemed, but also to show off a little. After having had so many of these tour buses blaze by me while walking and biking along the main road over the past year, it felt odd to be finally on one of them.

A group of young people in tight white, pink, and pale green polyester "Bai" attire greeted us at the pier—the boys beating cymbals and blowing horns, the girls clapping. We were the last group to arrive. There were already many people on board the large, white, three-tiered ship.

The ship's horn bellowed and we moved out into the river that leads to the southwestern tip of Lake Er, past a factory that smelled of chlorine, past some solitary fishermen floating in inner tubes, past groups of fishermen and women in small green metal boats, past old wooden sailing junks transporting gravel from the eastern shore of the lake to be used on Dali-side tourism construction sites.

Chinese tourists strolled on the ship's lower deck, relaxed in the lounge, and sang songs in the dining-karaoke room furbished with two video screens and two microphones. The tourists looked surprised to see a sole young foreigner (M. *xiao laowai*) aboard. I chatted with different groups and discovered that they were from all over China and their tour of Dali was part of different travel trajectories—Shanghai timber barons on their way to Tibetan forests, a northern couple on their honeymoon, Cantonese factory managers in the province for a meeting.

I peeked into a large room on the second deck. Approximately sixty tourists were seated in a semicircle in a low-ceilinged, carpeted room, with glass tea tables in front of them. The first of the day's "three-course tea" (M. *san dao cha*) performances had just begun. I recalled that one of my Bai teachers at the

Yunnan Nationalities Institute in Kunming had told me that the "three-course tea" was an "invented tradition" for the tourists (see Hobsbawm 1983). "Those three kinds of tea had been drunk previously—sweet, strong, bitter-sweet, but not exactly in the same way and not consecutively," she told me.

Young Bai teenage men in white pants with sea-green trim and sea-green vests, cloth sandals, white turbans, and tambourines began to perform, starting with a Mandarin "folk" song from the film *Five Golden Flowers*:

One time each year Third Month Fair	*Yinian yihui Sanyue Jie*
People arrive from everywhere	*Simian bafang you ren lai*
All nationalities greet with song	*Gezu renmin qi huan chang*
Race horses, sing songs, buy and sell.	*Saima changge zuo maimai.*

On this day there would be three morning performances. During the peak season of the Third Month Fair, when thousands of national and transnational tourists descend on Dali and the ship fills to capacity, there would be ten morning performances. The Third Month Fair (B. *sawa zi*; M. *sanyue jie*), held on the mountainside above Dali, starts on the fifteenth day of the third lunar month, which usually falls in April, and has been a horse trading and Tibetan medicine market for at least a millennium (Yuan n.d.). Just as the film *Five Golden Flowers* opens with scenes of the fair, so too would the performance start with songs from these opening scenes. The performers assumed that the tourists on board were familiar with the film and its characters. The actors called themselves "Ah Peng" and the actresses called themselves "Jinhua" (Golden Flower).

The performance followed the film's narrative: starting with the meeting of the protagonists, Ah Peng, a helpful village youth, and Assistant Commune Head Golden Flower on the opening day of the Third Month Fair; followed by Ah Peng's comedic efforts to find "his" Golden Flower among a garden of other village maidens named Golden Flower; and finally Ah Peng's and Assistant Commune Head Golden Flower's romantic rendezvous a year later at Butterfly Spring.[14]

Golden Flower:

Ai, nice views of Dali's Third Month Fair	*Ai, Dali Sanyue hao fengguang ai*
By Butterfly Spring I comb my hair	*Hudie Chuan bian hao shuzhuang*
Butterflies come to sip honey from the flowers	*Hudie feilai cai huami yue*
Little sister combs her hair for what affair?	*A Mei shu tou wei na zhuang*

Ah Peng:

Ai, the clear waters of Butterfly Spring	*Ai, Hudie Chuan shui qing you qing*
Toss in a stone to test its depth	*Diu ge shitou shi shui shen*
I pick a flower but I fear for thorns	*You xin zhai hua pa you ci*
Wavering, my heart is uncertain . . .	*Paihui xin bu ding ah yin yue . . .*

Out of all the song lyrics, these stanzas seemed most pleasingly famil-iar to the national tourists, and they smiled and sang or hummed along with the performers. The film obviously evoked strong emotions for them. Several tourists told me, "The *min feng* [popular sentiment] has not been the same since the 1950s. In the 1950s people's relations were more pure, and fake things were few, but the Cultural Revolution changed all that." The tourists were idealizing a time before both the turmoil of the Cultural Revolution and what they considered the fakery of the present reform era (Notar 2006).

Memory of the film evoked a nostalgia among the tourists that was part of a larger utopian nostalgia in China (see Rofel 1999). Su Yun, vice-director of the Changchun studio in 1960 and director of the studio after 1979, reflected on *Five Golden Flowers* after its re-release: "After seeing the film, it was like listening to emotionally expressive symphonic music, like drinking a cup of strong, pure, fragrant wine. One could cherish one's memories free of worry" (Su Yun 1985, 38).

Tourist nostalgia for the film springs from a juxtaposition of the film im-ages and the context of the current reform era. As Chinese metropolitans con-front the rush and insecurity of present market reforms—job layoffs, inflation, rising crime, counterfeits, and fake commodities (see Notar 2006)—the film represents a romance of a collective dream of socialism that was never real-ized. Nostalgia thus becomes "a means of establishing a point of critique in the present, calling to judgment the failures of the state and the mysteries of the market" (Bissell 2005, 239; see also Rofel 1999). As Ralph Harper writes: "Nostalgia is neither illusion nor repetition; it is a return to something we have never had. And yet the very force of it is just that in it the lost is recog-nized, is familiar" ([1955] 1966, 26). Harper's definition of nostalgia as a "re-turn to something we have never had" captures the sense of nostalgia as re-turn to a previously imagined experience.

Nostalgia is not new to China. At least since the Han dynasty (206 B.C. to A.D. 219), the terms *huaigu,* "thinking of ancient persons and events," and *huaijiu,* "thinking of past events and ancient persons," have been used in a melancholic way (Luo 1986, 7a: 786, 793). Since the Song dynasty (A.D. 960–

1279), the term *huaixiang,* "thinking of one's old homeland *(guxiang)*" (ibid., 791), has been employed in a way that approximates the meaning of nostalgia as used in 1688 by a Swiss doctor, Johannes Hofer, to describe the homesickness of "exiles far from their native land" who "languished and wasted away."[15]

Yet it would be a mistake to assume that the nostalgia of the Han and Song dynasties continues in China as the nostalgia of today. As others have observed, nostalgia is a product of a particular present: "its forms, meanings, and effects shift with the context—it depends on where the speaker stands in the landscape of the present" (K. Stewart 1988, 227). Moreover, nostalgia is a means of making sense of and "critically framing the present" (Bissell 2005, 216; see also Battaglia 1995; Nadel-Klein 2003, 169; Rofel 1999, 137). The nostalgias expressed in contemporary China are a reflection of current conditions there.

Chinese tourist nostalgia for the film *Five Golden Flowers* is somewhat analogous to American film audience fascination with the Western film genre, which reflects "a desire to get out of modernity without leaving it altogether; . . . to relive those thrilling days of yesteryear, but only because we are absolutely assured that those days are out of reach" (Rosenblatt 1973, 23).[16] I suggest here that Chinese tourist nostalgia is not for the time of the Great Leap Forward itself, but for the romantic dream of socialist utopia that the film depicted. Metropolitan Chinese tourists would not want to turn back the clock to 1959, but they seek the luxury of dwelling in the unrealized utopian dream that was promoted in the first heady days of the Great Leap.

This utopian nostalgia may be thought of as a form of what Fred Davis has termed "collective nostalgia": "Collective nostalgia . . . refers to that condition in which the symbolic objects are of a highly public, widely shared and familiar character, i.e., those symbolic resources from the past which can under proper conditions trigger off wave upon wave of nostalgic feeling in millions of persons at the same time" (1981, 222). Davis points out that in the twentieth century, mass media has played an increasing role in defining and shaping this collective nostalgia.[17] *Five Golden Flowers* provides an example of one such mass media event that shapes a collective Chinese utopian nostalgia in an era of market modernity.

This utopian nostalgia is not unique to China. Cultural critic and former Soviet exile Svetlana Boym has observed that after the dissolution of the Soviet Union, Russians of an older generation have expressed nostalgia during the sweeping economic changes that have left many in Russia without jobs, health care, or housing. Boym, however, fears that this utopian nostalgia can become "totalitarian nostalgia," a nostalgia for Stalin's state and "the longing for a total reconstruction of a past that is gone" (Boym 1994, 287).[18] Contra Boym, Chinese tourists in Dali did not express a desire to reconstruct the past; their nostalgia harks back to a romantic and unrealized dream of a socialist utopia during the current time of intense market competition.

Chinese cultural critic Geremie Barmé has drawn on Boym's idea of "totalitarian nostalgia" to describe "the revenant Mao cult of the early 1990s" and "a crude retro Cultural Revolution longing" (1999, 317). However, he notes that this "totalitarian nostalgia" has not been limited to these phenomena but more broadly has been "a nostalgia for a style of thought and public discourse" and "a nostalgia for a language of denunciation that offered simple solutions to complex problems" (ibid.).

"Totalitarian nostalgia" might be applicable to phenomena such as the construction of a revolutionary theme park in Mao Zedong's hometown of Shaoshan, in Hunan province, where tourists can follow in the footsteps of the "great helmsman" and the People's Liberation Army (Dutton [1998] 2000, 223; Han 2001). Or it might be applied to the former sent-down-youths (M. *zhiqing*) who now take return tours to the countryside (Guobin Yang 2003) and the "Cultural Revolution" restaurants in Kunming and other cities in the country (even around the world, in London, for example), where nostalgic former sent-down-youths can eat food reminiscent of hardship days.

Even in these cases, however, I am skeptical whether the term "totalitarian nostalgia" fits. Barmé posits that people "could indulge in Mao nostalgia because due to bans on remembering the past, they had forgotten its horrors" (1999, 321). People in Dali sometimes evoked Mao's stand against corruption and foreign imperialism as a means to critique current official corruption and what they saw as "selling out" to foreign corporations. But in evoking Mao, they had certainly not forgotten any of the horrors of the past (as we will see below). They were strategically using Mao as a symbol to critique the present. Likewise, it is possible for people to want to dwell on their hardships during the Cultural Revolution without wanting to reinstate any of the totalitarian practices of that time. Chinese tourists in Dali could safely indulge in a nostalgia for an imagined socialist utopia of the Great Leap because it was a dream of a romantic "return to something never had." Moreover, their nostalgia was not only melancholic; it was also "a romance with one's own fantasy" (Boym 2001, xiii) of the exotic.

Avoiding Authenticity

Two of the actors on board ship recognized me from a village wedding celebration a few weeks earlier, when a friend of theirs had married into the village in which I was living. I asked if he had adjusted to life at his mother-in-law's house. They shrugged and smiled, and invited me to sit down to talk with them. Two of the actresses were also sitting there.

It was not until the actors started to change their shirts and I heard female laughter from a room separated by a curtain opposite that I realized that I was sitting in the male performers' dressing room. This was an unusual situation. In the village I had little contact with men between the ages of twenty and fifty unless I was accompanied by my sixty-year-old research assistant, Teacher Du. But as long as the two other young women were sitting there, it seemed all right to stay and chat.

The performers told me that they had been recruited locally for their singing and dancing abilities, and had been working on the boat for three years. They were trained by Mr. Yang, who seemed about thirty, but it was difficult to tell because his face was covered with theater make-up—rouge, lipstick, eyeshadow.

Whereas I had assumed that singing and dancing for tourists every day would be exasperating, the young performers told me that they enjoyed their work. After all, it was much better than the back-breaking work of plowing, planting, harvesting, or shoveling gravel. And it was more fun than fishing. They saw the tourism-related work as both easier and more glamorous than the fishing and farming work of their parents. Plus, they had fun joking around backstage.

What the young people found odd about their performance work, however, was that they did not have much interaction with the tourists. Only rarely would a tourist make an effort to talk with them. Occasionally, a tourist would ask for their address and send a photograph. The tourists seemed to view the performers, like the place, as sights. In fact, the tourists seemed to view the young Bai performers as if they were characters in a film, to be gazed at and listened to but not to be engaged with in any meaningful form of human interaction.

The One-Day Tour was structured in such as way as to minimize any interaction between tourists and locals, except local tour guides. The tourists were visiting Dali because of the film and were not in search of any "authentic" experience with real Bai people. In fact, I observed that at brief moments of attempted interaction for souvenir sales and purchases, the tourists either avoided locals or fought with them.

When the ship docked at the northwest corner of the lake, the tourists, myself included, scrambled off the boat to the sound of the performers' cymbals, drums, and horns. Once on land, our guides led us to the buses that would take us to legendary Butterfly Spring. As we walked across the gravel parking lot, small groups of Bai women rushed forward to sell us souvenirs: embroidered pouches; indigo tie-dye scarves, hats, and table cloths; silvery bracelets, earrings, and necklaces. The women tried their best to surround and conquer but to no avail. The tourists kept moving steadfastly toward the bus, doing their best to ignore the women as if they did not exist.[19]

Romantic Reembodiment

Leaving behind the souvenir sellers, we moved along the tree-lined path toward Butterfly Spring. Excitement grew. This was the place where the film characters Ah Peng and Assistant Commune Head Golden Flower had first exchanged mementos of their love for one another and the place where they had finally found one another again. We were approaching the site of one of the most romantic scenes in Chinese film history. Hundreds of us converged on the spring simultaneously.

We entered a clearing at the center of which there appeared to be a small pond surrounded by a rock wall—the spring! A large tree with a crooked branch reached out over the water. We jostled with other tour groups to get closer.

In front of the rock wall separating us from the spring itself stood pairs of people. Each member of the pair was dressed in a different costume, immediately recognizable. One wore the costume of Ah Peng—a white turban and a black vest; the other was dressed in the costume of Assistant Commune Head Golden Flower—a multilayered headdress, a red vest, and an apron. The tourists laughed heartily and eagerly surged forward to rent costumes. Some young male tourists cross-dressed as Golden Flower, and some middle-aged women cross-dressed as Ah Peng. Camera shutters clicked.

This was the most spirited moment of the tour. The national tourists had reached their utopian destination, a place where it was possible to cross nationality and gender boundaries. It was a moment when they could play at being exotic minorities, play at being a different gender, or play at being a movie star. Just as the non-Bai actors and actresses had done for the original film,

National tourists transperforming for the cameras. (Photos by B. Notar, 1995)

the tourists dressed up as Bai and played parts for the cameras. It was a moment of transperformance, when the tourists could seem to become something other than they were.[20]

It was a ludic moment of play as well as a political moment (see Errington and Gewertz 1989). This kind of "mimickry" (Taussig 1993), "cross-ethnicking" (Robertson 1995, 975), "racial reembodiment" (Carlson 2002, 215), "ethnic masquerade," or "ethnic drag" (Sieg 2002, 218–219) is familiar from colonial and national imperial contexts, where public play at being someone else occurs in a context of inequality. During the time of British imperial expansion, British sailors mimicked native islanders (Taussig 1993, 76–78); during their conquest of Southeast Asia, Japanese troops "cross-ethnicked" as native Burmese (Robertson 1995, 975). North Americans of European descent have long dressed up to "play Indian" while Native American communities were being decimated (Deloria 1998). German hobbyists have "played Indian" in a romance of German colonialism, a form of anti-Americanism, a denial of their own genocidal past, or an escape from modernity (Carlson 2002; Lutz 2002; Sieg 2002; Zantop 2002).

In these instances of transperformance, internal or external Others who are impersonated or reembodied are not considered actual people but symbolic representatives. It is a form of "symbolic identification" where powerfully dominant groups attempt to "identify . . . with the other precisely at a point at which he is inimitable, at the point which eludes resemblance" (Zizek 1989, 109). This romantic reembodiment and symbolic identification can be seen as more about a sense of self than a sense of another (see Handler and Saxton 1988, 256).

Romantic reembodiment is not new to China. Elite men and women of the Tang dynasty, between the seventh and ninth centuries, dressed as Iranians in leopard-skin hats and tight-fitting bodices. Some Tang women cross-dressed in Turkish-style men's hats, riding clothes and boots. Other aristocrats went a step further, such as the prince Li Chengqian, son of emperor Taizong, who lived and entertained guests in Turkish sky-blue tents (Schafer [1963] 1985, 29). Unlike Tang times, reform era China is not a period of imperial conquest of "barbarian" lands. But it is the time of a vast national empire and of intensified "commercial expansion" into the borderlands (ibid., 30).

Of course, subordinated groups may parody dominant groups, but this usually happens in private, not public spaces (see Basso 1979; Lavie 1990). Or, if done in public, such parody occurs in contexts of carnival, where roles may be temporarily, symbolically, inverted (Bakhtin 1984). Moreover, while the tourists can "cross-ethnic" as a form of play, Bai villagers *must* cross-dress as a long-term strategy for achieving modernity through assimilation to dominant norms. When young Bai men and women leave the village to go to school in town or to work elsewhere in the province or the country, they cannot dress in village style—layered headdresses, silver and jade earrings, wool vests, aprons, embroidered sashes and shoes for women; or wide cotton pants and long, front-clasping cotton shirts and straw sandals for men. They don lycra stretch pants and fluorescent nylon jackets (women), or polyester suits and pointy shoes or sneakers and t-shirts (men). Chinese tourists can play at dressing down in "Bai style," whereas Bai youths, if they hope to appear modern, must dress up in an assimilated "Han" or globalized style.

Young Bai women and men, like the young Hui Muslim women whom Maris Gillette interviewed in the city of Xi'an, did not see this consumption of "Han style" attire as oppressive but as an opportunity to participate in modernity (Gillette 2000, 220). Yet it would be difficult for a Bai village woman to go look for a job in the city wearing Bai village clothes and not be romanticized as a "Golden Flower" or stereotyped as a "country bumpkin" (M. *tu baozi,* literally "earth bun"). While young Bai are enjoying dressing up in "Han style," they do not have the option not to do so if they are to be considered modern by the dominant culture.

A Mimetic Place

Soon savvy to reform era marketing techniques, local officials realized that national tourists were drawn to Dali because of the film *Five Golden Flowers,* and they began actively to use the film to promote Dali in tourism and investment literature, calling Dali in English "the Native Land of the Golden Flowers" or "the Home of the Golden Flower" (although most English speakers would not know the film reference) (M. Jinhua Guxiang) (Ou Yansheng et al. 1990, 1; Yang Yuan Jun n.d.). Officials went a step further and attempted to ensure that part of Dali as a place matched the tourists' film-framed expectations.

A few weeks after I participated in the one-day tour, my research assistant, Teacher Du, and I returned to Butterfly Spring to interview the vice-director. Vice-Director Tao, a pleasant man in his thirties, had been a former student of Teacher Du and welcomed us into his spacious reception room of marble floors and marble-topped tables. After pouring us tea, he told us that in 1978, with the start of China's reform era, Butterfly Spring had been made into a park. Then in 1982 the Dali Municipal Development Committee invested four million yuan (US$1.3 million at the official exchange rate, approximately US$400,000 at unofficial rates) to develop the park into a tourist site. The committee purchased land use rights from the village next door and relocated the ancestral tombs that surrounded the spring. He noted that the twenty-four members of the park staff who live on site sometimes felt a bit uneasy at night, since they are sleeping atop a former graveyard.

In 1994 the committee authorized construction of a Butterfly Museum and a state-of-the-art tourist toilet in the shape of a butterfly. Vice-Director Tao led us from the reception room into the Butterfly Museum, where dead butterflies and collages of dead butterflies adorned the walls and glass cases. He showed us the tourist toilet—"You can try it out later"—and then took us down to the spring itself.

It was late afternoon, past the peak hours, and only a few groups of tourists were posing and photographing by the side of the spring. Vice-Director Tao surreptitiously pointed to the large tree branch that reached out over the water. "This tree served as the model for the one that Golden Flower sat on in the movie," he explained, "but the main branch died. In order to maintain the feel of the spring, we reconstructed the branch. The branch is now a fiberglass one, covered with real bark." The importance of tourist nostalgia for the film was revealed in the vice-director's efforts to maintain the actual site so that it resembled as closely as possible the site as it appeared in the film: the actual site was to mimic its visual representation. Butterfly Spring as a place was supposed to match Butterfly Spring as represented in the film.[21]

Vice-Director Tao's efforts to re-create the tree branch from the film *Five Golden Flowers* bring to mind Stephen Fjellman's discussion of the Swiss Family Robinson tree in Florida's Walt Disney World, which inspired the title for his book on that theme park, *Vinyl Leaves*. Fjellman observes with amazement that "we have a fake tree holding a fake treehouse, representing a fake story . . . in an amusement park visited by 30 million people a year, most of who are, like myself, enchanted" (1992, 2). Whether the tree at Walt Disney World and the tree at Butterfly Spring are "fake" or "real" is not as important as whether or not the trees can evoke the feeling of the films that motivate tourists to journey to these fantasized places.

Despite Vice-Director Tao's best efforts, tourists with whom I spoke were still dissatisfied that the actual Dali did not mimic the film more. This might have been because, while most of *Five Golden Flowers* was filmed on location in Dali, the famous Butterfly Spring scenes, the most romantic scenes of the movie, were filmed on a film set at a studio in the northeastern city of Changchun.

Mimetic Magic

In the autumn of 2002 I visited the Changchun Film Studio. It was just after lunch, and not encountering a guard at the large main gate, I walked up the road to where I could see a white statue of Chairman Mao, arm upraised, standing before a low, gray brick building. It must be one of the few remaining Mao statues in the country, I thought. To the left I could see another brick building on whose face were faded slogans from the Cultural Revolution. I walked through the double doors into the main building. Two shabby red velvet boards displayed slogans in raised gold letters: "Let a hundred schools of thought contend!" and "Make better products to give to the world!" Inside the building the tall hallways with ochre walls and closed wooden doors were deserted. Like an apparition, a guard in an olive green uniform suddenly appeared at the end of a hallway and started waving at me. I approached him and said that I had come to visit the studio. "You have come the wrong way! Tourists must go around to the other side." He walked me back to the main gate and told me to walk around the corner to the "Film Palace" (Dianying Gong). I was disappointed not to be able to linger longer, but he was insistent.

Past bicycle repair stands, car washes, and a pink painted "massage center," I found a yellow-tile roofed gate and a booth selling tickets for tours of the Film Palace. I asked the woman behind the counter if the tour included anything about the film *Five Golden Flowers*. "Certainly. If you buy the all-inclusive ticket (M. *taopiao*) for 49 yuan (US$5.92), you will see something on the film." While waiting in the souvenir shop for the tour to begin, I bought video disk copies of *Five Golden Flowers, Third Sister Liu,* and *Glacier Guests,* two other films that formed part of the minority film genre in the late 1950s and early 1960s, and looked at a nicely illustrated history of the studio, which left out any mention of the Cultural Revolution.

A cute twenty-something tour guide in a ruby red fuzzy wool coat began the tour for our group: a middle-aged couple from Changchun, their three friends from Anhui province, and a group of ten from Guangzhou. Our guide led us down a cement walkway, cold in the late afternoon light, toward what looked like a large warehouse. I asked her about *Five Golden Flowers*. "Yes, part of it was filmed here. And then you know what happened to actress Yang Likun during the Cultural Revolution? Horrible." Her voice dropped to a whisper. She did not seem to want to say more about how the famous actress who played Golden Flower had been criticized and beaten and how she had been placed in an asylum.[22]

We reached a sliding metal door, two stories high, open a crack. Inside sat a small audience of tourists watching performers reenact Golden Flower and Ah Peng sing a duet on the set of Butterfly Spring. I couldn't help but smile and began to take photos, but a woman guard came rushing over: "No photos! You need to pay to take photos here!" I lowered my camera, and the couple reenacting the film scene finished their duet and exited the stage. Our tour guide said that we could have a photograph taken on the set, 7 yuan (US$0.85) with the studio camera, 3 yuan (US$0.36) with our own camera. I was the only one out of our small group who asked to have my photograph taken, perhaps because the others were ready to leave: it was cold in the room, getting close to dinner time, and the entire place had an eerie air of desolation. As we walked out, the woman from Changchun said to the woman from Anhui: "The pond was so small! From the film it looked much larger. And the flowers are all fake. I thought that it would be much nicer." It was as if seeing the set had ruined the magic of the film for her.

The following day I visited the privately run "Film City" (M. *Dianying Cheng*) down the street from the studio's official Film Palace. Buying my ticket at the booth, I asked the seller what the difference was between the two. "Our Film City is livelier; there is much more to do here," she answered enthusiastically. To the left of the main hall was a large room that exhibited blurry black-and-white photographs illustrating the history of film in general. "Quick, guests!" A woman's voice called out. "You should come to the outerspace room (M. *taikong shi*), which is starting now." Two other tourists and I docilely followed her to "outerspace."

We entered a rickety, cavelike hallway that ended in a small circular room and were the last to occupy seats. The door slammed shut behind us, and the room started to vibrate, then rotate as two video screens showed a rocket blasting off. Along with the older man next to me, I gripped the seat in front of me. Once we had blasted off into outer space, the video screens showed us landing on the moon. Then a young woman in a white bunny suit—the mythical rabbit on the moon—appeared on the screen dancing among clouds of mist. The woman faded, and a small central screen slid open to show us a diorama of the planets. "This gives more of the feeling of the universe," the woman to the other side of me observed aloud. The screen slid closed, the room started to shake and rotate again, and then a taped woman's voice said: "Your program ends here. Please come again." "I won't come the next time!" a man in the audience shouted. Another muttered: "That was terrible." We tumbled out of the circular room, down the cave tunnel into the main hallway.

It was just noon, and we rushed across the hall to the *Five Golden Flowers* room. The room was a replica of a film set, more elaborate than the real set

I had seen at the studio the day before. There was a larger pond, and instead of dirt, the floor was covered with green plastic astro turf. Mock-ups of Dali's Three Pagodas stood to the back (not in the original film scene), and a light show simulated the sun coming through clouds after a storm. A woman with a video camera, instead of a film camera, taped a young couple who came out to sing the famous Butterfly Spring duet. This gave the appearance of filming in progress.

The audience, all male middle school principals from Guangzhou, seemed more enthusiastic than the small tour group at the real studio the previous day. They laughed, took photos, and hummed along with the singers. Still, they were not as enthralled with the site as the tourists who traveled to Butterfly Spring in Dali.

After the Butterfly Spring duet finished, a guide ushered us into the room next door. We entered the simulated "set" of another minority film, *Glacier Guests*, set among the Tajik nationality. Instead of Film City performers singing the famous film duet, the guide asked for two volunteers from the audience. The Guangzhou principals pushed two of their colleagues to the front: one man played the male role of Ami'er (he was given a hat, vest, and stringed instrument), and another man played the female role of Gulandanmu (he was given a veil and skirt to wear). They lip-synched and hammed to the recorded music. The audience roared with laughter. This moment of transperformance more closely resembled the climatic gender and nationality romantic reembodiments of the tourists at Butterfly Spring.

It is not that everything mimetic has magic. The "outerspace room" in Film City was obviously a failure. Dali's Butterfly Spring, the studio's Film Palace, and the entrepreneurial Film City were all trying to cash in on the film *Five Golden Flowers'* mimetic magic and the utopian nostalgia for it but with different degrees of effectiveness. The real studio set where the Butterfly Spring scenes were originally filmed was too cold and too desolate for tourists to enjoy themselves. The most exaggerated site, the simulated film set in Film City, was more appreciated, but it lacked opportunity for participation. The actual Butterfly Spring, which the film set had copied and which in turn imitated the set, was better but still not as magic as the film. Yet, because both Butterfly Spring and the simulated set of *Glacier Guests* allowed for participatory transperformance, tourists were able to re-create some of their own mimetic magic. What the tourists enjoyed most was re-creating their own nostalgic theater, which they gladly paid to do.

Local Longing

As Teacher Du and I were biking away from Butterfly Spring after our interview with Vice-Director Tao that afternoon, he said to me: "You know, when I was a boy, there used to be hundreds of butterflies at the spring. They would hang in strings down from the trees. Now I never see them any more. The butterflies are gone (B. *goli deng mulo*)."

I opened this chapter in the Yao family living room, where villagers were viewing the video of *Five Golden Flowers*. While watching the video with the group that evening, villagers first pointed out themselves or relatives who had played bit parts in the film, especially in the Third Month Fair scenes—"Look, there I am!" or "Hey, look, there's Grandma Zhao!" Then the villagers began to direct my attention not to the characters in the film but to the scenery behind the actors. "Look, Na Peisi [my Chinese name], there used to be a row of trees along the shore there. Nice willows. You could lie in the shade after going for a swim in the lake. We miss those trees (B. *nga mi ze ya dua*)."

"The shore used to be nicer too. Clean water."

"Look, there wasn't any landfill yet. We could row boats from the end of our house to the villa on the island."

"There were many more fish in the lake. Bow fish (B. *gv nv*), shaped just like an archery bow, those were delicious. Now you can't even find one."

The film, meant to glorify socialist construction (M. *shehuizhuyi de jianshe*), for the villagers now documents the destruction wreaked on the local environment first during the Great Leap Forward, then the Cultural Revolution, and now during the reform era (about which I will say more in chapters 4 and 5). Since much of it was filmed on location, *Five Golden Flowers* captures what Dali's landscape looked like in mid-1959. Watching the video that evening, villagers expressed longing for a previous village landscape. This longing differed from the tourists' nostalgia.[23] It was not a desire for the "never had" but a desire for that which was once known, now lost—a longing for the landscape of the village before the worst of the Great Leap and Cultural Revolution destruction. For villagers the film represented a historical document of the former beauty of their place.

"To fuel the smelting furnaces during the Great Leap Forward, we cut down the forests—one large section after another," one village man explained. Another sighed: "It takes only a few minutes to cut down a tree; it takes a lifetime for it to grow back."

Dali's forests disappeared not only because they were being cut down for the Great Leap smelting furnaces, but also because people were spending more time up in the mountains engaging in "land reclamation" efforts to extend arable land. In December 1957 four man-made forest fires accidentally destroyed over 33,000 *mu* (5,436 acres) of forest. In September 1970, as part of the "Learn from Dazhai" campaign based on the model commune of Dazhai in Shanxi province, Dali villagers were sent up into the mountains to "open up wasteland" (M. *kai kendi*) and "create Dazhai fields" (M. *zao Dazhai tian*). In February 1973 a fire burned 40,000 *mu* (6,589 acres), and 2,500 people worked valiantly to put it out. In April 1973 another fire, accidentally started by commune members who had gone to "recover wasteland" from the mountain, burned another 5,000 *mu* (824 acres), including seedlings that had been planted by the Forestry Bureau in 1970 after a forest fire in December 1969, accidentally started by three commune members, had burned 15,000 *mu* (2,471 acres) (*DSZ*, 27–33; *DSLY*, 16–18). Altogether over 90,000 *mu* (14,830 acres) of forest had disappeared in forest fires between 1957 and 1973.

Trees disappeared not only to fuel the furnaces or through accidental fires, but were cut down surreptitiously to be sold or to prevent their use as hiding places during factional struggle. In 1964, in the recovery period between the Great Leap and Cultural Revolution, commune officials and members from one village had madly cut down 3,750 *mu* (618 acres) of forest—43,080 cubic meters (over 1.5 million cubic feet) of wood—before the forestry station investigated. The forestry station attempted to control further cutting (*DSLY*, 14), but it was difficult to patrol the entire mountainside. In 1968, during the Cultural Revolution, warring Red Guard factions cut down all of the trees that had been planted along the 36-kilometer stretch of road between Yangnan and Xizhou (*DSLY*, 16).

With the forests gone, wild game and birds disappeared. "We used to worry about wolves coming down into the villages," an old woman recalled, "but after the Great Leap Forward, the wolves were all gone." Charles Patrick Fitzgerald, a British researcher who had lived in Dali in the late 1930s, wrote about the bounteous wildlife that had inhabited the forests of Mount Cang then: "The wooded slopes of T'sang Shan are the safe retreat of pheasants, hares, partridges, wild goat, deer, and the animals which prey upon them, wolves, leopards, and possibly tigers" (1941, 39). Villagers commented that none of this wildlife had returned by the 1990s.

During the revolutionary era overly ambitious development projects were started and then discarded. In March of 1960, twenty-four tea plantations were planted, but by the end of the year they had been abandoned (*DSLY*, 13). In 1967 over 14,000 *jin* (15,430 pounds) of winter melon seeds were scattered in watery fields, but they failed to germinate (ibid., 15–16).

During the national "Learn from Dazhai" campaign to extend arable land, villagers were mobilized to "encircle the lakes to create fields" (M. *weihu zaotian*). They filled in the small lake next to their village as well as the shoreline along Lake Er. Similar to what Judith Shapiro has documented for Lake Dian in Kunming (2001, 116–135), this mobilization effort destroyed the natural beauty of the shoreline of Lake Er and created only swampy land that proved unsuitable for agricultural production. The elimination of the lake next to the village as well as the filling in of shoreline shallows disrupted fish breeding grounds. Villagers blamed this, combined with over-application of chemical pesticides like DDV (Dicrotophos, which villagers called *didiwei*), for the disappearance of indigenous fish in Lake Er. Villagers thought that the pesticides might have been partly responsible for the disappearance of butterflies at Butterfly Spring as well.[24]

The longing for the former village landscape expressed by older villagers while watching the film *Five Golden Flowers* that afternoon was a way that "sentiments" could "condense and coalesce" around place (Nadel-Klein 2003, 102). Villagers seemed not only to be longing for the landscape but to be allegorically mourning all those who had suffered and died in the first decades of the new nation.

On January 1, 1959, the provincial newspaper, *Yunnan ribao* (Yunnan Daily News), started the year optimistically: "Grasp This Year's Even Greater, Even Better, Even More Complete Great Leap Forward!" (*YNRB*, Jan. 1, 1959: 1). An article on the front page proclaimed that "under the general military line of Socialist Construction, our country's 500 million farmers, having passed through a year of brave struggle, have already begun to change the face of our country's agricultural production and have found the high-speed road of developing agricultural production" (Su and Xu 1959). The article conjured the image of communes as happily crowded buses, zooming along a "high-speed highway" (M. *yi tiao gao sudu de daolu*) into a bright socialist future. Early in 1959 the provincial news did not reveal concern about the speed of travel on the road to the future.

A September 1959 article on Dali in the *Yunnan Daily News* reminded readers of how bad things had been in the "old society" (M. *jiu shehui*) and how bountiful things were in the new. Before Liberation, the article roared, the eighteen streams that ran down Dali's Mount Cang "were like tears of accusation." "The waves of Lake Er, filled with lament and resent, could not wash away the crimes of the reactionary oppressors. At that time, the warm, laboring Bai peoples spent a life of hunger and cold." Before Liberation, "the grain in the fields was golden, but at home, mother died of starvation" (M. *tian zhong guzi huang, jia zhong ji si niang*). After Liberation, the article claimed, the Bai people sang a different song: "In the eighth month, the grain is a sheet of gold, around Lake Er, the harvest is busy; grain is piled into the waist of the clouds, grain piled higher than Mount Cang!" (Yan Liyun 1959, 3).

This article encapsulated a narrative form of "speaking bitterness" (M. *suku*) that the Chinese Communist Party had promoted as a way for the peasant population to come into revolutionary consciousness—to recognize their exploitation under the "old society" and their salvation in the new (Anagnost 1997, 263). In this narrative style, "the contrast between old and new had to be rendered absolutely black and white, so that it became an unequivocal moral drama between the forces of good and evil" (ibid., 267). Ironically, it was still the same old song during the Great Leap Forward, for the piles of golden grain did not go to the farmers, and mothers and fathers were dying of starvation at home. The great tragedy of the Great Leap could not be narrated at the time it was occurring because suffering was to belong only to the past. It has not yet been fully narrated, and in the 1990s people in Dali were still reluctant to talk about that terrible time.

During the Great Leap villagers were forced to engage in rural industrialization and socialist construction to the overall neglect of agriculture. Commune members smelted steel, chopped trees from the mountainside to fuel the steel furnaces, and engaged in massive construction projects—building reservoirs, roads, and hydroelectric stations. In Dali over 35,000 people were mobilized for these projects, and "only the old, weak, sick, and disabled were left to do agricultural production" (*DSZ*, 26).

When agriculture *was* remembered, the policies took on nightmarish forms. In 1958, in a campaign to protect crops and promote health, every person was told to try to kill nine rats or mice, eleven sparrows, one mosquito, and two flies, every day. In another campaign of June 1959, human hair and animal carcasses were declared efficacious as fertilizer. Women under the age of forty cut their long hair short and fifty thousand men shaved their heads. This hair was combined with the carcasses of three thousand dead dogs and spread out across the fields. At the same time, in an effort to create more agricultural land, ancestral graves were cleared from the mountainside and over ten thousand tombs were pried open (*DSZ*, 27; see also Mueggler 2001, 184). The tombstones were used to line irrigation ditches and pave work-site courtyards. The hair and dead dogs created a stinking mess in which nothing could grow.

The opening of the tombs unleashed the spirits of the ancestors, who could no longer rest in peace and protect the lives of their descendants in the valley below. The hair cutting symbolically and physically marked Bai villagers as new national beings. The tomb opening seems to have been intended not only to create more field space, but to further end villager beliefs in the magical power of the ancestral spirits and transfer this belief to the power of the state (see Siu 1989, 6). The state tried to destroy belief in superstition (M. *mixin*), but it recognized the power of symbolic manipulation.

While agricultural yields were decreasing, false reporting of increased agricultural production exacerbated the devastating famine that followed. In 1959 Dali officials falsely reported a grain yield of over 50 million kilos (over 110 million pounds) and gave the higher-level bureaucracy over 32 million kilos (70.55 million pounds) (*DSZ*, 27). There was nothing left for villagers to eat. One of the new radio songs of 1959 urged all too literally, "Give everything to the Party" (M. *Ba yiqie xian gei dang*).[25] Beijing and the party-state became like a "giant mouth," consuming the resources of the rest of the country (Mueggler 2001, 175, 198).

In the 1990s Dali villagers did not like to talk much about the famine deaths of 1960–1961, when Dali had the highest mortality rate of any prefecture in Yunnan province. Estimates of "excess" deaths nationally during the Great Leap Forward range from 16.5 million to 40 million persons (see D. Yang 1996; Mueggler 2001, 188). Yunnan was one of the worst-hit provinces during the famine (Kane 1988, 74–76), although not as badly affected overall as Sichuan, Guangxi, Henan, and Anhui provinces (Mueggler 2001, 188; Becker [1996] 1998). However, within Yunnan province, Dali was the worst-affected prefecture in 1960, at the height of the famine. In that year Dali prefecture had a *negative* population growth rate of 18.61 percent and officially recorded 60,059 deaths (as opposed to 30,237 births), which accounted for 35 percent of the deaths in the entire province (173,758) that year. Every district in Dali suffered. The worst population loss was in the districts of Eryuan, Jianchuan (-32.40 percent), and Heqing (-28.55 percent) to the north of the town of Dali and Nanjian and Weishan (-30.71 percent) to the south.[26] The famine in Dali was compounded by an unusual drought that year, itself perhaps exacerbated by the deforestation of the mountainsides to fuel the steel furnaces.

The term "swelling sickness" (M. *shuizhong bing*)—the swelling of the body, or edema, a symptom of starvation—became a euphemism for dying of starvation. The situation in the town of Dali was bad, but "swelling sickness" in the villages to the north and south was worse. Townspeople remembered villagers stumbling into Dali to beg for food. Some people tried to share a little, but there was not much to give. There were no proper funerals at the time. Instead of a regular funeral feast, the most one could do would be to buy a few packs of cigarettes and distribute one cigarette each to relatives and friends. A few young men would carry the dead bodies up to the mountain and bury them simply.

Beijing political elites and visiting foreigners were sheltered from the suffering. American film scholar Jay Leyda, who worked cataloging foreign films at the Film Archive during the Great Leap, recalls that "we were so well protected and so well fed in our comfortable hotel . . . that we couldn't believe anything serious or tragic was happening beyond the city walls. The occasional banquet had a few less courses, but there were still banquets for any official excuse. Chauffeured Buicks and Cadillacs continued to carry the children of big shots to and from school" (1972, 287). While villagers in Dali were immersed in revolutionary suffering, Beijing elites were enjoying bourgeois comfort.

Five Golden Flowers celebrated the Great Leap Forward, promoting the successes of collectivization and socialist modernization, while these idealistic projects were actually in the process of failing, taking their extreme toll on the population in Dali. Perhaps part of the popularity of the film among national audiences can be understood in that it displayed optimism precisely at a time of severe adversity; it presented a vision of a possible utopia, a classic function of film (Dyer 1985, 222). The film let people laugh and perhaps let them believe that the dream of socialism was succeeding somewhere, if not where they were. The film may also have convinced some viewers that certain aspects of their lives were already utopian (see Dickey 1995, 147–148), for example, working communally. Still, people in Dali could not pretend that the tragedy had not taken place, although the state has never officially recognized its role in the famine.

While older villagers never spoke openly about the human deaths of the Great Leap, they candidly expressed sorrow over the loss of other lives: trees, fish, and butterflies. This expression of sorrow four decades later might be viewed in terms of what Simon Schama, in *Landscape and Memory,* has referred to as "the craving to find in nature a consolation for our mortality" (1995, 15). In a context where public expressions of grief for former state-sponsored suffering are political, mourning must take an "underground" or delayed form (R. Watson 1994a, 1994c). For older Dali villagers the land has become the repository for memories of suffering (see also Basso 1996; J. Jing 1996; Rosaldo 1980; Santos-Granero 1998). In contrast to the tourists' utopian nostalgia, the villagers' longing might be thought of as a "responsibility to remember what happens" in a haunted landscape (K. Stewart 1988, 235).

In the reform era villagers found it ironic that so many tourists were coming to view the beauty of Butterfly Spring when they thought that the most beautiful days of the place were in the past. For older villagers, memories of the past cast "a dark shadow on the significance of change" (Lass 1994, 89) in the present. The massive influx of tourists was further changing the place, as graveyards were removed to make way for the Butterfly Museum and fields were covered with asphalt to create tour bus parking lots.

Cartoonist Li Kunwu, in his anti–travel guide *Humorous, Flirtatious Travels in Yunnan,* has mocked this massive rush of people to Butterfly Spring on the day of the "Butterfly Festival" when butterflies at the spring are supposed to be at their peak (see illustration).

1. Quickly now, one hundred hearings is not the same as one seeing-for-oneself; I hear this year there are more butterflies than last year.
2. Each year on the fifteenth day of the fourth lunar month, tens of thousands of butterflies gather at Dali's Butterfly Spring and hang from the trees, head to tail like streams of beautiful, colorful ribbons. This is the world-renowned wonder (M. *qiguan*) of Butterfly Spring.
3. Heavens, I have never seen so many people before!
4. There are painters, photographers, television crews, and film crews, all watching Butterfly Spring as they press forward.
5. There are singers, drink sellers, souvenir sellers, and monkey dancers who are all watching those who are looking at Butterfly Spring as they press forward.
6. Following those who are pressing forward are drivers, physicians, tour agents, and dance hall operators.
7. First crowding this way . . .
8. Then crowding that way . . .
9. Crowding up a dust ball.
10. Crowding up sweat showers.
11. Everyone is crowded flat. What shape have the butterflies been crowded into?
12. Reporter: You have just come from Butterfly Spring—are there many of those cute things?
13. Many, too many!
14. What kinds are there?
15. There are red ones, white ones, black ones, yellow ones, green ones, old ones, young ones, male ones, female ones. . . .
16. What? Are you talking about the butterflies?
17. Of course not, where are there butterflies that are that boisterous!

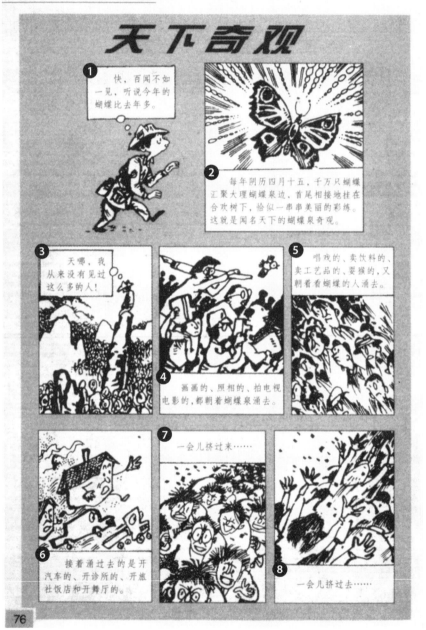

More tourists than butterflies. (From Li Kunwu 1999, 76–77)

天下奇观

9 挤得风尘滚滚。

10 挤得大汗淋漓。

11 人都被挤扁了。不知蝴蝶被挤成了什么模样?

12 你从蝴蝶泉来吧,那些可爱的小东西多不多?

13 多,多极了!

14 有些什么样的?

15 有红的,有白的,有黑的,有黄的,有绿的,有老的,有小的,还有男的女的……

16 什么,你是在说蝴蝶吗?

17 当然不是,蝴蝶哪有这么热闹!

18 但是我可以发明一种使蝴蝶和人一样热闹的东西——

19 不过需要一万年。

77

18. I can invent something that would make butterflies as boisterous as
people—
19. But that would take ten thousand years.

In this cartoon, Li Kunwu turns one of the natural "wonders" of Yunnan on
its head. Instead of the sight of thousands of butterflies, one sees thousands
of people: the tourists and artistic and mass media personnel—of which he is
one—come to document the butterflies (and the tourists) and all the others—
souvenir sellers, drivers, dance hall operators—who are hoping to profit from
those who have come to see the butterflies. The natural wonder has been
transformed into the human wonder of the tourist site phenomenon. This
human landscape is conveyed in the Chinese expression *renshan, renhai,* "a
mountain of people, a sea of people." In the second to last frame of Li's cartoon, he seems to be musing that since nature is no longer natural, he might
try to create larger-than-life artificial (perhaps genetically modified) boisterous butterflies.[27] Yet in the last frame he despondently realizes that this would
take forever (i.e., be virtually impossible).

Conclusion

Once depicted as a model place of the future, Dali has become a romanticized place of the past. When the film *Five Golden Flowers* was released in
1959, it used the people and place of Dali as illustrative of the success of the
Great Leap Forward and socialist modernization. By the turn of the twenty-
first century, however, Dali represented an unrealized dream of socialist utopia. The millions of well-off national tourists who journeyed there sought not
to return to the past but to remember a sense of communal spirit from that
time. In the reform era Dali became a place where national tourists could enact their collective utopian nostalgia as well as perform their own personal
fantasies of being (or acting as) a minority person for a day. As I have shown,
this romantic reembodiment has occurred in other times and places, where
culturally and economically dominant groups play at being "Indians" or "natives" and where minority people serve as symbols. The tourists drawn to Dali
because of *Five Golden Flowers* were not looking for the authentic but for a mimetic, where the people and place mirror what they had seen in a film.

Whereas the national tourists viewed the film *Five Golden Flowers* with
nostalgia and fantasy, younger villagers saw it as providing employment opportunities through tourism and a way out of the hard labor of farming and
fishing. Older villagers, in contrast, viewed the film with longing for a lost

landscape. For them the film served as a historical document of the destruction wreaked on their environment during the revolutionary era. In the reform era the film itself serves to transform the local landscape further, as local officials remove graveyards and pave over fields for parks and parking lots to accommodate millions of tourists.

Older villagers, in addition to viewing the film with longing for a place in the past, however, also viewed the film with pride that their place had been chosen for a celebratory national film. I never heard anyone express strong criticisms of the film's representations of Bai culture. Instead, people often joked about the film with me:

"Na Peisi, don't go back home. You can be our foreign Golden Flower, and we'll find a nice village Ah Peng for you."

"I already have a foreign Ah Peng."

"Never mind then. . . ."

CHAPTER 4

Heavenly Dragons

Commodifying a Fantastic Past

The past, like the future, is an eternally unfinished project,
constantly under construction. . . .

(Hue-Tam Ho Tai 2001, 3)

In 1994 I read an article in a Dali journal that intrigued me. The author, Zhang Nan, a Chinese resident of Dali, suggested that since Hong Kong author Jin Yong's martial arts novel *Heavenly Dragons (Tianlong babu)* "makes readers have wild and fanciful thoughts about Dali," developers could use it to market Dali to national and Overseas Chinese tourists (Zhang Nan 1994, 141). Zhang Nan urged developers not to just sit back and wait for the fans of Jin Yong's novel to arrive. Instead, they should actively develop the tourism potential of the novel and capitalize on it, following the model that other places have used: for example, the *Dream of the Red Chamber* theme park in Beijing and the *Romance of the Three Kingdoms* theme park in Sichuan.[1] He explained that since "scenery, historical sites, folk customs, and even the stories and plots of artistic novels have all become 'products,'" therefore, "*Heavenly Dragons* is the best way to attract investment" (ibid., 143).

Capitalizing on this literary "product," Zhang Nan proposed a detailed plan for developers to construct eight new tourist sites in Dali:

1. Open up a Heavenly Dragons Cave (M. Tianlong Dong). Include special lighting that makes visitors feel close to a mysterious place of the immortals.
2. Name the pool at the top of Lan peak "Sword Lake" after that which appears in the novel. This is where tourists on a one-day tour will eat a picnic.
3. Build a temple near Dali's Three Pagodas and call it Heavenly Dragons Temple. Create Buddhist statues like the ones described in the book.
4. Preserve the old town of Dali and reconstruct an imperial palace of

the Dali Kingdom. Let tourists "seek the serene and inquire as to the ancient."

5. Model Jinsuo Island after the retreat portrayed in the novel where King Duan meets his mistresses.

6. At the current Guanyin temple on the main road south of Dali, recruit monks and nuns to host tourists. Tell tourists that this is the place in the novel where Prince Duan's mother became a Buddhist nun.

7. Construct a Heavenly Dragons Amusement Palace. This site should include a wax museum, model clan temple of the Duan family, and martial arts performance ground.

And finally . . .

8. Construct a City-That-Never-Sleeps (M. *bu ye cheng*) along the shores of Lake Er. This entertainment area should include a karaoke pavilion, a laser disk film theater, a travel office, and a "Dali in miniature."[2]

Zhang Nan's plan struck me as quite preposterous. Rename places in Dali to match a martial arts novel? Build caves, palaces, and amusement parks? Zhang Nan was advising developers to shape reality to fit representation, making Dali a "simulacrum" (Baudrillard 1988)—a representation of a representation of itself. However, when I returned to Dali a few years later, I would discover, much to my amazement, that most of Zhang Nan's plan had been implemented.

This chapter explores the relationship between a third representation in popular culture—Jin Yong's martial arts novel *Heavenly Dragons*—and its material after-effects on the place of Dali. Like the Lonely Planet travel guide, which has drawn tens of thousands of transnational travelers, and the 1959 movie musical *Five Golden Flowers,* which has brought millions of national tourists, the novel *Heavenly Dragons* is attracting at least hundreds of thousands of national and Overseas Chinese tourists to Dali. In 2004 over 400,000 people—70 to 80 percent of whom were national tourists, mostly from the coastal cities of Beijing, Shanghai, and Guangzhou, and 20 to 30 percent of whom were transnational tourists, mostly Overseas Chinese from Malaysia and Singapore—visited the newly constructed Heavenly Dragons Film City, or "Daliwood," where much of a forty-part television series based on the novel was filmed.[3]

In this chapter we will observe the transformation of Dali into a place where, increasingly, the fictional blends with the actual. Dali officials in conjunction with transnational developers have begun to construct fantastic "historic" sites based on *Heavenly Dragons*. Dali is not alone in this process. In competition for tourist dollars, places around the world have been "seeking to distinguish themselves from each other through generating narratives of an imagined past" (Meethan 2001, 99). Dali officials do not need to generate a narrative, since the narrative has already been provided for them by Jin Yong's novel.

As we observed in chapter 3, Dali is becoming a place where tourists can actualize their status as consumers by playing out their fantasies. National tourists drawn to Dali by utopian nostalgia in a time of market competition can perform their individual fantasies of the exotic at Butterfly Spring. Overseas Chinese and a younger generation of mainland tourists are also drawn to Dali by a fantastic nostalgia for a distant fictional past. Tourist performance areas for this fantastic nostalgia now extend well beyond Butterfly Spring to encompass the entire Dali basin.

How have people in Dali viewed Jin Yong's novel and what might be called the theme parkization of their place? At the end of this chapter, we will meet Dali intellectuals who both applaud and critique *Heavenly Dragons*. Chapter 5 will investigate the divergent reactions of townspeople and villagers to the transformation of Dali.

From the Actual to the Fantastic

Brrnngg. At 5:30 a.m. a friendly attendant (M. *fuwuyuan*) gave me a morning wake-up call. I arose and walked the block from the guesthouse to the new airport in the dark, past the construction rubble. There were two flights to Dali that morning, one at 7:20, the other at 7:30. I stood in a long line at the check-in counter along with a group of middle-aged men. From the men's suntans, I thought at first that they were from Yunnan, but they turned out to be from Taichung, Taiwan. One man in a bright, short-sleeved print shirt told me that they had come to Kunming for the "Expo." Then they would spend two days in Dali and a day in Chengdu before flying home.

That summer the provincial capital of Kunming, with major funding provided by Yunnan tobacco companies, had launched a large exposition with exhibits of all the province's plants and products. The theme of the expo was "Man and Nature—Marching into the Twenty-First Century" (M. *ren yu ziran—zou xiang di ershiyi shiji*). I later came to think of this theme as highly ironic in terms of the changes in place that I was to observe in Dali. Provincial officials were expecting millions of tourists to visit Yunnan that summer.

My plane ticket indicated that the flight would take less than an hour. This was the first time that I had flown to Dali. The airport had opened in 1996, shortly after I had left after my first period of extended research.[4] For years I had taken various buses back and forth over the mountain roads from Kunming to Dali: the low budget, breezy, bumpy day bus, the mid-level reclining-seat day or night bus, or the high-end luxurious Hungarian sleeper bus, with real bunk beds. (This I usually took with friends or family who came to visit, but I was disappointed that they did not immediately recognize it as being "luxurious," perhaps owing to the blaring miniature television set showing Hong Kong gangster films or the guests who expectorated from the top bunks onto the floor below.) If I took a day bus, I could observe the undulating scenery, but I came to prefer the mid-level night bus, for then I would not see the trucks that had plummeted off hairpin curves into valleys far below. A bus trip would take anywhere from ten to fifteen hours, depending on how brazenly a driver dared to career the mountain roads in the dark or what business he or others had along the way. Sometimes drivers decided to pick up passengers or cargo (the fares or fees would go into the drivers' own pockets), or there would be military checkpoints. At checkpoints, security officers would flag down a bus, board it, and check our IDs, presumably in search of drug smugglers. Once a man in a silk suit boarded the bus with an aluminum attaché case handcuffed to his wrist. At a military checkpoint he and the officer had a long, low conversation, but the man in the suit remained on the bus.

I looked out the plane window. Narrow strips of rice fields gave way to wave upon wave of mountains. Suddenly, the snow-capped peaks of Mount Cang and the deep indigo of Lake Er came into view, and we landed lightly in Dali.

The Taiwanese men were met by local pennant-waving guides who escorted them to waiting tour buses. The few locals on the flight were met by eager relatives. I shared a cab with two Australians from the airport to the old town of Dali. On the way we passed through the prefectural city of Xiaguan. A grove of white-tile, blue-windowed buildings had sprung up in the four years since I had been away. The taxi driver turned onto a new highway (M. *gaosu gonglu*) that had been constructed in my absence. As we sped toward the old town of Dali, I noticed that the five-star hotel that had been under construction in 1995 had been completed. The hotel was the only one of its kind in the province and included an indoor swimming pool and a bowling alley. When I had interviewed the Taiwanese investor in the hotel in 1995, she noted that it was Buddhism that had initially attracted her to Dali. She hoped that her hotel would serve not only the Buddhist tourist, but also Overseas Chinese, Southeast Asian, and Japanese businessmen. A row of gleaming condominiums sat on the hillside below the hotel.

During my first few days back in Dali, I learned that, in addition to the condominiums, hotel, highway, and airport, a railway and a scenic road around the lake (M. *huan Er lu*) had been completed. Finally, I discovered that most of Zhang Nan's 1994 plan for promoting Dali based on Jin Yong's novel had already been implemented:

1. A Heavenly Dragons Cave had been opened north of Dali.

2. A French alpine-style cable car ran up the mountainside.

3. Behind the Three Pagodas a huge "tourist temple" was under construction (see illustration).

4. An imitation imperial palace had been built in the old town of Dali.

5. Jinsuo Island had been made into a palace-style resort and renamed "Nanzhao Island" after the place where the fictional King Duan meets his mistresses in the novel.

Tourist temple. (Photo by B. Notar, 1999)

The only parts of Zhang Nan's plan that had not yet been implemented were the amusement park and the "miniature Dali." Monks were hosting tourists at the Guanyin temple south of town, although not yet telling them a story from the novel.

Zhang Nan's plan to turn Dali into a simulacrum of the novel, I realized, was only part of a larger plan. At the Tourism Development Office one of the assistant directors handed me a large glossy brochure called in English the "Dali Provincial Travel and Vacation Region Investment Guide." The guide featured plans for an amusement park, a hunting field, tennis courts, a horse track, a regulation international eighteen-hole golf course with member club, a water park, and an "array of 250 flats and 200 villas, to be rented and sold for tourist use" (Yang Yuan Jun n.d.). Billboards along the main road advertised these development projects.

In order to understand this massive reconfiguration of Dali, we need to understand that the martial arts novel on which Zhang Nan's plan was based and the Hong Kong author who wrote it, although little known in the English-speaking world, are among the most famous books and authors on the planet.

The "King of Kung Fu"

To his millions of fans Zha Liangyong, the author who uses the pen names of Jin Yong in Chinese and Louis Cha in English, is the king of Chinese *wuxia*—"battle and chivalry"—novels. These historically based novels, such as *Heavenly Dragons*, emphasize the martial arts and feature numerous fighting factions, among which honor, duty, revenge, and indebtedness feature prominently.[5] Martial arts novels draw on a cultural and literary tradition of Chinese "knight-errants" or "gallants" (M. *xia*), Robin Hood–like swordsmen (Cao 1994, 238; Hamm 2005, 11–14; Ma and Lau 1978, 39) as well as a later literary tradition of "otherworldly and erotic" swordswomen (M. *nüxia*) (Hamm 2005, 15). One of the earliest recorded tales of a knight-errant is the story of Yü Rang that appears in the records of China's "Grand Historian" Sima Qian (c. 145–c. 86 B.C.). When Yü Rang's master is killed by Lord Xiang of Zhao, Yü Rang vows revenge. He disguises himself as a toilet-cleaning convict in order to try to catch Lord Xiang at a vulnerable moment. Yü's plot is revealed, but Lord Xiang orders his guards to let him go because he is "truly one of the world's worthy men" for wanting to avenge his master. Later Yü disguises himself as a leper to try again; the second time he fails again but is not forgiven (Sima Qian [c. 91 B.C.] 1978, 41–42).

The action for most contemporary martial arts novels takes place in the "landscape of the 'Rivers and Lakes' (M. *jianghu*)—the complex of inns, highways and waterways, deserted temples, bandits' lairs, and stretches of wilderness at the geographic and moral margins of settled society" (Hamm 2005, 17). The most popular of these tales in the English-speaking world is now Ang Lee's film version of Wang Dulu's novel *Crouching Tiger, Hidden Dragon* (*Wohu canglong*, 2000).

The global readership of these novels has been noted by one scholar who suggests that "wherever there are Chinese (M. *Hua ren*) there will be Jin Yong's novels" (Chen Fengxiang 1998, 179). It is estimated that over the past four decades one billion copies of Jin Yong's novels have been sold, and they have been read by at least double that number of people.[6] Jin Yong's novels as a form of print capitalism have helped to shape a transnational community of Chinese readers (Hamm 2002, 317).

When he began the novel *Heavenly Dragons* in 1963, Zha Liangyong, originally a native of Zhejiang province, was thirty-nine years old and had spent thirteen years in Hong Kong working as a film critic, editor, and script writer (sometimes under the other pen names Lin Huan and Yao Fulan). By 1955 he had embarked on an additional career as Jin Yong, author of martial arts novels. Between 1955 and 1963 Jin Yong wrote eight more serialized novels and novellas; *Heavenly Dragons* was to be his ninth (Leng Xia 1995). Between 1965 and 1972 Jin Yong wrote six additional novels and novellas, culminating in his final, and some say best, work, *Luding ji* (The Deer Cauldron Record) in 1972.[7] Fans have been hoping that Jin Yong will once again pick up his "precious pen," but the author has retired from literary life and entered political life (Ceng Huiyan 1998, 10). Yet, owing to the ongoing sales of both his newspaper *Ming Pao* and his books, he is among the top Chinese billionaires in the world (Yang Kuinie 1998, 209).

A Popular Novel among Popular Novels

Jin Yong's novels have been popular in Hong Kong and Taiwan for decades, but they only started to be printed and distributed in mainland China along with other formerly banned Hong Kong martial arts novels in the mid-1980s as part of China's "reform and opening" (Zhang Yaya 2002). This circulation of martial arts novels has formed part of a larger mainland interest in the products of Hong Kong and Taiwan (M. *Gangtai*) popular culture, an interest that may have been fueled in part by consumer desire for less ideological books, songs, and films, and one that was tolerated by the mainland government as a way to create a sense of a greater unified China (Gold 1993).

A survey conducted among five thousand people in the Beijing municipal area in 1993 found that the appeal of martial arts novels cut across age and educational groups. Of all the martial arts novelists, the vast majority of readers (85.7 percent) in the survey cited Jin Yong as their favorite (Zhang Yaya 2002). This interest in Jin Yong's martial arts novels has led to what one scholar has called a "Jin Yong fever" (M. *Jin Yong re*) on the mainland.[8]

Heavenly Dragons is one of the most popular of Jin Yong's fourteen novels. Jin Yong started it in September 1963 as a serialized novel in the Hong Kong newspaper *Ming Pao,* a newspaper he had established with his old middle school classmate Shen Baoshin in 1959. *Heavenly Dragons* ran in *Ming Pao* for two years between 1963 and 1965 as well as in Singapore's *Nanyang shangbao* (Southern Seas Commercial News) (Jin Yong 1978, 2126).[9] Since 1978 the novel has been reprinted numerous times in Hong Kong and Taipei.[10]

The appeal of the novel spans generations and geography. When I told a Chinese American friend about my interest in *Heavenly Dragons,* she divulged that her elderly parents (one from the mainland, one from Taiwan) had just finished reading the last of the novel's five volumes. "They were like kids," she related over the phone. "They stayed up all night reading it and couldn't put it down until they had read the last page." A university professor of history from the mainland who teaches on the West Coast told me that of course he had read the novel—"Jin Yong is great!" When Professor Wang Xiaoming, a neophyte to martial arts novels, asked his friends which of Jin Yong's fourteen novels he should begin with, they all recommended *Heavenly Dragons* (Wang 2000, 487).

Because of the novel's popularity, it can be difficult to find. When I looked for the novel at the University of Michigan Asia library, it was listed as "missing." I asked one of the Asia librarians about the possibility of the library's ordering a new copy, but he just shook his head. "Jin Yong's works are too popular," he said. "We've stopped trying to keep them in the collection. After a year or two, they always disappear." When I visited Cornell University's Asia library, I looked again. The library owned three sets of the novel, but all three were checked out, and all had holds placed on them. Again, I went to talk with the Asia librarian. "They are so popular," he said, "that they are never in the library. They are read so much that the books start to fall apart. Every three or four years we just order new sets and toss the old ones out." Not long after moving to Seattle in 1997, I found a Chinese book store in the International

District that had one complete five-volume set of the novel. On the same afternoon I discovered two Chinese video stores around the corner, both of which displayed large color posters advertising a recent Hong Kong video release of *Heavenly Dragons*. The posters displayed the novel's main characters in front of a Dali-esque snow-capped mountain landscape—images of an imagined Dali had appeared on the streets of urban America via Chinese popular culture.

A Buddhist "Wild, Wild West"

Heavenly Dragons has been described as a "masterpiece of eastern culture and art" (Chen Mo 1998, 56) and of all Jin Yong's novels "the one that most gives expression to human emotion" (Li Hongwen 1998, 119). Leng Xia, a biographer of Jin Yong, describes the novel as distinct from all the author's previous novels in that it is the first one in which Jin Yong used Buddhist thought to "oppose evil and transform the foolish" and used Buddhist teachings to guide readers about "eschewing greed, desire, and entanglements" (1995, 147). The title of the novel *Tianlong babu* (literally "Heaven, Dragon, the Eight Classes") represents the "eight classes of supernatural beings in the Lotus sutra"; that is, the devas, nagas, yakshas, gandharvas, asuras, garudas, kinnaras, and mahoragas (Soothill and Hodous [1937] 1977, 41). In his preface to the novel, Jin Yong briefly characterizes each of these strange and wondrous supernatural beings. The devas (M. *tianshen*), in particular Indra (M. *Dishi*), represent Buddhist belief in continual change and transformation. The nagas, Indian rain serpent deities (M. *longshen*), provide the source of inspiration for Chinese dragons, which can also be used to represent high-ranking monks. The yakshas (M. *yecha*) are usually evil, but some, especially the "eight great generals," protect the people. The gandharvas (M. *gandapo*) are vegetarian, teetotaling spirits who survive on incense smoke. They are Indra's musicians and represent all that is illusory. Of the asuras (M. *axiuluo*), the males are exceedingly ugly and the females extremely beautiful. They have temperamental and suspicious characters, and often battle with Indra but always lose. The garuda (M. *jialouluo*) is a giant, golden-winged bird who eats dragons and whose cries are bitter and tragic. The kinnaras (M. *jinnaluo*) resemble humans but have a single horn on their heads. They are also musicians of Indra. Finally, the mahoragas (M. *mohouluojia*) are the python deities who have human bodies and heads like snakes (Jin Yong 1978, 5–7). In reading the novel, one can see that Jin Yong has drawn on these descriptions to develop his fantastical characters.

A Buddhist "wild, wild West." (Cover of *Heavenly Dragons* DVD set, Jiuzhou yinxiang chuban gongsi, 2003)

In his preface Jin Yong further draws an explicit connection between Buddhism and the place of Dali. He notes: "The Dali Kingdom was a Buddhist country. The emperors all believed in Buddhism and often relinquished their reigns to become monks. This is a very strange and unique phenomenon (M. *shifen qite de xianxiang*) in our country's history" (1978, 7). In this statement Jin Yong not only makes a connection between Dali and Buddhism but describes Dali as a unique place where rulers would renounce power and wealth. My reprinted edition of the novel opens with photographs of Dali's famous Three Pagodas and reproductions of the painted scroll the *Long Roll of Buddhist Images,* depicting images of Dali's rulers set among Buddhist deities, monks, and fantastical creatures, for example, human bodies with frog or rooster faces.[11] The preface and the photographs set the scene: the reader expects Dali to provide a fantastical setting inhabited by strange and magical beings. Much of the novel's action takes place in eleventh-century Dali, and many of its fictionalized characters are modeled on the Duans, the ruling family of the Dali Kingdom.

Three male characters—Qiao (Xiao) Feng, Xu Zhu, and Duan Yu—stand out as the heroes of the novel. Qiao Feng, the main hero, is a more troubled character than the other two. He is raised by a family named Qiao who reside near the famous Shaolin Temple, the site of a sect of Buddhist warrior monks, and he secretly learns martial arts from an old temple monk. He later becomes a brave and fearless leader of a gang of beggars, a Robin Hood–like figure. Qiao Feng's main troubles begin when a woman who thinks he has scorned her, Madame Ma (Ma Furen), wife of a Muslim tea merchant, brings a letter to his gang that reveals that he is not Han but Khitan (a nomadic group of the northern steppes) and that he had been orphaned when a group of Han attacked and killed his parents at a mountain pass.

This revelation sends Qiao Feng spinning into an ethnic identity crisis. When he first hears the news, he denies it: "I am not Khitan! I am Han! (M. *Wo bushi Qidan ren, wo shi Han ren*)." He immediately retires as gang leader— some of the gang members call him a "Khitan dog" (M. *Qidan gou*) when they hear the news—and he sets off to find out whether or not the content of the letter is true. When he discovers that indeed (most of) it is true, he changes his family name from his adopted name Qiao to his natal Xiao and sets off to avenge the deaths of his parents. His vengeful quest, guided by misinformation, concealed identities, and mixed loyalties, leads to some unexpected turns of events.

The second hero, Xu Zhu, is an orphan who has been raised as a monk at the famous Shaolin Temple. He unwittingly receives magical martial arts powers and becomes the ruler of Spirit Vulture Palace and the imperial son-in-law of the Xixia, a nomadic group of the northern steppes.

The novel commences with the story of the third hero, Duan Yu, Prince of the Dali Kingdom.[12] He has run away from home because he does not want to learn the martial arts that his (supposed) father, the brother of the King of Dali, wants to teach him. Prince Duan is a good-hearted character, but his childlike irreverence and outspokenness get him into tight spots, whereupon he must rely on his wits and the aid of strong women to rescue him. For example, Zhong Ling, a perky teenager, keeps poison snakes up her sleeve, and Mu Wanqing (also called Wan'er), a sullen and suspicious maiden, veils her face and shoots poison darts out of her sleeve. Their interactions with Duan Yu involve a form of slapstick sadism that is common in Disney cartoons (see Fjellman 1992, 262). Prince Duan's wanderings over the Dali landscape and his encounters with strange characters propel the novel's initial storyline. Critic Chen Mo suggests that Duan Yu is "an observer" for the reader, the novel's "cute guide," and the fictional "embodiment of the author" (M. *zuozhe de huashen*) (1998, 58–59).

The novel is popular among younger readers, especially male, partly because it represents a coming of age story of the three main heroes. They struggle with finding their identities, realizing their martial arts skills, and recognizing romantic interests. Part of the reason for its popularity among older readers may be that the novel is replete with the characters' conflicting loyalties, which lead to complex plot twists and turns. That two of the heroes, Qiao Feng and Duan Yu, are not Han Chinese and that Xu Zhu marries into a non-Han family also allows the author a certain exotic and romantic leeway that would not be as feasible with Han Chinese characters. The popularity of such a novel is analogous to the popularity for German readers of Karl May novels, which give a romanticized portrayal of Native American Indians and has led to the formation of Indian hobbyist clubs and German tours to the American Southwest (Calloway, Gemünden, and Zantop 2002).

Jin Yong's novel *Heavenly Dragons* and its film, video, and television versions have emblazoned the place and people of Dali in the popular imagination of Chinese readers and viewers worldwide in much the same way that the film *Five Golden Flowers* has captured the popular imagination of moviegoers nationwide (see chapter 3). While the film *Five Golden Flowers* has been used to market Dali to an older generation of national tourists, Dali officials and developers have begun to use the novel *Heavenly Dragons* and its film and video versions to market Dali to Overseas Chinese, a "major force" in China's tourism development (Lew 1995, 155), and to a new generation of mainland youth.[13] They realize that a younger generation of mainlanders will not be nostalgic for the Maoist-era romantic movie musical *Five Golden Flowers* in the same way as their parents (see chapter 3), but they will be familiar with Jin Yong's novel (Zhang Nan 1994), especially because of the recent (2003) airing of a forty-part television series based on it, much of it filmed on location in Dali. Moreover, new second-year high school textbooks include excerpts from the novel (along with excerpts from Wang Dulu's *Crouching Tiger, Hidden Dragon;* see Yang Li 2005). We may ask then, what has it meant for Dali as a place that it is the setting for one of the most popular martial arts novels in the world?

Capturing History, Cashing In on Popular Culture

In June 2002 a major construction project commenced on the mountainside above the old town of Dali. Covering over 325 *mu* (21,678 square meters or 53 acres) of land, containing 25,000 square meters of architecture, and costing over 111 million yuan (over US$13.4 million) to build, the site would become the set for the forty-part television series version of *Heavenly Dragons*. The site had been selected by the well-known director and producer Zhang Jizhong, who filmed earlier popular television series based on the classic novels *Sanguo yanyi* (The Romance of The Three Kingdoms) and *Shuihu zhuan* (Water Margin). Initial investment was provided by the prefectural government and the Dali Holiday Resort Area Management Committee. Mr. Song Hongrong of Beijing designed the layout and architecture based on the famous Song dynasty scroll by Zhang Zeduan *Qingming shanghe tu* (Qingming Festival on the River). The site, dubbed in English "Hollywood East" or "Daliwood," would include four main sections: the Dali Kingdom market street and palace, the Xixia Kingdom, the Liao Kingdom, and the Jurchen tribal land. Construction was completed by December 2002.[14]

The television series was one of the most expensive in China to date, the cost of production reaching an estimated 28 million yuan (US$3.38 million). However, broadcasting rights were sold well in advance: to Zhejiang province alone for 2.8 million yuan (US$338,000), to Hong Kong for US$1 million, and to Taiwan for US$400,000. Zhang Jizhong produced the series, and the once renegade, now mainstream fifth-generation director Zhou Xiaowen (*Ermo, The Emperor and the Assassin*) directed it.[15] Broadcast in 2003, the television series situated Dali and its connection with Jin Yong's novel even more firmly in the Chinese and Overseas Chinese popular imagination.

Over 50 percent of the scenes from the *Heavenly Dragons* television series were filmed in Daliwood and around Dali.[16] Once produced, the series included some stunning "exotic" footage of Dali: for example, the scene where Prince Duan and his mother bring Mu Wanqing home to meet his father. An overhead shot shows an impressive imperial palace with golden Buddhist stupa-like towers against the emerald mountains to the west. The dress of the three characters evokes the ethnic exotic: Prince Duan wears a white robe, while a turquoise clasp holds part of his long hair in a topknot; his mother dons a diaphanous white veil with royal blue trim; Mu Wanqing has a simple black and white cotton dress, while long beaded coral earrings dangle from her ear lobes. As the three enter the city gate on horseback, thousands of townspeople gather to greet them with lion and bamboo stick dances, some playing bamboo flutes. This scene strangely resembles a scene from the 1959 movie *Five Golden Flowers*: the thousands of extras who greet the trio are dressed like Bai minority villagers of the 1950s, the women in layered headdresses, shirts, aprons, and pants; the men in white turbans, cotton vests, and wide cotton pants. There is an intervisuality at work here, the director expecting the television-viewing audience to be familiar with the "ethnic" costumes of Dali from the 1950s movie, whether or not they resemble those of the eleventh century. A familiar past of the 1950s is transmuted back to a distant past of the eleventh century.

After filming for *Heavenly Dragons* had been completed, the site was turned into a tourist "film city" theme park, and "Daliwood" opened to the public in February 2003. In February 2004 the Dali Travel Group Co., Ltd., which also operates Dali Three Pagoda Park, Butterfly Spring, Nanzhao Style Island, Erhai Lake Park, and Erhai Lake Cruises, took over operation. Although there are fourteen other "film cities" in China, this is the only site that is the "birthplace of the story" (M. *gushi de fasheng di*), the place where the story is actually set.[17]

Daliwood shares several of the characteristics of Walt Disney World that anthropologist Stephen Fjellman has identified in his in-depth analysis of that park, namely, the park is geared to middle-class consumers; it contains "authenticity within inauthenticity" (i.e., great attention is paid to re-creating fictional detail); it presents a pedestrian-only space; it offers opportunities for both spectatorship and play; tourists arrive already familiar with narratives presented in the park; and the park blurs reality and fantasy (Fjellman 1992). Let us examine these theme park characteristics in more detail.

That Daliwood is geared toward Chinese middle- and upper-class consumers is apparent in its ticket price, a hefty 82 yuan in 2005. While this is reasonable in U.S. terms, only $9.90, in Dali prefecture it was slightly more than half of a farmer's average monthly income.[18] For 82 yuan one could take forty-one bus rides, eat twenty bowls of noodle soup, or buy approximately eight paperback books.[19]

While a new place, Daliwood seeks to re-create the old. The approach to Daliwood is via a newly constructed cobblestone road that winds around the mountain from the top of the Third Month Fair grounds. A massive fortress-like gate with flying orange flags marks the entrance. Most tour buses plan to arrive just before nine in the morning or two in the afternoon so tourists can view the "opening" of the gates. At these times, performers playing the King of Dali and his consort, wearing golden robes and elaborate crowns, accompanied by their entourage of armored palace guards carrying spears and ladies-in-waiting in satin gowns, officially welcome tourists as "guests" and allow them to enter through the gates. No cars or buses are allowed through. Once inside, tourists are pedestrians, leaving behind the "modern" world outside and entering into a fictional eleventh century.

The park draws on tourists' familiarity with the novel's narrative and ex-

pertly combines and alternates between tourist participation and observation. The first day that I visited Daliwood, I arrived with a group of tourists
from the southern metropolis of Guangzhou. After passing through the gate,
the first performance we observed was that of "a maiden of the Duan family throwing an embroidered ball to find a husband" at the "betrothal building" (M. *cailou*). The start of the performance was announced by a young man
in a burgundy robe, accompanied by gongs and drums. We gathered around
the base of a two-story building on the market street, while a narrator in a
long beard and golden brocade robe set the scene for the mini-drama to be
enacted—a maiden of the Dali imperial family was searching for a husband
to marry into her family (we as tourists might have heard that matrilocality
was more common here at the borderlands). She would toss an embroidered
ball off the second-floor balcony, and whoever caught it would be her mate.
The maiden and her handmaidens tossed a large red cloth ball, almost a foot
in width, over the balcony, and male tourists in the crowd below jostled to
catch it. One young man managed to wrestle it away from the others. "Aha!
A mate has been found," the narrator announced. Guards in armor drew the
young man apart from the rest of the crowd and led him into the building. The
crowd laughed. He appeared a few minutes later on the balcony in long robes
and hat. The narrator commented that the young man "appeared to have a
girlfriend below, but no matter." We laughed some more. The young man was
ordered to bow nine times to his new bride and drink a cup of wine.

Daliwood is structured in a series of scenes in which both professional
performers and tourists participate. This is similar to the structuring of Walt
Disney World into cinematic scenes, as Fjellman has observed: "As we move
around we enter into a series of activities constructed as movie scenes. We
are in the middle with the action taking place all around us" (1992, 11). To
elaborate on Fjellman, the scenes in Daliwood are not structured as if we are
watching a film but as if we are in the process of making a film, as if we are
on a film set (which, in fact, we are). Yet this kind of structuring of performative participation predates cinema. Vanessa Schwartz, in her discussion
of the rise of popular amusements in late-nineteenth-century Paris, has observed that in wax museums "spectators commanded the spectacle: they participated in it at the same time that they believed it was constructed for them"
(1998, 131). Spectators could "literally dissolve the boundaries between self
and spectacle—to blur reality and representation" (ibid., 132). This blurring
of self and spectacle, reality and representation seems key to tourist enjoy-
ment at Daliwood.

After the "marriage" of one of our group to a Dali princess, our guide hur-

Stilt dance at Daliwood. (Photo by B. Notar, 2005)

ried us through the Song dynasty–style market street. No matter that it was based on the river town of Kaifeng in Henan province, it was impressively constructed and created an aura of an "authentic" historic street. There were shops selling souvenirs on both sides—Dali tie-dye cloth, tea, and wooden swords for children—but we didn't have time to shop. We could do that on the way out, our guide said. Ahead another performance was starting, the stilt dance (M. *gao qiao*). On an open-air stage between the market street and the Dali imperial palace, long-legged dancers twirled and spun zanily while a band of drums, gongs, and reeds urged them on. One performer in particular captured audience attention, a man who cross-dressed and danced in silky pink pajamas as an older woman smoking an exaggeratedly large pipe. We clapped and laughed. We also gasped and cheered for a younger man who was able to hold and twirl three women about his waist at once, despite his (and their) being on stilts.

Later that day, during one of their breaks, I lingered to see if I could talk with some of the performers. A thirty-something woman, who had dressed as a man for the afternoon performance, was rinsing out two beer bottles. "You performed very well," I commented. "Come in and chat with us," she said.

Inside was a single room, which felt cool after the mountain sun outside. In the middle of the room hung two racks of clothing, one of men's outfits, one of women's. On the right side of the room, most of the male performers lounged bare-chested, smoking or drinking water. On the left side of the room, a single male performer was playing cards with the other female performers. I was about to go to the left side of the room, but the woman led me to a bench on the right side and sat beside me. A younger man flopped down on the bench next to me, and a middle-aged man, flushed from the recent performance, pulled up a chair. He was the one who had performed the old woman smoking the pipe, and he, I found out, was the troupe leader, Mr. Wang. I directed most of my questions to him and the woman sitting next to me, Ms. Zheng.

Their troupe was from far northeastern Liaoning province and had been recruited to perform at Daliwood by the Dali Arts Troupe. They had trained in stilt and other dances since they were children. Some of the other performers in Daliwood came from other places; for example, the jugglers had been recruited from Wuqiao in central Hebei province, and some of the martial artists had been recruited from world-renowned Shaolin Temple, located in Henan province and the base of one of the protagonists in the novel, Xu Zhu. Troupe leader Mr. Wang said that they earned about 1,000 yuan per month (although I expected that he as troupe leader earned more). "Not bad," I said. "Yes, not bad," he nodded. They were given room and board, and stayed in a dormitory nearby.

"Don't you get homesick?" I asked.

"Yes, of course, we miss our families. And the food here is too spicy! We miss northern food, especially *jiaozi* [pork dumplings]," said Ms. Zheng.

When I asked how much longer they would be staying, Ms. Zheng said, "Ask our troupe leader."

"We'll probably stay until after the new year," Mr. Wang replied. "Then those who wish to stay can renew their contracts. Those who wish to return can go back home." Their contracts were from six months to one year, and some had renewed them two to three times.

These were Han Chinese performers from the far northeast, recruited to work in Dali to perform "exotic" dances for other Chinese tourists from the east coast. Like the actors in the television series and the tourists I have described in chapter 3, they cross-dressed and "cross-ethnicked" (Robertson 1995, 975). Shortly, we as tourists would have our own opportunity to cross-ethnic and cross-dress.

As the stilt dance concluded, our guide ushered us ahead to the majestic Dali imperial palace. Up a flight of steep stone steps, we found ourselves in a temple-like throne room. Facing us, three women in beautiful satin robes sat giggling on a golden throne. Our guide informed us that here we could rent costumes for 10 yuan (US$1.21) and take our own photos. About half of our group, both men and women, delightedly dressed up as Dali royalty (see illustration) and waited a turn to take the throne.

This was the opportunity for us to perform our own fantasies based on

Tourists transperforming as Dali royalty. (Photo by B. Notar, 2005)

our nostalgia for Jin Yong's novel and the television series based on it. We could further engage in playful nostalgia for other historical novels or dramas we had read or seen. It allowed us to put our imaginations into practice. There were other places in Daliwood where we could do this as well. For example, when we first entered the city gate, there were posters of wanted criminals, the "Four Great Wicked Ones" (M. *si da e'ren*) from the novel, and a wooden "prisoner" cart. The second day I visited Daliwood along with a group of tourists from Xiamen, in Fujian province, a group of young women went directly to the cart. One pretended to be a caught criminal, while the others pretended to be guards, leading her away. There was also an archery range, where both children and adults could try their hand, under supervision from some of the performers, at bows and arrows and crossbows.

In Daliwood tourists playfully perform the past based on their previous reading and viewing of fictional historical narratives. It has been suggested that "the closer that life in the tourist resort comes to resemble the pure play form, the more will tourists flock to visit" (Rojek and Urry 1997b, 11). This may not hold true for all tourist resorts, but in the case of Daliwood, allowing adults to play out some of their fantasies is key to the success of the site.

"Heavenly Dragons Hero" performed in front of the Daliwood palace. (Photo by B. Notar, 2005)

After our own mini-performances as Dali royalty, our guide informed us that we should wait on the stone railing seats by the main plaza where we had seen the stilt dance. There we would see our final performance of the afternoon, a scene from the novel and television series that the theme park called "Heavenly Dragons Hero."

Blue smoke emanating from a carved stone (styrofoam) dragon head at the base of the palace steps announced the start of the performance. Instead of live music, a soundtrack played over the loudspeakers, and the actors mimed their performances, reenacting the scene where Ma Furen and Quan Guanqing expose Qiao Feng as being not Han Chinese but of Khitan descent. Once his ancestral "impurity" is exposed, Qiao Feng's authority over his band of beggar brothers is challenged, and he leaves. Shortly thereafter, however, when the band is attacked by the Xixia, Qiao Feng returns to save them. This scene was not explained to us. It was assumed that we were already familiar with the narrative.

When the Xixia attacked, the actors engaged in stylized martial arts combat. As the Xixia and Qiao Feng's band fought, they cracked open "stone" pedestals, clearly made of styrofoam. When one of Qiao Feng's men severed one of the Xixia men's heads, the (false) head went flying, and "blood" spurted out from the neck. It was so clearly exaggerated and over the top that the crowd laughed and cheered. There was no pretense of reality, only of an enjoyable performance.

It has been argued that in a world of simulations, "it is increasingly difficult to differentiate between the simulated and the real. . . . In such a world, the tourist would not know an 'authentic' experience even if one could be found" (Ritzer and Liska 1997, 107). I disagree that tourists would not know the difference between the "authentic" and the "inauthentic"; I am more in accord with the appraisal that "people may still be able to tell the difference between reality and artifice, but increasingly they don't care which is which" (Fjellman 1992, 254). Clearly our group could differentiate between a real battle with real injuries and a performed one with fake injuries, and certainly we knew that Daliwood was not the real Dali Kingdom. But did we care? What difference did it make if this was a film set and not a real historical site? We were enjoying ourselves. Moreover, we could "take a certain comfort in artifice" (ibid., 300), for example, that the battles were exaggeratedly false.

Yet is there no problem "when the imagineered logic of Disneyworld becomes the logic of the rest of the world" (Relph 1991, 104)? Fjellman suggests that there are two "dangers" to Walt Disney World, which I think are also applicable to Daliwood. First, he asks: "If the truth value of parts of the past is indistinguishable from the truth value of fantasy and futurology, then what is history but crafted amusement?" (Fjellman 1992, 62). In other words, if we come to associate fantasy as being as "true" as reality, then what does it matter what actually happened in the past? Dali intellectuals have something to say about this, which I discuss below in relation to a conference held in Jin Yong's honor. Second, Fjellman cautions that in parts of Disney World, "we learn to think of other nations as theme parks" (ibid., 240). In the case of China and Dali, we can say that tourists are being taught to think of other nationalities (M. *shaoshu minzu*), the minority peoples of China, as leading a theme-park-like existence.

Theme Park Fever

Since the 1970s officials and developers across Asia have constructed hundreds of theme parks for political and economic purposes (Hendry 2000; Oakes 1997, 44; Oakes 2006). To tap into the "theme park fever" (M. *zhuti gongyuan re*) (Oakes 1997, 50) sweeping the rest of China, Dali officials and developers have not only constructed Daliwood, but have implemented Zhang Nan's plan to transform the Dali basin based on Jin Yong's novel. To implement this plan, Dali government and party officials have actively solicited transnational investors to fund these projects: French, German, Japanese, Taiwanese, and Thai companies have agreed to sign on.[20] While some scholars have seen more of a tension between transnational capital and China's party-state earlier in the reform era (ibid., 134; Ong 1997, 172), in Dali, transnational investors, government officials, and Communist Party cadres have cooperated profitably.[21]

The Dali plan has drawn on elements from four types of theme parks: parks based on a representation in popular culture such as a novel, re-created historical towns, the "nation in miniature," and a variation on this, the "folk villages." However, the Dali plan has differed from previous parks in that it has not been limited to a confined space but has extended across the entire Dali basin. Dali itself can become a theme park.

The first type of theme park, that based on representations in popular culture, has been constructed by officials and developers who seek to commodify a preexisting interest in a novel or film. I have mentioned the *Dream of the Red Chamber* theme park in Beijing and the *Romance of the Three Kingdoms* theme park in Sichuan province, which inspired Zhang Nan's plan for Dali. In addition to these, there exist at least twenty-three *Journey to the West* parks in China (Oakes 1997, 50) based on the classic novel that recounts the adventures of a mischievous monkey king. The overall plan for Dali fits within this type of theme park, yet it also draws inspiration from three other types of parks.

The main market street, city walls, and imperial palace of Daliwood fit the type of the re-created historical town. They are an attempt to re-create the capital of the Dali Kingdom, but this re-creation has extended beyond the walls of Daliwood itself.

In 1998 most of the old main street of Dali had been torn down and rebuilt into a replica of its former self. The two-story faded wooden storefronts, built on stone foundations and topped with gray clay-tile roofs, had been demolished. In their place had appeared concrete foundations on top of which sat gleaming crimson painted storefronts. Like a pedestrian street in a theme park (Fjellman 1992, 12), the old street was repaved and closed off to motor traffic. Perhaps to emulate the competitor Naxi minority tourist town to the north, Lijiang, a stream of water was added along the new street. In 1995, between the south gate at one end of the main street and the intersection with Foreigner Street, roughly in the middle of the main street, there had been a mix of shops for townspeople, souvenir shops, and residences. By May 2005, however, of the 291 shops I counted between the south gate and Foreigner Street, 92 percent were souvenir and film shops.[22] Only the second half of the street, between Foreigner Street and the north gate, provided shops that catered primarily to residents. The "creative destruction" (Zukin 1991) and reconstruction of Dali's main street looked beautiful, but it no longer felt like the old town.

Other cities in China have constructed "old towns" (M. *fanggujie*), literally "streets emulating the old." For example, city officials in Nanjing have ordered buildings surrounding the Confucian temple, Fuzimiao, to be razed. In their place have been constructed "picturesque" old-looking buildings that now house shops and restaurants (Anagnost 1997, 167). The city of Shengyang in northwest China has created a "Qing Dynasty Street" (Bai Lian 2001, 237–255), and I have observed that the city of Beijing has similarly razed and rebuilt the old arts street of Liulichang for tourist consumption of a literati past.

Still other theme parks in Asia have sought to re-create a general historic time period, such as the Chu Kingdom theme park in Wuhan, the Tang dynasty village in Singapore, and the Song dynasty village in Hong Kong (Oakes 1997, 44, 135). One park has even attempted to re-create the life of a specific individual: the Chairman Mao theme park in Hunan traces the Communist leader's life journeys and in so doing narrates a national history (see Dutton [1998] 2000, 234; Han Min 2001, 215–236).

The destruction and reconstruction of Dali is opposite to the preservation approach that some places have chosen. For example, the town of Lijiang, north of Dali, was recognized as a UNESCO World Heritage Site in 1997 (McKhann 2001, 147–166; Peters 2001, 313–332), and efforts there have focused on preservation. Michael Herzfeld (1991) has described the Cretan town of Rethemnos in Greece, where residents have been required by local officials to maintain their homes in "traditional" style for the purposes of preservation for tourism. Similar preservation projects have begun along the Ping Shan Heritage Trail in Hong Kong (S. Cheung 2001, 257–270) and in the southeastern Chinese coastal city of Quanzhou (Nilsson and Tan 2001, 289–312).

The third type of theme park is what might be called the "nation-in-miniature." Daliwood not only contains an imagined replica of the Dali Kingdom, but also includes mini Liao and Xixia kingdoms, and Jurchen tribal lands. In actual geography, the distance between Dali and the northern steppes is great. But for the purposes of filming and touring, these distances are shrunk and encapsulated.

Perhaps the best known of the nation-in-miniature type of theme park in Asia is "Beautiful Indonesia," which opened in 1975. The park presents a unified and sanitized version of the nation and was a pet project of President and Mrs. Soeharto (Pemberton 1994, 150–160). In China theme parks illustrating the nation in miniature have proliferated since the late 1980s. These parks "construct a landscape in which the 'essence' of a nation is represented" (Oakes 1997, 34). "Splendid China" (Jinxiu Zhonghua), a thirty-plus-hectare park located in the southern special economic zone boomtown of Shenzhen, miniaturizes China's most famous sites, such as the Great Wall and the Tibetan Potala Palace (Anagnost 1997, 160). For those tourists and business people entering the mainland from the gateway city of Hong Kong, the park serves as an introduction to future potential tourist itineraries in the rest of China. For those who do not have the time or means to journey elsewhere in China, the park provides an "I was there" illusion. Posed properly and from certain camera angles, one can appear to be standing in front of the real Great Wall or Potala. Splendid China presents "a timeless identity" (Anagnost 1997, 165) within the "supermodern" (Augé [1992] 2000) setting of the city of Shenzhen.

These national Chinese theme parks are reminiscent of the Qing dynasty imperial hunting and leisure grounds at the summer capital of Chengde, north of Beijing (see Dutton [1998] 2000, 231). Set amid rolling hills, Chengde includes replicas of structures from around the empire, such as a Tibetan prayer hall based on the Potala in Lhasa and a southern Chinese style garden and pagoda. In his in-depth analysis of Chengde, Philippe Forêt suggests that the imperial park "formed a composite landscape that reproduced the map of the Manchu empire" (Forêt 2000, 18). From their villas the Manchu Qing rulers "contemplated their empire by observing a microcosmos that acted as a synecdoche for the entirety of their domains" (ibid., 18). The imperial park at Chengde reproduced a "microcosmos" of the empire, just as the Splendid China parks reproduce a "microcosmos" of China's present national empire. Yet, while the imperial park was reserved for emperors and their entourages, the current theme parks are open to a paying public. In the former, the emperors could contemplate their empire; in the latter, the paying public gazes upon the national empire with which they are intended to identify. The theme parks reinforce the conceptual boundaries of the national empire.

The fourth type of theme park focuses on the "peoples" more than the places of the national empire. The Chinese Folk Culture Villages (Zhonghua Minsu Wenhuacun) in Shenzhen, the Chinese Ethnic Culture Park in Beijing (Zhonghua Minzu Yuan), and the Yunnan Nationalities Villages (Yunnan Minzucun) in Kunming exhibit China's "minority nationalities" in re-created ethnic villages. These villages highlight stereotypical elements of each minority group: The Dai (Tai) village in Kunming contains a Buddhist stupa, and tourists can participate in a water-splashing festival. The Bai village holds a temple containing a grotesquely exaggerated *benzhu* (local tutelary) deity. In the minority village of the Wa, a group stereotyped as one of the most "savage" of the Chinese borderlands, barefoot women dance wildly, shaking their long hair.

In an interview I conducted in 1995 with Mr. Mu, the manager of the Kunming park, he informed me that he tried to give tourists a clear concept of each minority group and found that the most popular "villages" in the park were those that were clearly categorized. "The Dai are popular," he explained to me, "because they are a 'water nationality' (M. *shui zu*). They are rather unique and give people a very beautiful feeling. The Bai are popular because they have been greatly influenced by the Han and because they have developed to an advanced stage (M. *fazhan de bijiao xianjin de*). People like the Wa because their character is as hard as steel. They are fierce and violent. When they dance, they are like America's Indians."

Mr. Mu suddenly stood up and mimicked how he thought a Native American Indian would dance, shuffling and shouting, shaking his head. I was startled and couldn't help but laugh. He laughed too, then sat back down behind his desk and continued: "In the future, I would like us to follow a Japanese marketing concept and be able to categorize each nationality clearly by a three-part categorization so that when people think of a nationality they immediately call to mind this categorization. This will be excellent for advertising purposes. Each nationality should have one essence, one object, and one action (M. *yi jing, yi pin, yi dong*). For the Bai this would be as follows: they worship the color white, they produce Dali marble, and they celebrate the Third Month Fair." Manager Mu hoped that his categorization would operate like a familiarizing brand concept for tourists so that they would know what to look for and what to purchase in each village.

The Folk Culture Villages in China uncomfortably bring to mind the nineteenth- and early-twentieth-century world's fairs and expositions of Europe and the United States. At these fairs "primitive" and "exotic peoples" were on exhibit for millions of visitors. In "native" costumes, the peoples on exhibit performed quotidian and ritual activities for millions to see. In his history of the U.S. world's fairs between 1876 and 1916 (held in Philadelphia, Chicago, Seattle, and so on), Robert Rydell has argued that they served to "alleviate the intense and widespread anxiety that pervaded the United States" during a time of great socioeconomic change and "offered millions of fair goers an opportunity to reaffirm their collective national identity in an updated synthesis of progress and white supremacy" (1984, 4). Similarly, the Folk Culture Villages in China encapsulate the national empire at a time of great anxiety about socioeconomic change. Through their act of representing "exotic" minority peoples, the Folk Culture Villages serve to solidify metropolitan Chinese tourists' sense of their superior status and metropolitan progress relative to the more "backward" peoples of the borderlands.[23] It is this contrast (see Foster 2002, 47) between the "traditional" minorities and the "modern" urbanites that creates a sense of "progress."

In order to tap into tourist revenues, actual villages have attempted to mimic the mimetic theme park villages. For example, in an ironic twist, some theme park workers from Guizhou province have returned home to their real villages and attempted to establish their own village-level "folk" theme parks (Oakes 1997, 182; Oakes 2006). In other cases village officials in Guizhou, Yunnan, and Hainan have attempted to open village parks, with more or less success depending on their relationships with higher-level officials, the extent to which higher-level officials seek to control tourism development and revenue, and the extent to which villagers retain decision-making power (Oakes

1997, 182; Oakes 2006; Yang Hui et al. 2001, 167–177). Zhang Nan's plan to transform Dali based on Jin Yong's martial arts novel *Heavenly Dragons* extends these theme park characteristics beyond a village or park to apply to the entire Dali basin.

The danger in creating these tourist theme park playgrounds, however, is that tourists may come to think of all minority communities as places where they can play out their own fantasies and to view minority peoples as there to serve them. A growing trend of sex tourism in minority areas points in this direction (see Hyde 2001; Swain 2005; Walsh 2001, 2005). Minority peoples become objectified in this process (Sofield and Li 1998, 384). Moreover, the theme parkization of the past, where "the past is presently available mostly as commodity, as pieces of history as pastiche designed and marketed to assuage our nostalgia" (Fjellman 1992, 60), does not lend itself to an understanding of past histories of conflict and discrimination. It is this history that borderland scholars sought to bring to light at a Dali conference held in author Jin Yong's honor.

Talking Back

In April of 1994, the prefectural head of Dali, Li Yingde, sent a letter to author Jin Yong, thanking him for writing *Heavenly Dragons* and inviting him to visit Dali as an honored guest. Jin Yong was busy, but finally, after representatives from Dali visited him in Hong Kong, he agreed to come to Dali in 1996 (Shi and Zhang 1998, 225). Amid a sea of photographers and reporters, prefectural head Li presented Jin Yong with a golden key to Dali and made him an honorary citizen. The author was taken on a tour of Dali, laden with souvenirs, and fêted.

During his visit an international scholarly conference was organized in the author's honor, and its proceedings were later published in a conference volume, *Jin Yong yu Dali* (Jin Yong and Dali; Shi and Zhang 1998). Conference presenters came from Beijing, Hong Kong, and Yunnan (ten from Yunnan altogether, with seven scholars from Dali constituting the majority).

The Dali conference forms part of a larger phenomenon of the emergence of *Jin xue*, "Jin Yong studies" or "Jinology" (Hamm 2005)—international scholarly conferences and publications dedicated to analyzing the author's writings.[24] These conferences point to a growing global scholarly interest in analyzing popular culture in general, and martial arts novels and films in particular. In the case of Dali, the conference was officially staged to use the author's fame to promote Dali, another example of borderland officials attempting to tap into the products of global popular culture for profit-making purposes (Oakes 1997). Yet the Dali conference had an officially unintended function: it offered a forum whereby borderland scholars could "talk back" (hooks 1989) to the author and coastal elites in attendance. Much has been written about the ways in which Chinese and Europeans have represented the Chinese borderlands (e.g., Diamond 1995; Harrell 1995c; Litzinger 1995; McKhann 1995; Swain 1995b), but scholars have only begun to pay attention to the ways in which borderland intellectuals view themselves and their own communities (Bulag 2002; Litzinger 2000a, 2000b; Schein 2002; Swain 2001). While it has been argued that minority elites are often complicit in perpetuating dominant stereotypes of the borderlands (Schein 2002), here we see an example in which some elites (officials) are attempting to perpetuate stereotypes for profit-making purposes, whereas other elites (intellectuals, but also state employees) are attempting to challenge such stereotypes for educational purposes.

At the conference several of the Dali scholars expressed gratitude to Jin Yong for creating a more positive image of borderland men. For example, Yang Guangfu noted that Jin Yong "abandoned the Han Chinese imperial orthodox prejudicial perspective toward minority nationalities usually found in battle and chivalry novels, and replaced it with a perspective of equality" (Yang Guangfu 1998, 200). Yang attributed Jin Yong's "many doting minority nationality readers" to the fact that the author "takes nationality equality as a key note" (ibid., 203). Another Dali scholar, Yang Guoqiong, praised Jin Yong's depiction of the character of Duan Yu, who exhibits a "kind of person-to-person emotion, pure platonic love, and a chivalric sense of justice" (Yang Guoqiong 1998, 199).[25]

While praising Jin Yong's depictions of borderland men, the Dali and Yunnan scholars were more critical of Jin Yong's representation of Dali's past. Liu Ts'un-yan has suggested that the "magic" (M. *moshu*) of Jin Yong is that he takes events based in historical fact and makes them "vivid" (M. *huoling huoxian*). A novel "cannot . . . be so woodenly identical to an official history (M. *zhengshi*) or local history (M. *fangzhi*)," Liu has argued (2002, 565). The popular success of a historical martial arts novel may well be in the "magic" of exaggeration and manipulation of historical events and characters. Indeed, Jin Yong's novels captivate readers through their magical settings and fantastic characters.

However, Dali and Yunnan intellectuals at the Jin Yong conference critiqued the novel's historical representation of their place. Their critique of these representations implicitly challenged official versions of historical events and borderland-center relations. They encouraged elite scholars from the "interior" (M. *neidi*, i.e., central China) to learn more about the past from a borderlands perspective and to rethink legitimating myths of national imperial conquest. Two conference presenters in particular, Dali scholar Shi Lizhuo and Yunnan author Tang Shijie, took the opportunity to try to educate their coastal colleagues.

Dali historian and editor Shi Lizhuo told the conference attendees that "naturally, artistic creation and actual life (including historical reality) are not the same, but understanding historical reality is beneficial to the reading of a related novel" (1998, 215).[26] Shi Lizhuo emphasized the glories of Dali's past as a kingdom that stretched from what is now northeast Myanmar to the eastern part of China's Guizhou province and from current Xichang in Sichuan province to northern Vietnam. He described the splendor of Buddhism in the Dali Kingdom and the wealth of Dali's elite, as depicted in Zhang Shangwen's A.D. 1180 *Long Roll of Buddhist Images,* which has become important to the study of Buddhism in general (see Chapin 1972; Li Lin-ts'an 1982; Zhang Xilu 1999, 47–54).

Shi Lizhuo also reminded conference attendees that borderland and central relations were not always cordial. When Tang dynasty troops advanced on the Nanzhao Kingdom, the Nanzhao ruler's son Feng Jiayi and the general Duan Jianwei overwhelmingly defeated the Tang in a battle at Xi'erhe (now the city of Xiaguan). Shi Lizhuo further noted that Chinese Song dynasty founder Zhao Kuangyin had wanted to expand to the south and conquer Dali, but "his wild ambition (M. *yexin*)" was constrained by historical circumstances and troubles to the north. It was not until 1252, when Kublai Khan's army conquered Dali, that Dali became part of the Mongolian Yuan dynasty empire.

Through his discussion of conflict and conquest, Shi challenged the Chinese state ideology of "nationality unity" (M. *minzu tuanjie*) whereby all borderland "nationalities" have belonged within the bounds of the empire from an indefinite historic past and all have coexisted peacefully. Contrary to imperial narratives that assumed culture flowed only from the center out to the borderlands, Shi Lizhuo emphasized that the Dali Kingdom contributed much to the "interior" Song dynasty. From Dali came Buddhist texts, herbal medicines, knives, swords, and wool felt.[27]

Similarly, Yunnan author Tang Shijie underscored the high level of development of the Dali Kingdom, emphasizing that it was a "famous political power" and that "the Dali Kingdom's agriculture, animal husbandry, handicrafts, and metallurgy were advanced (1998, 184). Tang challenged narratives that Chinese culture was necessarily more developed than borderland culture. In addition, Tang noted that the Dali Kingdom was not isolated but connected to South Asia and beyond through extensive trade networks. Mule trains traveled to what is now Tibet, Nepal, India, and Persia (ibid., 185).

Shi Lizhuo's and Tang Shijie's discussions certainly displayed local historical pride, but in addition to this they encouraged the other conference participants and the broader audience of the published volume to think of Dali not only as a fantastic place of the past, but as an actual place in the past, one that controlled a large territory and had a highly sophisticated spiritual and material culture. They emphasized that material and cultural goods did not just move one way, from the center out to the borderlands, but that Dali provided the center with many cultural and material resources. In providing this narrative, Shi and Tang countered a national imperial narrative of the necessity of a Chinese civilizing presence in the imagined "barbaric" borderlands.

Borderland intellectuals used the opportunity of the Jin Yong conference to highlight Dali's glorious past to counter a national imperial mythology of "nationality unity" and to contest the idea of a one-way transmission of culture from the center out to the borderlands. In this sense the borderland intellectuals resembled Yao minority intellectuals about whom Ralph Litzinger (2000a) has written: they are attempting to show their centrality to the nation, not their marginality.[28]

Despite the explicit and implicit criticisms of continuing national imperial biases toward borderland history, the conference itself was circumscribed within the larger goal of using the novel and its author to market Dali. A final theme expressed by scholars at the conference was praise for Jin Yong's business acumen and gratitude to him for writing a novel that could be used to promote Dali's development. In his paper "Jin Yong yu jingshang" (Jin Yong and Commerce), Yang Kuinie praised the author. Yang suggested that Jin Yong's combination of culture and commerce (he is a novelist and a billionaire) is a kind of "Confucian commerce" (M. *Ru shang*) and should be a model for Dali and for all of China to follow into modernity.

Yang further emphasized how "Jin Yong's novels have become Dali's cultural resource" (M. *renwen ziyuan*) and that "the novel has promoted and accelerated economic development; it has been a matchmaker, a bridge builder" (Yang Kuinie 1998, 209–210). In his praise Yang was comparing the novel both to a traditional matchmaker who arranges a marriage between locals and tourists, and to a spatial and temporal bridge, between Dali and the outside, the local and the global, the underdeveloped and the economically developed. This literary text would allow the place and people of Dali to cross over into prosperity. Yang Kuinie's praise of Jin Yong and his novel as a cultural resource was not empty talk, for local officials and transnational developers had already begun to market Dali as a tourist site to Jin Yong fans.

Conclusion

Scholars have debated whether people seek out "the simulation of historical worlds," as in Civil War reenactment, because they seek an "authentic world" of "narrative coherence" that their own "everyday, alienated lives lack" (Handler and Saxton 1988, 243) or whether people "living in a post-modern world dominated by simulations increasingly come to want, nay to insist on, simulations when they tour" (Ritzer and Liska 1997, 107), that is, "many tourists today are in search of inauthenticity" (ibid.). I have suggested here that people delight in historical simulations in Dali not because they are explicitly searching for authenticity or inauthenticity but because they are seeking a place and time that allows them to indulge in and perform their own fantastic nostalgia based on previously consumed narratives. This fantastic nostalgia is similar to the utopian nostalgia I discussed in chapter 3 in being framed by narrative, but it differs notably in that an older generation of tourists is able to remember the 1950s themselves, whereas no tourist alive can recall the eleventh-century setting of the novel *Heavenly Dragons*.

In earlier chapters I illustrated that the Lonely Planet guidebook has tapped into a colonial nostalgia for transnational travelers and the 1959 film *Five Golden Flowers* has drawn on a utopian nostalgia for national tourists who seek to recapture idealism in the midst of the cynicism of the reform era. In both of these cases, travelers and tourists have sought to consume Dali as an exotic place of contrast: transnational travelers have considered themselves privileged observers of a rapidly disappearing "authentic" minority culture; national tourists have viewed Dali as a currently "backward" minority place in the process of development. Like the transnational travelers and other national tourists, the new middle classes in China who have the luxury to travel and Overseas Chinese elites who are martial arts novel fans can heighten their own modern status by consuming what they imagine to be the nonmodern. In this chapter, the tourists who come to Dali because of their familiarity with the martial arts novel *Heavenly Dragons* are seeking an exotic borderland place that not only is lagging behind other "modern" places, but is a fantastic place of the distant past.

Yet in the process of providing a tourist playground based on Jin Yong's novel *Heavenly Dragons*, Dali is increasingly becoming a "hyperreal" place, a place "sheltered from . . . any distinction between the real and the imaginary"

(Baudrillard 1988, 167), a classic characteristic of theme parks such as Walt Disney World (see Eco [1967] 1987; Fjellman 1992). We observed this phenomenon of blending representation and reality in the previous chapter with the movie musical *Five Golden Flowers* and Butterfly Spring, and in this chapter we have seen its intensification. The blurring of the real and the imaginary is no longer contained to a single spot, however, but is being extended to an entire region, so that Dali itself is becoming like a giant theme park. Inherent in this process of theme parkization is the danger that tourists may come to think of Dali and the people there as leading only simple, theme-park-like lives. Moreover, in providing tourists with a playful place of a fantastic past, where tourists can "indulge the fictional in the landscape of the real" (DeLyser 2003, 896), historical events are subsumed by imaginative ones, and the actual is subsumed by the fictional.

I concluded this chapter with comments by borderland intellectuals at a Dali conference in Jin Yong's honor who praised the author's depiction of minority men and critiqued his fictional representation of Dali's past. Both their praise and their critique, I have suggested, served as a form of "talking back" to stereotypical Chinese representations of Dali as a politically "marginal" and culturally "backward" place. In the following chapter I turn from the discussion of representations in popular culture and tourist nostalgia to examine in greater depth the divergent perspectives of townspeople and villagers on the transformations of the place of Dali. We will examine more closely the relationship between "talking back" and place, as townspeople and villagers strive to achieve prosperity in China's reform era.

CHAPTER 5

Earthly Demons

Displacing the Present

*But to care for a place involves . . . a real responsibility and
respect for that place both for itself and for what it is to your-
self and to others.*

(Relph 1976, 38)

The local television station announced the opening of the tourist cave on
the evening news.[1] Bright flags flew outside while prefectural, township, and
village-level officials cut a red ribbon. The site was called, as Zhang Nan had
proposed in his development plan for Dali based on Jin Yong's martial arts
novel, "Heavenly Dragons Cave" (Tianlong Dong) and had been constructed
halfway up the mountainside not far from Butterfly Spring. Several villagers I
knew visited the cave shortly after it opened. They described their experience
there as "strange." One woman told me that she was terrified going through
the dark places and had held her friend's hand the entire time.

Not long after the cave opened, it closed for inspection. Rumors ran rife in
the village. According to one rumor, a woman had been killed by a bandit who
was hiding out there. Another rumor related that the cave had been formed
when a bolt of lightning struck. The lightning split open the mountain. From
deep inside the earth, a giant serpent crawled into the cave. The serpent lay
in wait for unsuspecting tourists, whom it would swallow whole. The cave did
not reopen before I left Dali in the summer of 1995.

In his novel *Heavenly Dragons* Jin Yong depicts Dali as a place of mysti-
cal creatures and unearthly events where one should always expect the unexpected. Could the cave closing have been a promotional ploy on the part of
municipal authorities, one meant to enhance Dali's reputation for the "strange
and mysterious"? This is highly unlikely—village rumors would not reach the
ears of tourists. It is more likely that there was some technical difficulty in the
cave—unreliable electricity for the "eerie" lighting, a leak, or a slippery spot.
Why then the village rumors?

The rumor of the serpent in the cave continues a long tradition of serpent
stories in Dali. One well-known tale tells of a giant serpent who lived in the

mountains. This serpent would capture and eat any woman who came into the mountains to collect firewood or visit temples. Finally, a poor village hero, Duan Chicheng, slew the giant serpent by sacrificing himself. He tied knives to his body, then allowed the serpent to swallow him whole, thus stabbing the serpent from the inside.[2]

Old serpent legends reflected a reverence for the powers of place and the supernatural. The mountainside where the new tourist cave opened is home to both beneficent and malevolent spirits (ancestors, ghosts, and strange creatures such as serpents). Many temples stand on its slopes. The recent rumors continued this reverence for place and the supernatural. As one village woman told me: "They shouldn't have opened the cave there. That place on the mountain was struck by lightning. No good could come of it." While old serpent legends may have served to make a moral commentary on women who wandered too far into the mountains by themselves, the recent rumors seemed to make a moral commentary on the disruption of a supernatural place for the sake of development.

While these village rumors did not constitute resistance (see Scott 1985, 1990) to Dali's development, they did challenge the official logic of what constitutes the "rational." As Jean-Noël Kapferer has pointed out: "Rumors are not necessarily 'false': they are, however, necessarily unofficial. Marginalized and at times in the opposition, they challenge official reality by proposing other realities" ([1987] 1990, 263). Village rumors underscored that the opening of a tourist cave on the mountainside was not only inappropriate, but downright dangerous given the potential to unleash the mountain's supernatural powers.

The rumors themselves were not enough to close down the cave, but the rumors provided a running critique on the development of tourist sites that did not take into consideration the very place and people themselves. These rumors pointed to the views of at least some villagers that new tourist places posed potential threats to human well-being.

In chapter 4 we saw a divergence between official appropriation and promotion of Jin Yong's martial arts novel *Heavenly Dragons* to market and transform Dali, and challenges by some Yunnan scholars to the novel's fictionalized representation of Dali's past. In this chapter I turn to the broader issue of what the transformations of Dali as a place mean for the people there. As geographer Timothy Oakes has highlighted, "The experience of tourism becomes a fundamental component of people's senses of place and ethnic identity" (1997, 66). We will see in this chapter that this sense of place and identity is not unified at the local level: townspeople and younger and older villagers increasingly vary in their views regarding the future of their place.

In particular, we will examine the divergent views of townspeople and younger and older villagers toward tourism industry construction. Anthropologist Marc Augé has described "air, rail and motorway routes . . . airports and railway stations, hotel chains, leisure parks" as "nonplaces" (non-lieux), spaces that are not initially "relational, or historical, or concerned with identity" (Augé [1992] 2000, 77–79).[3] These nonplaces of "transport, transit, commerce and leisure" are intended to be passed through quickly, not lingered in or inhabited (ibid., 86, 94, 104). The proliferation of these nonplaces, he suggests, represents a condition not of "postmodernity" as some geographers have suggested (Harvey [1989] 1990), but one of "supermodernity," where the focus is on movement. This idea of nonplaces of supermodernity applies well to the new kinds of structures that have appeared in Dali.

Time over Place

In 1999, when I returned to visit my town host family, Teacher Zhang and Teacher Duan spoke excitedly about Dali's rapid changes. The new buildings— the hotels and condominiums—and the newly constructed "old" buildings on Dali's main street made Dali look more beautiful than ever. Dali as a place was modernizing—xiandai hua—literally "transforming into the present."

The teachers spoke of speed conquering space: "Whereas before it would take ten to twelve hours on the bus to get to Kunming, with the new highway, it takes only four hours. Or, we can take the new overnight train, which arrives in just six hours. And with the new airport, one can fly to Kunming in about an hour!" Modernity meant getting places faster. Geographer David Harvey ([1989] 1990) has spoken of our current era as one of "postmodernity" characterized by a "time-space compression": people, products, and information can move increasingly more quickly over greater distances. Teacher Zhang and Teacher Duan celebrated the time-space compression that was taking place in Dali, but they saw nothing postmodern about it—it was finally allowing Dali to become modern. As Scott Lash and John Urry have observed: "The paradigmatic modern experience is that of rapid mobility often across long distances. . . . This mobility is not something that has simply existed but it had to be developed and organized" ([1994] 1996, 253; see also Urry [1995] 1997, 141). The airport, railway, and highway were organizing this modernity, or supermodernity, in Dali. As we have seen in previous chapters, this time-space compression and rapid modern mobility have allowed millions more tourists from farther away to come to Dali.

Yet it was not only tourists from elsewhere who took advantage of the new transportation infrastructure. Dali townspeople themselves began to travel to other parts of China and even to Southeast Asia. Teacher Zhang decided that since she was retired and had time, and since she had spent her entire life in Yunnan, she should "go take a look" (B. *bei hahaze*). Teacher Zhang left Teacher Duan alone at home to smoke cigarettes and tend his flowers while she began to go on group tours with some of the other women in their apartment building. First, she and her neighbors visited classic Chinese historical sites: the Forbidden City in Beijing, the gardens of Suzhou and Hangzhou. Then they traveled to scenic nature spots located in other minority areas such as Jiuzaigou, a Tibetan nature reserve in Sichuan province. Finally, they journeyed down to northern Thailand. Teacher Zhang showed me photographs from her travels. She posed for the camera much like the other Chinese tourists; however, as a very tall Bai minority woman, she usually stood above most of the other people in the photos.

Moreover, like the Chinese tourists whose one-day tour seemed to validate their "hometown feeling" (M. *jiaxiang gan*) and sense of modern status relative to what they saw as the "backward" place of Dali (see chapter 3), Teacher Zhang's trips seemed to heighten and reaffirm her hometown feeling and her status relative to others. "Northern food is not as good as our food," she would comment. Or "those other places are too crowded and noisy; they don't have the fresh air that we have here." Or "Thailand is not as developed as I thought it would be. There are some backward places there." Her travels solidified her confidence that despite being a minority woman living at the borderlands, she lived in a better and sometimes more developed place than others did.

Teacher Zhang's appreciation of Dali's new transportation infrastructure and her reaction to other places allied her more closely with coastal elites than with nearby Bai villagers. To travel quickly, and to solidify her status in relation to others made her feel more "modern." As Lash and Urry have noted, new forms of mobility produce new forms of subjectivity and apprehensions of place ([1994] 1996, 255–256; see also Urry [1995] 1997, 141). Through her travels Teacher Zhang had developed a new understanding of herself in relation to other peoples and places.

When I asked another townsperson, Mr. Dong, the Bai manager of one of the new "boutique" hotels in Dali, what he thought about the recent changes, he responded: "Modern culture (M. *xiandai wenhua*) and nationality culture

(M. *minzu wenhua*) will form one body (M. *yiti*); they will create a culture circle (M. *wenhua quan*)." He saw no contradiction between the "modern" and
the minority but saw them forming a "circle" like the green and white colors
of a jade ring, where one blended into the other. He himself was an example:
a minority man who managed a hotel, elegantly dressed in a tailored beige
suit. We sat talking in the glass and chrome lobby of his hotel, while a young
woman played classical music on an ebony baby grand piano in the back-
ground. He continued: "Because of Jin Yong's novel, everyone will know about
Dali, both nationally and internationally. Tourism development will ameliorate Dali's backward face (M. *luohou de mianmao*), change our socioeconomic
structure, and change traditional backward perspectives (M. *gaibian chuan-
tong de luohou de guannian*)." According to Mr. Dong the allegorical "face" of
Dali would be improved by the new transit and leisure infrastructure.

In contrast, most older villagers with whom I spoke viewed the rapid
changes in Dali from a different perspective than the teachers, Manager Dong,
and most other townspeople. Instead of celebrating time-space compression
and rapid modern mobility, they mourned the disruption of local places, bemoaned the creation of nonplaces, and lamented the proliferation of haunted
places.

"Rational" Displacement

It was a sunny May day in 1999 when I went back to visit my former research
assistant, Teacher Du, to see how he and his family had been faring since I
had last seen them. After four years away I had forgotten exactly how to get
to his village home and spent a few hours walking down dirt roads and across
narrow rice paddy paths until I thought I was in the general vicinity. There a
"grandfather" I asked kindly led me to Teacher Du's home.

Lanky Teacher Du was alone in the courtyard, hanging his grandsons'
blue socks on the clothesline to dry in the strong afternoon sun. "Oh, Na
Peisi [my Chinese name], you have come back! (B. *bei da ya lo*)." Teacher Du
smiled, surprised to see me. Although I had written to tell him that I hoped to
return to Dali in May, I did not know exactly when I would arrive. Once I was
in Dali, I could not call him, because he did not have a telephone. He invited
me and the grandfather up to the second floor of the new wing that he had
added to his house. The blue glass windows kept out the angry late spring flies
and created cool pools of light on the unfinished wooden floorboards.

Teacher Du insisted on boiling water for tea, so the grandfather and I
went back downstairs with him into the kitchen, watching as he placed wood

in the clay stove and drew water from the urn for the pot. When the water had boiled, Teacher Du handed us each pungent green tea in old glass jars, offered the grandfather a Gold River brand cigarette and then ushered us back up to the blue-windowed reception room.

Teacher Du and I inquired about the health and well-being of each other's families. His grandchildren were doing well in school; my parents were enjoying their retirement. Teacher Du's wife soon came home, and the grandfather excused himself. I brought out small gifts—an illustrated book of U.S. national parks for Teacher Du, postage stamp sets for his grandsons, lip balm for his wife and daughter. Teacher Du's wife went back down to the kitchen, and I knew that she would be cooking an afternoon snack. She would never let a guest come from afar and not be fed.

I asked Teacher Du about the new addition to his house. He said that he had used up three *fen* (0.05 acres) of their family's allocated three *mu* (0.49 acres) of land and had to pay a fee of 10,000 yuan (US$1,208.00) to the village office. "Even though we paid a building fee and now only have 2.7 *mu* (0.44 acres) of land, we still have to pay the same amount of grain tax as before. Out of our harvest of 4,000 *jin* (4,409 pounds), we pay taxes of 200 *jin* (221 pounds) and we must sell 600 *jin* (661 pounds) to the state at prices below market value. The other 3,200 *jin* (3,527 pounds) we eat ourselves, and if there is any left, we sell it. Our land has shrunk but our tax has not," Teacher Du explained.

We then talked about the new construction in the Dali basin—the airport, railroad, and especially the highway that ran right by the village. Teacher Du said that the engineering efforts on the highway had been substantial. "For months there were hundreds of workers and trucks here. Most of the workers were brought in by the Transport and Engineering bureaus, but some local men were hired on a part-time basis. They had to bring in truckloads of dirt and gravel. You see, the new highway is three meters higher than the surrounding land. Some people lost their farmland during construction. They were not allocated new land and were forced to give up farming and try their hand at other things. Some people even lost their homes—the highway went right through them! They were given a little money by the village office, but not enough to build a new home."

"Did anyone try to stop the construction or to get the highway route changed?"

"Of course they did. They went to the village office to complain, but it didn't work. The new highway couldn't twist and turn around every house. Once there was a plan, there was a plan."

I remembered when Teacher Du and I had gone to visit one home in another village four years earlier. On a hot, dry afternoon in April 1995, Teacher Du and I had knocked on the courtyard door as part of our random sample household survey. The man who answered the door, Mr. Li, agreed to be interviewed and ushered us into a newly constructed room off a courtyard shaded by a pomegranate tree. We all sat down on low wooden stools. Teacher Du offered Mr. Li a cigarette, and Mr. Li poured hot water from a crimson thermos into cups of tea leaves. After asking the man questions about his family size, educational level, land area, and crops, we came to the open-ended questions on the last page of the survey. When Teacher Du asked, "Have there been any problems in the reform era?" Mr. Li sighed, dragged on his cigarette, and leaned back on his stool.

"Look around you," he gestured. We looked around at the reception room—noting the finely carved wooden doors, the smooth cement floor, the freshly painted white walls. "I have been working hard these past few years of reform and have saved money so that I could build this new addition to my house. But now," he said, leaning forward on his stool, his voice taking on a different edge, "they are planning on building a new road, and they tell me that this road will run right through my house. Can you believe it? All of these years of working and saving, and soon it will all be gone."

How could they build a road through his house? Was there no recourse? Would he not be compensated? we asked.

Mr. Li shrugged his shoulders. He had gone to the village office and argued his case. He had tried to convince them to follow another route. Village officials told him that he would be duly compensated. However, construction had already begun on the road, which was slowly inching toward his house, and as of yet he had neither been compensated nor allocated land elsewhere. He was still undecided about what to do if and when the road construction crew finally reached his house.

The anticipated loss of his house without compensation touched a raw cultural nerve for Mr. Li. Two things in life are especially important for Dali farmers: land and a fine house. Without land, one is no longer a farmer, and without a fine house one's status in the village remains low.

Dali villagers construct homes or additions to homes with great patience and ceremony. After masons lay the foundation and floor, they allow it to settle for at least one year. Then, if its finances are in order, the family building the house will hold a beam-raising ceremony and a feast. Carpenters erect nine support pillars, each carved from a single pine tree. Male members of the family then choose an auspicious date to hoist high the three roof beams, si-

Continued highway
construction and house
destruction. (Photos by
B. Notar, 2005)

multaneously tossing coins and steamed buns to neighborhood children for good luck and sprinkling water from the beams to ward off any future fire. Depending on the family fortunes, a Daoist orchestra might be invited to play before the ceremony. In any event, the family would most certainly invite several tables of family and friends for a feast of fresh pork, preferably prepared in eight different ways. Sometime after the beam raising, construction would begin on the body of the house.

Several years later, once construction had been completed and enough money saved, a family would hold a house "birthday" party. The most spectacular house birthday party I attended lasted four days and three nights. On the first day a Daoist priest invited the water spirit, village deity (B. v ni; M. benzhu), and family's ancestors to attend. On the second day the ancestors, deity, and spirits were invited to celebrate along with eight hundred guests for a feast, after which a large Daoist orchestra played. On the third night the family invited male performers, who dressed as the Earth Mother, Earth Father, and other deities, to sing and dance until the wee hours of the morning. On the fourth day the Daoist priest asked the ancestors, deities, and spirits to go home, back to the ephemera. Although people did not speak of houses as having personalities, such as those described by Daniels ([1984] 1987) among Tamil villagers, these house birthday parties marked houses as beings, like humans, who matured and came of age.

All working adult villagers I knew who had not already built a new home or an addition to a home were saving money to do so. Even children, in a game resembling hopscotch, played at "building a house" (B. *cv ho*), where the winner was the one who completed a house first.

Houses clearly represented a village family's status in the reform era. Some new village homes—with their brightly painted front gates, spacious courtyards, and elaborately carved wooden doors and windows—rivaled former landlord mansions from the 1930s and 1940s. That Mr. Li would not receive any compensation for his newly expanded home was almost unthinkable. Later Teacher Du explained to me that prefectural and municipal authorities had allocated compensation funds, but these funds had not trickled down past the township, county, and village levels. If the road did indeed proceed through the man's house, he would be left homeless and possibly without compensation.

When farmers wanted to build a house, they were required to obtain permission from the village office. Some farmers were allowed to build on a large tract of land, some were allocated a small plot of land, and others were not allowed to build at all, depending on their family's specific relations (M. *guanxi*) with village officials (see Kipnis 1997; Y. Yan 1996; M. Yang 1994). However, when village and higher-level officials wanted to expropriate land for construction, they did not need the permission of other villagers.

Most villagers in Dali told me that they had warmly welcomed the "household responsibility system" (M. *baochan daohu*) of the reform era even though some households received more and better land than others. In 1984 the Party had formally ordered communes across the country to be disbanded and for land once again to be distributed to individual households. Land was redistributed according to the number of people in a household and according to the amount of land available per production team (M. *shengchan dui*). Some production teams had more land than others, so land was not distributed equally across the Dali basin. Villagers drew straws for specific parcels of land, some receiving excellent valley land, some swampy landfill, others rocky mountain land.

By 1994, however, only a decade after the communal land had been redistributed to households, local officials were already expropriating parcels of land for tourism industry construction, exercising the state's right to eminent domain. Legally, local officials, as representatives of "the state," could determine the "rational use of the land." But villagers, as representatives of "the people," often questioned both the official rationale and the process of this land reclamation.

In Dali's densely populated and cultivated prefecture, there is no "empty" land except that near the mountain peaks. Mountainous terrain constitutes 93.4 percent of the prefectural land and valleys only 6.6 percent of it (DZNJ 2004, 31). In the Dali basin, villages and fields sit both in the valley and on the mountain slopes. Farther up the slopes lie ancestral tombs and temples. On the mountainside stretch cattle pastures, and above these stand clumps of forest from which villagers gather mushrooms and firewood for cooking. People use every bit of land except that rising above the tree line. In the three villages where Teacher Du and I conducted surveys, household landholdings were only two to three *mu* (0.33 to 0.49 acres). From this small parcel of land, households would grow beans and wheat in the winter, and rice or corn in the summer, enough to feed their family and animals, and to pay their taxes in kind.

Available arable farmland was not only at a premium but was shrinking. In 1992 almost 3 million *mu* of fields (494,200 acres, nearly 200,000 hectares) were planted in the prefecture. By 2003 the area of planted fields had shrunk by over 146,000 *mu* (24,050 acres, nearly 10,000 hectares) (see table below). In the Dali basin (Dali municipality), in 1992 over 200,000 *mu* (32,950 acres or 13,355 hectares) of fields were planted, but by 2003 this had shrunk by 33,513 *mu* (5,521 acres or 2,234 hectares). The Dali 2004 yearbook records that available farmland had decreased by 1,291.3 hectares (3,191 acres or 19,370 *mu*) between 2002 and 2003. Of this "the state" (*guojia*) had appropriated 263.53 hectares (651 acres or 3,953 *mu*) for construction, "others" (which could include both developers and private individuals) used 661.9 hectares (1,636 acres or nearly 10,000 *mu*) for construction, and 366 hectares (904 acres or 5,490 *mu*) were returned to forest (DZNJ 2004, 266). Averaged out over the entire population, or even the entire farm population, the per capita decrease in land does not seem particularly significant. However, it is important to keep in mind that some farm families would be adversely affected—losing all of their land and their homes, while others would not. Furthermore, while the percentage of farmers relative to the overall population had decreased, the overall number of farmers had increased (see table).

This shrinkage of farmland is a growing national problem in the context of officially sponsored rapid real estate development. In China's reform era,

Changes in Dali's Population and Farmland, 1992 to 2003

	1992	2003	Change
		Dali prefecture	
Total population	3,085,500	3,358,300	(+272,800)
Farmers	2,793,800	2,943,300	(+149,500)
Percent farmers	91	88	-3
Fields in *mu*	2,963,200	2,816,477	(-146,723)
Fields in hectares	197,645	187,859	(-9,786)
Mu per capita	0.96	0.83	(-0.13)
Mu per farmer	1.06	0.95	(-0.11)
Hectares per capita	0.06	0.06	(0)
Hectares per farmer	0.07	0.06	(0.01)
		Dali municipality[a]	
Total population	448,211	535,556	(+87,345)
Farmers	304,701	325,295	(+20,594)
Percent farmers	68	61	-7
Fields in *mu*	200,230	166,717	(-33,513)
Fields in hectares	13,355	11,120	(-2,235)
Mu per capita	0.45	0.31	(-0.14)
Mu per farmer	0.66	0.51	(-0.15)
Hectares per capita	0.03	0.02	(-0.01)
Hectares per farmer	0.04	0.03	(-0.01)

Source: *DZNJ* 1993, 37, 39, 291; *DZNJ* 2004, 31–32, 266, 339.

[a]In 1992 Dali municipality was composed of two townships (M. *zhen*), Fengyi and Xizhou; eight districts (M. *xiang*), Wanqiao, Yinqiao, Chengyi, Qiliqiao, Wase, Haidong, Taiyi, Xijiao (the "suburbs" of Xiaguan); and two administrative areas (M. *banshichu*), Dali and Xiaguan. In 2003 the size of the municipal area had remained the same but the names of some of these units had changed: Wanqiao, Yinqiao, Qiliqiao, and Wase had become townships (M. *zhen*), as had Dali (into which had been merged Chengyi) and Xiaguan (into which its suburbs had been merged). Only Taiyi was still a district. By 2005 the municipal area was expanded to include Eryuan county (M. *xian*) at the northern end of Lake Er.

three problems in particular influence land control and management: (1) the ambiguity of the legal language, (2) a general unfamiliarity with the law, and (3) corruption (see Cai 2004, 664; Ho [2000] 2003, 94).

Articles 9 and 10 of the "General Principles" of the revised 1982 constitution of China contain the core of land management law. The first half of Article 9 states that "mineral resources, waters, forests, mountains, grassland, unreclaimed land, beaches and other natural resources are owned by the State, that is, by the whole people, with the exception of the forests, mountains, grassland, unreclaimed land and beaches that are owned by collectives in accordance with the law" (*PRCY,* 101). This long sentence can be broken up into three parts. First, "mineral resources, waters, forests, mountains, grassland, and so on," refer to any nonagricultural, uncultivated land. Much of China's borderlands, where the majority of minority people live, comprises this kind of uncultivated land (see Ho [2000] 2003, 108; Yeh 2000). Second, and this is where much ambiguity lies, the article states that these areas are "owned by the State, that is, by the whole people." In other words, "the State" equals "the whole people" but, as we see in the last part of the sentence, does not equal "collectives." Who exactly constitutes "collectives" (M. *jiti*) and how they differ from "the State" (M. *guojia*) leaves much room for interpretation, which, the article tells us, will be clarified by later laws.

Article 10 of the constitution provides further information on land management:

1. Land in the cities is owned by the State.
2. Land in the rural and suburban areas is owned by collectives except for those portions which belong to the State in accordance with the law; house sites and privately farmed plots of cropland and hilly land are also owned by collectives.
3. The State may in the public interest take over land for its use in accordance with the law.
4. No organization or individual may appropriate, buy, sell or lease land, or unlawfully transfer land in other ways.
5. All organizations and individuals who use land must make rational use of the land. (*PRCY,* 101)

In this article we again see a distinction between "the State" and "collectives" as well as a further distinction between these two categories and "organizations" and "individuals." The drafters of the constitution aimed to distinguish between national-level control and local-level control.

Mark Selden and Aiguo Lu have observed that even after the state officially disbanded communes in 1984, the word "collective" did not disappear from land management law. They point out the ambiguity of the term but suggest that we substitute "village" where "collective" appears (Selden 1993, 194). Selden and Lu also provide a useful five-point elaboration of the concept of "ownership" in relation to the land:

1. Formal landownership rights.
2. Use rights: over the cultivation, investment, industry, mining, and construction on the land.
3. Transfer rights: over the purchase, sale, rent, contracting, or inheritance of the land.
4. Product rights: over the consumption and sale of products of the land.
5. Labor rights: over the labor power of those attached to the land. (Selden 1993, 188)

In Dali the household responsibility system gave individual households limited use, transfer, product, and labor rights to the land, but formal landownership and final decision-making power still belonged to the collective, that is, the village office and higher-level authorities. That is to say, Dali farmers can decide what to plant, when to work, and what to sell at the market as long as they can fulfil their annual tax quotas either in kind or in cash. Farmers in Dali may even hire day laborers to help them in busy agricultural seasons, or they may rent out an entire section of land to another family who has less land. Farmers can also pass along their land use rights to their children. Individual farm households cannot, unless they have village office approval, build a house on their designated farmland or sell the land to an outsider. Farmers can decide what to do with their land only as it relates to farming activities.

The village office and higher-level officials, for their part, have the power to determine overall land use. Article 10 of the 1982 constitution specifies: "The State may in the public interest take over land for its use in accordance with the law." The constitution grants "the State" leeway to determine what is in "the public interest" and what is not. Moreover, the last sentence in Article 10 stipulates that people must make "rational use" of the land. Again ambiguity exists as to what constitutes "rational use." Is construction of an amusement park more "rational" than maintenance of a rice paddy? It is up to the authorities to decide.

On March 14, 2004, amendments were added to the constitution on land

and private property. An amendment to the third clause of Article 9 stated that while the state continued to have the right to "expropriate or take over land for public use," it was obligated to "pay compensation in accordance with the law" ("Land Administration" 2004). The constitution also contained a new article on the protection of private property:

1. The lawful private property *(siyou caichan)* of citizens may not be encroached upon.
2. The State protects by law the right of citizens to own private property and the right to inherit private property.
3. The State may, for the public interest *(weile gonggong liyi),* expropriate or take over private property of citizens for public use, and pay compensation *(geiyu buchang)* in accordance with the law. (ibid.)

Here we see that while the state now protects private property rights, it simultaneously guarantees itself the power to take that property away "for the public interest" as long as it makes compensation. However, as anthropologist Katherine Verdery has pointed out in the context of postsocialist Romania, property rights mean very little in the abstract unless they guarantee *"effective ownership"* for farmers (2003, 355; her italics).

The terms by which the state should compensate those whose land has been expropriated are elaborated upon in the "Land Management Law," first adopted in 1986 and most recently amended in 1998 (another draft law on property rights is currently under discussion) ("Land Management Law" 2004; "Revising Draft Property Law" 2005). Article 47 stipulates that compensation should include a subsidy for resettlement, compensation for crops already in the ground, and compensation for the land itself. The latter "shall be six to ten times of the average annual output value in the three years prior to requisition" ("Land Management Law" 2004). Apart from the issue of how the output value is calculated, there is the issue of the land being worth much more to a real estate developer than the value of its crops. The value of a home is not calculated. While the Land Management Law claims that the state "protects cultivated land and strictly controls turning cultivated land into noncultivated land" (Article 31), it also "protects the legitimate rights and interests of developers in accordance with law" (Article 38). Whether the "State" (i.e., officials at the local level) will "protect" farmers' land or "protect" developers' "rights and interests" will depend on the interests of the officials themselves, an issue that I will address shortly.

In addition to ambiguities in the language of the law, there exists a second problem of unfamiliarity with the law. In 1992 the Dali prefectural government recognized the problem of unfamiliarity and cited its promotional efforts as follows:

provided 215 film and video showings
made 78 television announcements
gave 319 slide shows
made 2,614 radio announcements
wrote 3,350 long-term educational slogans
wrote 21,026 short-term slogans
designated 125 uses of promotional vehicles
distributed 369 video cassettes
held 248 meetings
made 32 street and wall announcements
posted 351 notice boards
distributed 130,000 pages of materials
educated 1,321,800 people
trained 110 land management law inspectors (*DZNL*, 1993, 159)

Clearly this illustrates a bureaucracy in action. Yet we do not know the content of these efforts, whether any farmers attended the meetings or saw the posters, and what they learned. The almanac itself, the official annual guide to Dali, does not include a copy of the land laws.

Corruption was a third major problem with regard to land management. Although the state is required to compensate villagers for lost land and crops, compensation does not go directly to villagers but to "the production team or village" office and then to village families or individuals.[4] Beginning in 1995, but more vociferously in 1999, villagers in Dali began to complain to me that compensation for expropriated land had not trickled down past the level of the village office. Nor had they received any displacement compensation.

Official expropriation of land for development projects caused particular controversy in the village where Mr. Li lived. The village was located in a spot where higher-level officials had authorized the construction of a new road that would enable tourist buses to make a complete and scenic circle of Lake Er. To promote the construction of the road, village officials had written signs on the blackboards that lined some of the village streets: "If the people want to achieve prosperity, [they] must first build the road" (M. *Renmin yao zhi fu, bixu xian xiu lu).* Many villagers, such as Mr. Li, who was worried about the road coming through his house, did not have any say in the new project and certainly did not welcome the new road enthusiastically. Other anthropologists have noted the important connection between political voice and place. For instance, Jolly and Rodman in Vanuatu have observed that those who "lacked the power to voice their objections also lacked the power to regain their land" (Rodman 1992, 648).

While some villagers were not compensated at all, others received compensation well below market value. For example, local officials would give a household so much money for land, say 100,000 yuan (US$12,077.00) but then would turn around and sell the land use rights (M. *shiyong quan*) to a private company for 400,000 or 500,000 yuan (US$48,309.00 to US$60,386.00). The private company would in turn build shops and rent out the space to make more money. None of this extra wealth would "trickle down" to the original farm family. They would not share in the profits from the land they had once occupied. Teacher Du taught me a Bai proverb that I often later heard with regard to official corruption at the village level: "A cat rests and eats spicy meat; a water buffalo works and eats dry straw (B. *anni hoxian ye la gair, xuinge zuji ye ga ma*)." Farmers are like the buffalo, he explained, while officials are like the cat.[5]

Yongshun Cai, in his comparative analysis of land compensation and corruption in China, has argued that village-level officials have much to gain by continuing to expropriate land and by excluding villagers from decision-making processes: "Once self-serving people become village cadres, they may use power to pursue personal interest by usurping more land, selling land to others and pocketing the money, or even allotting land to some people as gifts. Their control over resources like land also enables them to establish personal connections with higher-level cadres which may help them obtain personal benefits and even provide protection for their corrupt activities" (Cai 2003, 667; see also Guo 2001, 426–427; Ho [2000] 2003, 108).

Not all officials in Dali were like corrupt cats, however. One conscientious village official confidentially expressed his concern to me that soon there would be homeless villagers. "Where will villagers go who have been displaced and who have not been compensated with land or money?" he mused. "What will they do?" Urban officials have focused on the problem of China's rural-to-urban migrants, who they fear are "flooding" the cities (see L. Zhang 2001), but they have only begun to see this problem as related to rural displacement ("China's Land" 2005, 40).

Ghosts on the Road to Reform

Teacher Du's wife came back up the stairs carrying two steaming bowls, each containing two fried eggs and sticky rice flour disks floating in a pork fat, sugar, and ground walnut broth. This was one of those dishes that had been difficult for me to learn to like but that I had missed greatly while I was away. "I am off to chant Buddhist sutras," she said, "but you can stay here. Rest at our house tonight."

I knew that Teacher Du's wife was the "sutra mother" (B. *jiain mo*), the woman who led the Lotus Pond Society, the group of older women who chanted at the village temple (B. v *zao sei*).[6] However, it was not the first or fifteenth day of the lunar month, when older women of the society usually gathered, so I asked why she was chanting today.

"You see," Teacher Du explained, "someone was killed a few days ago on the new highway. They are chanting for him. There have been several accidents on this new highway. Three other villagers were killed just a few weeks ago."

"How did this most recent accident happen?"

"It was at night. Duan Long was coming home, driving a putt-putt tractor (M. *shoufu che*). He turned down from the highway onto the village dirt road. There was a truck driving on the road too quickly, coming from the other direction. The truck driver didn't see the tractor. Duan Long's body was split in half—not across the stomach but from his groin to his head. His head was split in half." I grimaced, and we sat quietly for a moment. Teacher Du lit a cigarette.

"Did anyone from the village see the accident?" I asked.

"Yes, and the truck driver stopped too. If no one had seen it happen and the truck driver had not stopped, then that would have been the end of it. But the truck stopped. From the village office they called the Transportation Police. They came pretty quickly from Dali."

"Was the family compensated?"

"Well, the law only requires 7,000 yuan (US$845.00), but that isn't very much. The family wanted more, and the driver paid. I'm not sure how much. Do you want to go see them chanting?"

"Yes."

I followed Teacher Du and his wife up a village alley to a house just a few doors away. Upon entering the courtyard, I saw a cup of wine, a cup of water, and a cup of tea on the ground, surrounded by a circle of radiating incense sticks. Bamboo leaves had been spread atop wooden benches arranged in a half moon shape. I asked Teacher Du what this was.

"That is the bridge that his spirit must cross to come home. They want to call his spirit home tonight and then send it off again properly so that it does not forever wander the highway."

"What if his spirit does not come home?" I asked quietly.

"Aiya, who can say that there is a spirit? That is just a village superstition. Scientifically there is no spirit." Teacher Du momentarily switched back into his former schoolteacher role.

We walked through the courtyard to the main part of the house. Offerings covered a table at the front of the reception room: fried shrimp chips, burning incense, bowls holding broken pieces of straw. On the back wall of the reception room hung the family's genealogical scroll and below that a large black-and-white photograph of the deceased. "He was a young man!" I exclaimed.

"Only twenty-eight," Teacher Du nodded.

On the left wall hung a string of paper clothes for the deceased and above them a string of *jiama* ritual papers depicting *ku shen,* the spirit of mourning as a woman, her tears falling like rain on an umbrella below her (see illustration).[7] A young woman wearing the white cotton turban of mourning—Duan Long's widow—stood forlornly nearby.

On the right side of the reception room stood a Daoist priest who had set up a table with a bronze bell, a small gong, cymbals, and ritual texts printed in Chinese characters. An elderly man, he wore a brown felt fedora and a long blue cotton robe. He remembered me from four years before and pulled my old name card out of his robe. The priest briefly showed Teacher Du's wife how to play the cymbals in rhythm with his small gong—*beng, beng, beng*—then turned to Teacher Du's wife, two other Lotus Pond Society women, and Duan Long's older brother, who was also wearing a white mourning turban, and said, "*Bei*" (Let's go).

"They're going up to the highway where the accident happened," Teacher Du explained.

We walked up the dirt road to the new highway. As Teacher Du had told me earlier, the highway was higher than the village land around it. An air-conditioned tourist coach and a Mitsubishi sports utility vehicle zoomed by above us.

The Daoist priest and the three Lotus Pond Society women debated about where to conduct the ritual. In theory, it should be done on the exact spot of the accident. But what if they went up onto the road and became accident vic-

Mourning the dead: *jiama* ritual paper. (Purchased at weekly market)

tims themselves? In the end they decided that they would have to sacrifice some of the efficacy of the ritual for their own safety and would conduct the ritual near where the village road met the highway (see illustration).

Duan Long's older brother placed bowls filled with broken straw, fried shrimp chips, and fuschia incense sticks in a pile beside the highway while the Daoist priest and Teacher Du's wife hit the gong and cymbals in unison. After a few minutes they all turned to walk back to the village. Teacher Du asked if I wanted to stay overnight, but, thinking that it was an inconvenient time for them, I said I would go back to the town of Dali and visit them

Calling back the wander-
ing spirits of the road.
(Photo by B. Notar, 1999)

again later. Teacher Du waited with me by the highway for a minibus. Tourist minivans, sleek private sedans, and lumber trucks flew by. A few tractors
chugged past. After about twenty minutes a private minibus finally stopped
when Teacher Du waved it down.

Riding the minibus, I realized that the new highway had become a metaphor for different perspectives on Dali's reform era modernity. For provincial
and local officials, the highway was a symbol of progress, a route to the future.
For local officials, international investors, and local entrepreneurs, the new
highway was the key to making money by exporting local resources and im-
porting tourists. For Dali townspeople, the road allowed them to experience
time-space compression and to develop a modern identity.

For many villagers, in contrast, the highway represented a threat. The first threat came in the form of their displacement from land and homes as the highway moved through the Dali basin. It did not wind around villages and homes like a dragon; rather, it sliced right through them like a sword. Like the truck that had severed Duan Long's body in half from groin to head, the road cut the Dali basin in half from what villagers called the river's "tail" (B. *gvn ngv*), at the northern end of Lake Er, through the body of the mythical dragon of Dali (B. *nv wai*).[8] Furthermore, once displaced, villagers were not adequately compensated with land, money, or new homes. They might no longer be farmers, might have to move in with relatives, or might have to leave the area altogether to look for work elsewhere.

After the highway had been completed, it posed a second threat by claiming the lives of villagers and producing wandering spirits. Might not these restless wandering spirits, if they refused to return home and then leave peacefully, start to wreak more havoc on the highway? Particular parts of the highway could become haunted by the ghosts that wandered them.[9]

Like the truck that killed Duan Long, higher-level officials, tourists, and townspeople moved mostly north and south along the road to travel between towns and tourist sites, while villagers often moved laterally, east to west across the basin, from the lake to the mountains. Villagers followed dirt roads and paddy paths to climb into the mountains to attend major temple festivals, bury relatives, pay respects to ancestral tombs, collect firewood, or graze cattle and goats. To carry on these important ritual and economic activities would now require crossing the new highway and endangering one's life.

The villagers were supposed to embrace the road as a symbolic and economic route to reform; yet how were they to make the leap from the slow dirt road onto the high-speed highway without getting injured in the process? This was a different kind of leap from the Great Leap Forward that they had been asked to make four decades earlier. Yet, as before, this leap emphasized speed at the villagers' peril.

A few days after I visited Teacher Du and learned of the village accidents, I went to visit another village family, the Zhaos. I had met the Zhaos' daughter when she was studying in the United States, and she had asked me to bring a few things back to her family. Since I had never been to the Zhaos' village or home before, they were afraid that I might get lost trying to find it. Therefore, they met me in Dali in a shiny red taxi, and we rode back to the village together along the new highway. Before I could ask them what they thought of the highway, Mrs. Zhao said, "Oh . . . this road is bad."

"This road is not bad at all," said the taxi driver. "Look, there are two wide lanes. It is very smooth, with nice shoulders, so much better than the bumpy old road that we used to call the 'highway.' What is bad about this road?"

"There are too many accidents on it," Mrs. Zhao replied. "Just last week a group of people died."

"Because people drive too fast?" I suggested, hoping that the taxi driver would slow down a bit.

"Perhaps, but it is the road itself. There are too many intersections," Mrs. Zhao pointed out. Near the town of Dali, there had been signs indicating the intersections, but as we moved out into the countryside, the intersections between the highway and the village roads were unmarked.

While the taxi driver agreed that the design and construction of the road were problematic, he viewed the villagers themselves as even more problematic. "They don't have *renshi* [knowledge, understanding]. They'll ride their bicycle or tractor out onto the road and won't even look. They won't check if there is any traffic coming, they'll just turn the handlebars (M. *longtou*) in the direction they want to go." He shook his head. He thought that local officials should close off the road to village traffic in order to make it safer.

Whereas the villagers saw the road as a danger, the taxi driver saw the villagers as endangering efficient movement because they lacked sufficient knowledge. However, instead of providing the villagers with this knowledge (M. *renshi*)—such as how to cross the highway and how to calculate the speed of an oncoming vehicle—or giving them safe access in the form of traffic bridges and crosswalks, the driver suggested banning them from the highway altogether. One village official expressed a similar perspective: "Some villagers have a low educational level and their perspective is too narrow. Our process is one that must move from being inflexible to flexible (M. *bu linggeng dao linggeng*)."

The relationship between the villagers and the road in Dali underscores the larger issue of the relationship between villagers, townspeople, and city dwellers across China. Roads are not only metaphors, they also contribute to the formation of socioeconomic relations (Flower 2004; Thomas 2002). In the reform era process driven by the phenomenal growth of the coastal cities, should "narrow-minded" and "inflexible" villagers who cannot move at the proper speed on the road to reform be removed from that road altogether? What will happen to those who are left behind?

Disputing Displacement

Lack of compensation for land expropriation is not unique to Dali. It is estimated that in China every year, tens of thousands of disputes erupt over official expropriation of farmland ("China's Land" 2005, 40). Farmers across

China have been expressing anger over expropriated land and lack of compensation for it. Indeed, since land is the primary guarantee of farmers' future prosperity, "disputes over land use have been one of the most important reasons for peasants' collective action" (Cai 2003, 663, 672). Although the constitution was amended on March 14, 2004, to include guarantees regarding private property and China's prime minister, Wen Jiabao, has called for a temporary ban on "non-urgent conversion of agricultural land" ("China's Land" 2005, 40), official expropriation of land has continued, as have farmers' complaints. When farmers have dared to take collective action, their efforts have often been met with violence by police or hired thugs.

For example, between 2002 and 2004, villagers from Sanchawan in Shaanxi province staged a sit-in of a planned development site and their village's Communist Party headquarters in order to protest pending land expropriation without adequate compensation. They had tried petitioning local government offices and even sent representatives to Beijing but to no avail. Early in the morning of October 4, 2004, paramilitary police attacked the village and arrested twenty-nine farmers. In January 2005 twenty-seven of the farmers received stiff sentences of between two and fifteen years in prison (Ramirez 2005; Yardley 2004). In May 2005 two thousand villagers who were demonstrating against inadequate land compensation clashed with seven hundred police in Zigong, Sichuan province. Eighty villagers were detained. In response, a local official said that they would not increase land compensation, only increase "'propaganda work'" ("Police" 2005, A7). In June 2005 in the village of Shengyou, Hebei province, south of Beijing, farmers clashed with approximately three hundred thugs who were hired to clear the way for a waste-processing plant. Six farmers died, and fifty went to the hospital ("China's Land" 2005, 40). Also in June 2005 farmers of Maxingzhuang south of Beijing protested displacement to make way for the 2008 Olympic Aquatic Park ("Farmers" 2005). In July 2005 thousands of farmers from Sanshangang village, in Guangdong province, China's manufacturing hub, tried to stop bulldozers from leveling 670 hectares (1,656 acres) of land ("Thousands" 2005). In December 2005, in yet another conflict over construction and compensation, farmers from Dongzhou village in Guangzhou battled security forces, leaving dead and wounded (French 2005). As Yongshun Cai has argued, "in the use of rural land, the state tends to assume a predatory role in the sense that the local state and its agents often ignore the basic interests of the peasantry" (2003, 663). Since many local officials see their interests allied with private and higher-level state development projects, they do not represent the concerns of their rural constituents.

Chinese farmers are not unique in their protests over official expropriation of land. Hundreds of thousands of people protested their homes being razed to construct the "Beautiful Indonesia" theme park (Pemberton 1994, 152). Mexican farmers in San Salvador Atenco attempted to halt the construction of an airport outside of Mexico City by staging mass demonstrations and taking hostages (Thompson 2002). However, protests in China may be particularly intense at this time because of both the rapidity of real estate development and the population pressures on land.

In China not only have people protested land expropriation and lack of compensation, they have also protested traffic accidents. For example, in the spring of 2003, many Chinese Internet chat rooms were filled with indignation over the case of a BMW car owner who ran over an onion farmer. Authorities closed some of the chat rooms and message boards (Marquand 2005). In July 2005 thousands of people protested in Chizhou, Anhui province, after a car owner beat up a bicyclist who had scratched his car ("Thousands" 2005).

These protests reveal a growing tension between the new "haves," who can afford to buy cars, and the "have nots," who cannot. In the spring of 2005, a Mitsubishi Sport sports utility vehicle was advertised in the *Yunnan Daily* for 189,900 yuan (US$22,826.00) for a manual transmission and 309,000 yuan (US$37,319.00) for an automatic (*YNRB* April 29, 2005, 11). Yet in 2003 the average farmer's annual income in the Dali basin was only 3,291 yuan (US$397.00) and in the prefecture as whole, only 1,959 yuan (US$237.00) (*DZNJ* 2004, 32, 266). Unless a farmer has productive sideline industries or children who have gone to college and work at well-paying white-collar jobs, owning such a car would be a dream. The average working townsperson in the Dali basin earned a salary of 14,061 yuan (US$1,698.00), four times more than that of a farmer. A townsperson's average annual income in the prefecture as a whole was 8,339 yuan (US$1,007.00), more than double that of a farmer, although still modest compared to that of coastal elites. A townsperson might have to buy food, whereas a farmer could grow his or her own, but for any other items that were markers of "modernity," such as clothing, farmers would pay more, either in increased transportation costs into town or in the higher prices charged by the entrepreneurs who brought such items to rural markets.

In the Dali basin I neither observed nor heard of any acts of collective resistance against the construction of the new nonplaces and the increased incidence of traffic accidents.[10] Nor did I hear of Dali villagers holding meetings and sending representatives to higher-level authorities, as villagers have done elsewhere in Yunnan (Guo 2001). Certainly Dali villagers complained to and argued with local officials and took some cases of real estate development, corruption, and embezzlement to prefectural court. But perhaps older farmers in Dali were tired of years of political struggle. Or perhaps they had little faith that higher-level officials would intervene on their behalf if village officials had already refused to do so. Moreover, many younger Bai villagers saw their futures as being tied to the airports, railways, and highways leading to the towns and cities, "concrete embodiments of hope" (Flower 2004, 652), rather than to the dirt roads leading to the villages.

Conclusion

In earlier chapters I investigated what postcolonial scholars have called "symbolic displacement" (see Bammer 1994; Chow 1994)—the separation of representations from what they represent. The Lonely Planet guidebook, the film *Five Golden Flowers,* and the novel *Heavenly Dragons* all portray the people of Dali; yet once created, these representations circulate without the control of people in Dali. Furthermore, these representations may come to be used for very different purposes, as we saw in particular with the film *Five Golden Flowers* and the novel *Heavenly Dragons*. The film was originally intended as propaganda, and was later used to market Dali; the novel, originally intended for readers' pleasure, four decades later was also used to market Dali as a tourist destination. The chapters further illustrated the material after-effects of these representations—the formation of Foreigner Street, the transformation of Butterfly Spring, and the increasing theme parkization of Dali. Here I have examined more explicitly the connection between the symbolic displacement of representations from what they represent and the economic displacement of persons from place. While this connection has been suggested as a possible avenue of inquiry (Spivak [1988] 1994, 86), it has remained largely unexplored.

In this chapter we have seen that there exists a marked difference between the ways in which townspeople and younger and older villagers view the transformations of Dali as a place through tourism industry construction. Most Dali officials and townspeople, and many younger villagers, have viewed tourism-related development—the creation of an airport, railway, and highway; of Daliwood, the new "old" town, fantastic palaces, and tourist temples—positively, as bringing them closer to market modernity. Older Dali villagers, in contrast, have critiqued the commodification of historic sites and the construction of new nonplaces as displacing them from their past and present, and increasingly leading to a haunted future.

This divergence in perspectives between Dali townspeople, younger villagers, and older villagers reveals a divide between those who are profiting in China's market reform era and those who are not. While there is a growing gap between metropolitan coastal prosperity and peripheral poverty in China, it is more complicated than a simple center-periphery split (cf. Frow 1991). Most townspeople in Dali have been thriving in the reform era, and many younger villagers hope to.

While I observed no form of collective resistance to official confiscation of land and demolition of homes for new construction projects, villager rumors and narratives of traffic accidents have subverted official discourse as to what constitutes "rational" development and the "public interest." Like Yi minority villagers to the east of Dali who have used ghost stories to "produce an oppositional practice of time and an alternative mode of history" (Mueggler 2001, 9), Dali villagers have used narratives of supernatural serpents and haunted highways to challenge the current creation of nonplaces and have attempted to assign these new nonplaces unofficial, malevolent meanings.

As Marc Augé has noted: "Place and non-place are rather like opposed polarities: the first is never completely erased, the second never totally completed; they are like palimpsests on which the scrambled game of identity and relations is ceaselessly rewritten" ([1992] 2000, 79). Like a palimpsest—a piece of parchment from which the original writing has been partially erased and then written over—the original homes and fields where villagers had resided and labored were being erased and built over by new nonplaces of transit and leisure. In the process of using and visiting these new nonplaces, the villagers imbued them with new meanings, as happens with nonplaces, transforming them into places over time (ibid., 78). In this case the new meanings were malevolent.

In Dali there has been an official triumph of time over place.[11] Officials have emphasized rapid movement by car, bus, train, and plane, so that Dali can be more conveniently connected to urban centers. With the construction of highways, railways, airports, hotels, and parking lots, there has also been a triumph of new nonplaces of transit and leisure over former places of residence and labor. Local officials, in an effort to move quickly into a bright future, are marketing Dali as a place of a fantastic past and shaping Dali into a simulacrum of representations in popular culture. Townspeople who are prospering in this context are willingly leaping onto the road to reform. Meanwhile, many villagers, who have been viewed by some officials and townspeople as "inflexible" and lacking in proper "knowledge," fear they are being excluded from the new "capitalist road" into the bright future.

CHAPTER 6

Off and On the Road to Reform

"It was as if they had cut off our tongue," Yang Lanhua, a Bai village woman told me. She was referring to a small spit of land that had stretched from her village out into Lake Er. A few months earlier, village officials, in the hopes of attracting tourists, had decided to sever the spit of land from the shore, dig a canal for pleasure boats, and construct a scenic half-moon stone bridge over it. The new stone bridge, while not unsightly, was inconvenient for fishing families who had to carry their supplies and catches up and over the steep and slippery bridge each day. Officials had promised the fishing families that they would be able to make money giving boat rides to tourists, but the tourists, who rode the large cruise ships around Lake Er on the one-day tour, had yet to come to the village.

Yang Lanhua's comment was more than a complaint over inconvenience. Villagers had not had a say in whether the bridge and canal would be constructed. They had not had a say in the decision-making process with regard to their place—it was as if their tongues had been sliced off. In her analogy, if the peninsula was the villagers' tongue, then the place of the village was like the villagers' head and body, an embodied place.

Yet, the tongues of Dali villagers have not been completely cut, for they have narrated their past and present in relation to place and have critiqued official policies that have led to the disruption of local places. While millions of nostalgic national tourists visit Dali to reenact romantic scenes from the 1959 movie musical *Five Golden Flowers* and while local officials attempt to reshape parts of Dali to mimic the film, some older Dali villagers have viewed the film as a visual historic document that captures the beauty of their place before the ravages of the Great Leap Forward and the Cultural Revolution. While watching the film, villagers pointed out to me scenes that were actually filmed in Dali (not on a film set), scenes that captured forested hillsides before deforestation, a tree-lined lake before swampy landfill, and clear lake water before pesticides and pollution.

In addition older Dali villagers have critiqued the current reform era "creative destruction" of old places and the formation of new "nonplaces" of transit and leisure. Over the past decade, Dali officials and transnational developers have increasingly drawn upon Jin Yong's popular martial arts novel *Heavenly Dragons* to market Dali as a fantastic place of the past to Overseas Chinese tourists and a younger generation of mainland martial arts novel fans. In so doing they have not only constructed the theme park "Daliwood," but have also sought to transform much of the Dali basin to match its representation in the novel, turning Dali into a fantastic theme-park-like simulacrum, a representation of a representation of itself. This marketing and transformation process has involved immense destruction and construction projects: tearing down and rebuilding Dali's old main street, demolishing homes to make room for highways, and uprooting fields to clear space for airports, railways, tourist temples, and parking lots.

Geographer David Harvey has suggested that "place-bound politics . . . is doomed to failure" (1993, 24). Because Harvey defines "place" as "fixed capital embedded in the land" (ibid., 6), he sees place-based resistance as useless against capital. Yet for fishers and farmers whose past, present, and future are intimately tied to place, it is difficult to imagine that another kind of politics could serve as an equally powerful arena from which to speak, organize, and act. As population and development pressures consume more land, the politics of place can only intensify in China.

Dali villagers have not yet engaged in mass protests or sit-ins, as have villagers elsewhere in China. Why farmers in some places decide to take collective action against land expropriation, lack of compensation, and corruption deserves further in-depth research. However, older Dali villagers have attempted to subvert official justification for "rational" development through rumors of the supernatural and narratives of a haunted highway formed by the wandering spirits of villagers killed in traffic accidents.

Older villagers have not been the only ones to "talk back." I have shown that at a conference officially intended to honor author Jin Yong and promote Dali based on his novel, intellectuals from Dali and other parts of Yunnan criticized the author for fictionalizing Dali's past. In so doing, they issued a broader critique of long-standing Chinese representations of the borderlands as backward places in need of a Confucian civilizing influence. By praising Jin Yong's positive portrayals of minority male characters, they implicitly criticized other long-standing negative stereotypes.

Not everyone in Dali has been critical of the policies of the reform era, however. Younger villagers in the Dali basin have welcomed the employment opportunities that the tourism industry has offered. Instead of the backbreaking manual labor of hoeing, planting, weeding, harvesting, and threshing, or hauling fish nets, they have preferred performing for tourists, working as tour guides, or serving as waitstaff. This kind of work brings them out of the villages and into the towns, and provides some disposable income for consumption of the accoutrements of modernity, such as "Han style" clothing and music.

Minorities within Dali, especially Muslim families who had suffered discrimination dating back to the brutal imperial suppression of the Pingnan Kingdom in the late nineteenth century, welcomed the entrepreneurial opportunity to "jump into the sea" of private business in the early reform era. Many of these families were the first to open backpacker cafés catering to transnational travelers who followed the Lonely Planet guide into Dali. The café owners provided a "home away from home" for these travelers, who ironically, although explicitly seeking "authentic" culture "off the beaten track," spent much of their time in Dali drinking coffee, eating pizza, and listening to reggae, as they might back home. The colonial nostalgia of the lonely planeteers for an enclave of familiar food and music led to the creation of "Foreigner Street," a transnational place within the town of Dali. However, both café owners and transnational travelers expressed concern that Dali was becoming "just like" other touristed places. While anthropologists have pointed out the ways in which people localize global processes, I have suggested that is also important to pay attention to people's *perceptions* of homogenization as a way of understanding their experience of globalization. Both the travelers and the café owners have recognized their participation in the early stages of a global process whereby Dali was becoming structurally similar to other touristed places, if not homogeneous in content. As Dali became more accessible to mass tourists, the transnational travelers began to look for more "out-of-the-way" places to the north of Dali. This started a subsequent decline in backpacker business for the café owners and a rise in catering to well-off Chinese tourists.

In general, Dali townspeople have been the most satisfied with the changes of China's reform era. Unlike many older villagers, most townspeople have embraced the conquest of time over place and the creation of new nonplaces of transit and leisure. The construction of an airport, railway, and high-speed highway not only brings tourists into Dali, but has allowed townspeople with adequate means to travel themselves, to "go see some things." They have enjoyed the speed of travel and the comparative perspective that travel brings. Better purchasing power and recreational travel opportunities gives this new "native leisure class" (Colloredo-Mansfield 1999) a "modern" sensibility that has more in common with Chinese coastal elites than with

Bai villagers nearby. The construction of hotels, condominiums, and a new "old" town has given Dali a "modern" yet picturesque look of which they are proud.

The divergent perspectives among Dali townspeople, younger villagers, and older villagers reveals a growing gap between those who see themselves as secure and flourishing in the later reform era, those who hope to prosper, and those who fear that they will be left on the side of the road to reform or even injured while trying to travel on this road. A pressing concern for Chinese Communist Party policy makers will be how to bridge this gap ideologically and materially as they negotiate ongoing reform in the twenty-first century.

The people of Dali do not stand alone in negotiating the material aftereffects of representations in popular culture on themselves and their place. As officials and developers from other marginalized places try to tap into a global tourist market, popular films and novels provide convenient marketing tools. As these processes unfold, it is particularly important to examine representations in practice—investigating the contradictory meanings and uses of representations over time and their delayed material after-effects on peoples and places, sometimes decades after original production. Borderland and minority peoples must contend with the transformations that the influx of new people, capital, and structures can bring as they strive to survive and successfully define their own futures.

Author Jin Yong had not yet been to Dali when he started writing *Heavenly Dragons* in 1963. He had no way of knowing then that his serialized martial arts novel would become so popular or that decades later Dali officials and developers would see it as the key to Dali's future economic development through tourism. He could not have predicted the relationship between his symbolic appropriation of Dali as a setting for his novel and the delayed material after-effects that the novel would have for people there. Nor could the scriptwriters and filmmakers of the 1959 movie musical *Five Golden Flowers* have predicted that decades later millions of national tourists would journey to Dali to reenact film scenes. Only the Lonely Planet travel guide writers could have predicted, based on the earlier appearance of backpacker enclaves in Thailand and Nepal, that their representation of Dali might lead to the formation of a "Foreigner Street." This book is yet another representation of the people and place of Dali. It differs from the three popular narratives I have discussed in that it is based on the input of Dali villagers and townspeople. Still, as with any representation, there are dangers that it may be used in unintended ways. I can only hope that it will do no more harm than good.

Notes

Chapter 1: With the Sign Begins the Search

1. "No Sign . . ." 2005, 39–40. In response to those who describe China as "post-socialist," Smart reminds us that "the fastest growing economy" is "located in a Marxist fossil" (1998, 428). Babb's (2004) term "postrevolutionary" therefore seems more apt.

2. *ZTNJ*, 623; "China Tourism Statistics" 2005. International tourism receipts dropped 15 percent from 2002 to 2003 owing to fears of SARS (Severe Acute Respiratory Syndrome).

3. Geographer Tim Oakes (see 1995, 1997, 1998, 2006) has contributed the most to discussions of tourism and place in China. This book draws inspiration from and builds on his work by analyzing the relationship between representations in popular culture and transformations in place.

4. Dali has not always been represented as an "exotic" place, however. In his 1948 monograph *Under the Ancestor's Shadow,* anthropologist Francis L. K. Hsu described the people as "typically Chinese." I discuss scholarly representations of Dali elsewhere: see Notar 1992, 1999.

5. Other translations of *Tianlong babu* include *The Demi-Gods and Semi-Devils, Eight Demi-Gods and Semi-Devils,* and *Demi-Gods and Half Devils.*

6. Statistic courtesy of the Dali Tourism Bureau. My thanks to Yang Guocai and Zhang Ji for assistance.

7. "Number of Visitors" 2006 (The Official Site of the Eiffel Tower); "India Tourism 2004 Statistics, Facts and Figures" 2006.

8. See Basso 1988, 1996; Boas 1934; Feld and Basso 1996; Harkin 2004; Relph 1976; Rodman 1992. I use "place" to refer to both geographic locations and cultural constructions of them. The term "landscape" has been defined as a "cultural process" (Hirsch 1995, 23) or as physical geography (Basso 1988, 100). In Mandarin the terms for landscape are *jingse; fengjing,* literally "wind and scene"; or *shanshui,* literally "mountains, water." Land itself is called *tudi* (earth) or *tiandi* (fields). The word *difang,* "earth location," refers to a geographic place. In Bai, *ji* refers to both field and earth, and *jifv* to place.

9. Adler (1989) has noted the performative aspects of tourism but goes too far in describing these performances as "art." My use of "performance" follows the sense of "performativity" of daily life (see Butler 1993). In an unpublished paper, Kershaw has argued that "reminiscence" should be used in place of "nostalgia" where tourists perform the past (cited in Rojek and Urry 1997b, 14). However, to reminisce means to remember something that one has experienced, whereas nostalgia, as it has come to

be used, does not need to be based on actual experience. Because the performances I discuss are not all linked to memories, I prefer the term "nostalgia."

10. Much important research on China's borderlands explores constructions of gender and ethnicity: e.g., Blum 2001; Brown 1996; Bulag 2002; Chao 1995; Chien and Tapp 1989; Du 2002; Friedman 2004; Gladney 1991; Harrell 1995a; Litzinger 2000a, 2000b; Makley 1999; Pang 1992; Schein 2002; Swain 1990, 1995a, 2005; Walsh 2005; White 1997.

11. See Blum 2001; Bulag 2002; Chao 1995; Cheung 1996a, 1996b; Diamond 1988, 1995; Gladney 1994, 1995; Harrell 1995a, 1995b, 1995c; Hostetler 2001; Khan 1996; Litzinger 1995, 2000a, 2000b; McKhann 1995; Pang 1992; Swain 1995b.

12. Diamond 1988, 1995; Gladney 1994; Harrell 1995b; Litzinger 1995; Lopez 1998; McKhann 1995; Swain 1995b.

13. Some anthropologists have begun to undertake research on fan culture (Robertson 1995, 1998), "talking back" to media representations (di Leonardo 1984, 185–190), and manipulation of outside images (Adams 1996), but much remains to be done.

14. Yunnan is 380,000 square kilometers and California 411,033 (158,700 square miles). There has been heated debate as to whether to translate *minzu* into English as "race" (Berry 1992) or "ethnic group" (Crossley 1990, 19–20; Heberer [1984] 1989; Yingjing Zhang 2002, 152–157). This debate illustrates what Lydia Liu has termed the "hypothetical equivalence" of all translation (1995, 259). To avoid viewing the Chinese context through an American lens, I prefer to use "nationality" for *minzu*. This is more familiar in the Canadian context, where the term "First Nations" is used to refer to the native peoples of the country.

15. See Backus 1981; *BJS*; Credner 1935; Dai and Chen 1990; Dodd 1923; Fang 1957, 1984; Fitzgerald 1941; Hsu [1948] 1967; Lacouperie [1885] 1985; Mackerras 1988; Parker 1890; Pelliot 1904; Wang Shuwu 1988; Wu 1989, 1990; Yang Kun 1957; You 1980.

16. The prefectural population was 3,296,552 according to the 2000 census (*YNRK*, 1:85); 3,358,300 by 2003 according to the prefectural yearbook (*DZNJ* 2004, 31).

17. Atwill 2003; Cordier [1909] 1927; Jing Dexin 1986, 1991; Notar 2001; Rocher 1879, 1880; T'ien 1981, 1982; Wang Jianping 1996; Wei 1974; *YHSLD*.

18. This was the real name of a café that closed. Other café names used here are pseudonyms.

Chapter 2: Lonely Planeteers and a Transnational Authentic

1. Numerous terms have been used for this form of traveler. However, the standard term has become "backpacker" (see Elsrud 2001; Loker-Murphy and Pearce 1995; Richards and Wilson 2004c), owing to the large hiking backpacks these travelers carry with them.

2. Margary met an unpleasant end—he was killed in the town of Manwyne on

February 21, 1875, two months after leaving Dali. His journal entries and letters to his parents were published posthumously.

3. "Burmese Prime Minister Vacations in Yunnan," *Peking Review* 4.15 (April 14, 1961), 23.

4. In 1992, 27,095 transnational tourists visited Dali. Of these, the majority were from Asia (8,037 from Hong Kong and Macao, 3,345 from Taiwan, and 2,339 from Japan). From Europe came 6,697 tourists and from the Americas 2,081. Other places accounted for 2,509 tourists (*DZNJ* 1993, 156–157). Most of the tourists from Hong Kong, Macao, and Taiwan came on group tours, not as individual travelers.

5. Out of twenty-three travelers from around the world (Australia, Belgium, Canada, Denmark, Japan, Poland, Spain, Sweden, and the United States) that I distributed a survey to at a café in the spring of 1995, all but two of them used the Lonely Planet as their guide. Of these two, one used no guidebook at all, and one used the Japanese guidebook *Chikyū no arukikata* (How to Walk the World).

6. Only when later editions of the guidebook started to list more places or when guided on an "adventure tour" did backpackers start to go to other places around Dali.

7. Fang Guoyu and Lin Chaomin have examined textual evidence from books and stone inscriptions to verify that Yachi is present-day Kunming and Carajan includes the area of Dali more broadly as well as the town of Dali (1994, 22–26).

8. For example, a Guide Madrolle (1939) includes Yunnan as part of Indochine du Nord.

9. Letter dated Peking, May 1, 1877, by Hugh Fraser. In Baber [1878] 1915.

10. Café owners told me that in 1985 the rent was only 120 yuan per month (US$40.00 at the official exchange rate, US$12.00 at the unofficial rate). In 1995 the rent for a small café or shop had risen to 500 yuan (US$60.39) for an old shop or 1,000 yuan (US$120.77) per month for one of the first-floor shop spaces in the new building. By 1999 two of the larger cafés paid monthly rents of 3,000 yuan and 7,000 yuan (US$362.32 and US$845.41).

11. Three Japanese long timers—a jade merchant, a gangster following the merchant, and a researcher searching for the origins of the Japanese people in Yunnan, a common myth in Japan—are depicted in Takashi Miike's 1998 film *The Bird People* (*Chūgoku no toribito*). In a survey I distributed to twenty-three travelers one morning at a café in the spring of 1995, they described their activities in China as follows: "visiting girlfriend" (1), "tourist" (2), "traveling" (4), "studying Chinese" (5), "teaching English" (11). Of the travelers, one wrote that he was "looking for good places where I might live in the future." These travelers fall into the three main groups: a long-term traveler (1; 4 percent), short-term travelers (6; 26 percent), those studying/working elsewhere in China (16; 70 percent). Since I distributed this survey at the time of Chinese New Year, I expect that there were more expatriate teachers and students on vacation than if I had distributed it during the summer, when there would likely have been more short-term travelers.

12. Philip Deloria makes a similar point in the U.S. context, where Anglos desired "authentic Indians" to counter modernity. In this context, assimilated Indians become "negative Others," while "unassimilated Indians" become "authentic" Others (Deloria 1998, 94).

13. Directed by Dennis O'Rourke, 1987. MacCannell provides an in-depth analysis and critique of the film (1992, 17–73).

14. This is contrary to what Richard Wilk has observed in Belize. He notes: "Tourism has also played a role in the emergence of Belizean cuisine. When the tourism boom began in the mid-1980s, Belizeans were initially unprepared. The tourists wanted to eat local foods, but the hotels and larger restaurants served only Chinese or badly cooked American foods. . . . As a nation, Belize was supposed to have distinctive and exotic cuisine. What had previously been a point of shame quickly became a marketing opportunity" (Wilk 1993, 311).

15. Pei-yin-shan (Bei yinshan) was possibly located near present-day Neijiang in southern Sichuan province (see Tan Qixiang 1989, 40).

16. Jonathan Friedman has noted: "The old saying, 'you are what you eat,' once a characterization of a vulgar ecological view of humanity, is strikingly accurate when it is understood as a thoroughly social act. For eating is an act of self-identification, as is all consumption" ([1990] 1997, 314).

17. From the song "All I Want," written by Joni Mitchell, 1971.

18. Erik Cohen describes similar types of travelers in Thailand who "seek a way to opt out from the modern world" (1996, 221).

19. This is different from Thailand, where it has been suggested that "households that were initially better off tend to profit most from the tourism business" (E. Cohen 2001, 40).

20. Gates has also observed that "remembered knowledge of prerevolutionary custom" (1991, 13) was helpful for the success of women entrepreneurs in Sichuan.

21. See He [1993] 2003, 294–304, for another description of opening a café.

22. Interview with Dali Tourism Bureau, 1999.

Chapter 3: Five Golden Flowers

1. PDDY; "Smash the Old World" 2003, originally in Shoudu chubanjie geming zaofan zongbu (Capital Publishing World Rebel Headquarters) 1967, 33–37; Su Yun 1985.

2. Marion (1997) lists thirty-five films on minorities and another four films that are set at the borderlands between 1949 and 1965. Yau states that between 1949 and 1965 approximately fifty films were made about minorities in total (1989, 119). See also Clark 1987a, 95–101.

3. The films included *Neimeng renmin de shengli* (Victory for the People of Inner Mongolia), 1950; *Caoyuan shang de renmin* (People of the Grasslands), 1953; *Caoyuan chenqu* (Morning Song of the Grasslands), 1959; *Muren zhi zi* (Son of the Herdsman), 1957; *Jin Yuji*, 1959; *Lusheng liange* (Love Song of the Calabash Pipes), 1957; and *Bi-*

ansai fenghuo (Beacon Fire of a Border Hamlet), 1957 (Uradyn Bulag, personal communication; Marion 1997, 541; Su Yun 1985, 36–38).

4. On the Jingpo was *Jingpo guniang* (Jingpo Girl, 1965), on the Qiang was *Qiang disong* (A Song for the Qiang's Whistle, 1960), and on the Yi was *Daji he tade fuqin* (Daji and Her Fathers, 1961) (Marion 1997, 541; Su Yun 1985, 41–44).

5. These films have been re-released on video by the German Institut für den Wissenschaftlichen Film Göttingen. Thank you to Charles McKhann for this reference.

6. "Yinmu jinxi" (The Silver Screen Yesterday and Today), *YNRB*, Sept. 27, 1959, 5.

7. The Chinese characters used to represent the names of two of these groups were particularly derogatory and dehumanizing, the name Di including the written Chinese symbol for "dog" and the name Man containing the symbol for "insect." See Ecsedy 1974, 331, note 6; Notar 1992, 16–18; Schafer 1967, 57.

8. Henrietta Harrison records that a five-bar flag was originally used by the Qing dynastic navy for "certain lower-ranking officials." It was declared the national flag in January 1912, but amidst controversy (Harrison 2000, 101). National founding father Sun Zhongshan later declared that the five-bar flag was a "decrepit bureaucratic flag" for depicting the overthrown imperial Manchus equally with the Han Chinese and ordered this flag replaced by the Nationalist Party "blue sky and white sun" flag, which Fitzgerald suggests symbolically signaled the arrival of the single-party state in China (1996, 180–183). There is some disagreement regarding the color symbolism of the five-bar flag. Fitzgerald suggests the color representation as follows: red for the Han, yellow for the Manchus, blue for the Mongolians, white for the Tibetans, and black for the Hui Muslims (ibid., 180). C. A. S. Williams interprets the colors as red for the Manchus, yellow for the Han, blue for the Mongolians, white for the Muslims, and black for the Tibetans ([1941] 1975, 190–191).

9. Dreyer notes that initially two hundred researchers were sent, with more sent later (1976, 141, 147). Mackerras says that in total over one thousand researchers were sent to fifteen provinces: Fujian, Gansu, Guangdong, Guangxi, Guizhou, Heilongjiang, Hunan, Inner Mongolia, Jilin, Liaoning, Ningxia, Qinghai, Sichuan, Tibet, and Yunnan (1994, 142–143, 301, note 11). Dreyer includes a useful summary of Fei Xiaotong's and Lin Yuehua's discussions of the difficulties of applying Stalin's criteria to China's nationalities (1976, 142–146; see also Stalin 1934; Fei 1980). The research project continued in Dali until the 1960s. However, the wealth of data that the investigation teams collected remained largely unpublished until after the turmoil of the Cultural Revolution. See the "Chuban shuoming" (publisher's foreword) and the "Hou ji" (editorial afterword) in *BSLD1*.

10. Harrell 1995c, 3–36; see also Diamond 1995; Hostetler 2001; Litzinger 1995; McKhann 1995; Swain 1995b.

11. For investigation dates, see the end of each report in *BSLD1*, 78, 98, 122, 176, 190, 221, 232. See also He 2003. One source (Zhong Xiu 1983, 60) tells of a documentary film, *Ten Thousand Golden Flowers Face the Sun,* made the same year by the Cen-

tral Documentary Film Studio, "about the accomplishment of Bai women in various fields." I have not yet seen this film.

12. The call to combine revolutionary realism with revolutionary romanticism (M. *geming xianshi zhuyi yu geming langmang zhuyi*) in cultural production was first used by Zhou Yang in "Xin minge kaituole shige de xin daolu" (New People's Songs Have Opened a New Road for Songs and Poetry), *Hongqi* (Red Flag), 1 (June 1958): 33–38, as quoted in Clark 1987a, 57, 63.

13. Unpublished figures from 2004 courtesy of the Dali Tourism Bureau. Figures from 1998 and 1999 published in Doorne, Atlejevic, and Bai 2003, 5.

14. One piece of the performance was not from the film—a duet sung in Bai during which the actors danced *bawangbian*, the bamboo stick dance—but it was stylized, exaggerated, and taken out of its usual temple festival context.

15. Johannes Hofer used the term *Heimweh*; see Lowenthal 1975, 1.

16. As quoted in Lowenthal 1985, 7.

17. "Private nostalgia," Davis explains in contrast, "refers to those symbolic images and allusions from the past which by virtue of their resource in a particular person's biography tend to be more idiosyncratic, individuated, and particularistic" (1981, 222).

18. Boym uses "utopian nostalgia" in earlier writings (1994) and "restorative nostalgia" in later work (2001). She refers to private nostalgia as "ironic nostalgia" in earlier writings and "reflective nostalgia" in later writings (see Boym 1994, 2001).

19. I observed this not only with national tourists, but also with transnational tourists on group tours.

20. When I accompanied national tourists to Butterfly Spring in 1999 and 2005, their transperformances were similarly enacted.

21. Rojek has used a computer metaphor to describe this process: "Cinematic events are dragged onto the physical landscape and the physical landscape is then reinterpreted in terms of the cinematic events" (1997, 54).

22. I provide a much longer discussion of the story of Yang Likun elsewhere. See Notar n.d. b.

23. My use of "longing" differs from that of Susan Stewart (1984), who uses it interchangeably with "nostalgia."

24. See Yin et al. 1981, 177, for mention of the loss of butterflies due to pesticides.

25. "Zhongguo changpian, 1959 di yi qi xin pian" (China's Songs: The First New Songs of 1959), *YNRB*, Jan. 3, 1959, 3.

26. See Yunnan Sheng tongji ju renkou ban 1990, 377–395. I thank Erik Mueggler for lending me this source. Mueggler records that where he conducted research in Dayao county, the mortality rate reached 41.8 per thousand, higher than any other area in Chuxiong prefecture (2001, 188–189).

27. Thank you to Wang Ying for discussing this interpretation.

Chapter 4: Heavenly Dragons

1. *Dream of the Red Chamber* (*Honglou meng*, also called *The Story of the Stone*) is an eighteenth-century, Qing dynasty, novel by Cao Xueqin; *The Romance of the Three Kingdoms* (*Sanguo yanyi*) is a Yuan dynasty (A.D. 1279–1368) novel by Luo Guanzhong.

2. Paraphrased from Zhang Nan 1994, 144–145.

3. In 2003 only 100,000 tourists visited Daliwood because of SARS. Figures courtesy of the manager of Daliwood (*Tianlong babu yingshicheng*), Mr. Zhao Jian, May 3, 2005.

4. The State Council and the Central Military Commission had approved construction of the airport in 1992 (*DZNJ* 1995, 103, 159).

5. King-Fai Tam, personal communication.

6. "Jin Yong: Kungfu Novel Master" 2001.

7. Three of Jin Yong's novels have been translated into English to date: *Luding ji* (The Deer and the Cauldron) by John Minford, *Shujian enchao lu* (The Book and the Sword) by Graham Earnshaw, and *Xueshan feihu* (Fox Volant of the Snowy Mountains) by Olivia Mok.

8. See Li Hongwen 1998, 119. Of course not everyone is a Jin Yong fan. For example, in 1999 mainland novelist Wang Shuo wrote a scathing critique of Jin Yong's writing in the widely read *China Youth Daily* (*Zhongguo qingnian bao*) as well as a lament over the "flood" of imported Hong Kong and Taiwanese culture (Hamm 2005, 250–260).

9. When Jin Yong traveled to Europe in May and June 1965, his friend Ni Kuang filled in for him. Upon his return to Hong Kong in July, Jin Yong then took up the story where Ni had left off (Leng Xia 1995). When the novel was republished in book form in 1978, Jin Yong rewrote the parts that Ni had originally written (Jin Yong 1978, 2125).

10. My edition is a reprint of the 1978 edition published by the Wuxia chubanshe in Hong Kong. Wen Rui'an has written an entire monograph titled *In Praise and Appreciation of Tianlong babu* (*Tianlong babu xinshang juyu*). This monograph forms part of a twenty-three-volume series of appreciative writings on Jin Yong, a series known as the Jin Studies Research Collection (*Jin xue yanjiu congshu*), published by Yuanjin in Taipei, Taiwan.

11. For reproductions and discussions of this scroll, see Chapin 1972; Li Lin-ts'an 1982.

12. Film and video versions start the story differently.

13. Another of Jin Yong's novels, *Shediao yinxiong zhuan* (The Legend of Eagle-Shooting Heroes), also features Dali in part. However, this novel has not yet been adopted by Dali officials.

14. This information is based on my interview with the manager of the *Tianlong babu yingshicheng* on May 3, 2005, as well as on two untitled promotional pamphlets and two press releases he gave me: "Dali *Tianlong babu* yingshicheng fazhan qing-

kuang jieshao" (An Introduction to Dali Heavenly Dragons Film City's Development) and "Dali *Tianlong babu* yingshicheng jianjie" (A Brief Introduction to Dali Heavenly Dragons Film City).

15. "Louis Cha's *Kung Fu* Tale Retold" n.d.

16. In addition to *Heavenly Dragons*, other television series have been filmed at Daliwood: for example, *Women de yanjing* (Our Eyes) and *Cha ma gudao* (Ancient Tea Mule Road). World-renowned director Zhang Yimou plans to film another series soon. Interview with film city manager, May 3, 2005.

17. Interview with film city manager, May 3, 2005.

18. The average annual income for a farmer in Dali prefecture was 1,959 yuan (US$236.59) (*DZNJ* 2004, 32). One month's income would be 163 yuan (US$19.69).

19. Dali residents, I learned later, often negotiated a cheaper entrance fee to Daliwood, as little as 10 yuan, or US$1.21.

20. Interview, Dali Tourism Bureau, May 1999.

21. David Wank (2000) and Jing Wang (2001a, 2001b) have observed this for other parts of China. Jean Michaud (1993) notes that the collaboration between transnational capital and state officials for tourism development has been a close one in Ladakh, India, and northern Thailand.

22. Shops broke down as follows: tie dye and batik clothing (62), Heqing silver jewelry (56), jade (52), Pu'er and other tea (24), purses (14), Dali marble (13), trinkets such as wood placards with Naxi minority style Dongba characters or minority dolls (11), packaged snacks (11), wood carvings (10), compact disks and gourd flutes (7), film (6), and primitivist paintings (2). The other shops could cater to both tourists and residents: books (5), pharmacies/clinics (5), sporty clothes and shoes (5), cell phones (3), eyeglasses (2), department store (1), watches and watch repair (1), cigarettes (1).

23. They have even been described as "human zoos" (Bulag [2000] 2003, 243).

24. Conferences have been held in the author's home county of Haining, Zhejiang province; at Hangzhou University; in Taipei; in Beijing; as well as in Boulder, Colorado. See Jin Yong 2000, 23–28; Wang Qiugui 1999; Wu Xiaodong and Ji Birui 2002.

25. Representations of gender and ethnicity in *Heavenly Dragons* deserve a much more in-depth discussion, which I have begun elsewhere (Notar 1999; Notar n.d. a). For discussions of gender and ethnicity in Jin Yong novels, see, for example, Chen Fengxiang 1998; Chen Mo 1998; Feng Xiaoran 2000; Hamm 2005, 83–88; Huang 1999; Jin Yong 2000; Song Weijie 2000.

26. The following historical overview of the history of the Dali Kingdom is paraphrased from Shi Lizhuo 1998, 214–224.

27. Schafer [1963] 1985 describes in detail some of the luxurious tribute items the Nanzhao sent.

28. Expressions of local historical consciousness have extended beyond the space of the conference and the edited volume, and have been expressed in more popular forms. A recent Chinese-language guidebook of Dali that was edited in Dali includes maps of the Nanzhao and Dali kingdoms, showing the extent of their rule. However,

the kingdoms are still temporally and spatially retained within the Chinese empire, for the maps are labeled as the Tang (dynasty) Nanzhao Kingdom and the Song (dynasty) Dali Kingdom (Bao 1996). Another example of local historical consciousness was expressed by Mr. Wang, a high school history teacher I knew. On his weekends Mr. Wang began to follow Chinese tour guides around Dali's sites. If he thought that the guides were leaving out important aspects of Dali history, he would interrupt them and insert his own historical narratives.

Chapter 5: Earthly Demons

1. This was in the spring of 1995.

2. See the tale as told by Yang You in *BZSH*, 172–174; also Yang Zhengye 1994, 113–115. For translations of some Bai and other Yunnan folktales, see Miller 1994.

3. It seems Augé must have been influenced by Relph's earlier work: "Roads, railways, airports, cutting across or imposed on the landscape rather than developing with it, are not only features of placelessness in their own right, but . . . have encouraged the spread of placelessness well beyond their immediate impacts" (Relph 1976, 90).

4. According to Selden and Lu, "when the state appropriates land it pays compensation to the production team or village" (Selden 1993, 198).

5. Katherine Verdery (1996) reports a strikingly similar situation in postsocialist Romania, where villagers who try to reclaim presocialist landholdings must negotiate or bribe their way through corrupt local officials.

6. For discussions of Bai village deities, see Yang Zhengye 1994; Yokoyama 1991.

7. As elsewhere in China (Wang Shucun 1992), Bai villagers used *jiama* papers— woodblock prints with images of different deities and spirits. These papers are used both to represent and to communicate with the supernatural world. Some *jiama* were displayed for an entire year, for example, the kitchen god pasted by the stove or the image of the spirit of the six animals (M. *liu xu zhi shen*) pasted on the pig shed. Other *jiama* were displayed or burned for ritual occasions.

8. For elegant accounts of the relation of body to place, see Basso 1988; Thornton 1997, 2004.

9. Michael Mayerfeld Bell has suggested that "although the cultural language of modernity usually prevents us from speaking about their presence, we constitute a place in large measure by the ghosts we sense inhabit and possess it" (1997, 813).

10. Why farmers in certain places decide to take collective action, while others do not deserves in-depth research.

11. In his discussion of the "battle" over "the future of the past" (Herzfeld 1991, 5) in Greece, Michael Herzfeld has conversely observed the "triumph of place over time" (ibid., 11).

Bibliography

Adams, Vincanne. 1996. *Tigers of the Snow and Other Virtual Sherpas*. Princeton: Princeton University Press.

Adler, Judith. 1989. "Travel as Performed Art." *American Journal of Sociology* 94.6: 1366–1391.

Anagnost, Ann S. 1997. *National Past-Times: Narrative, Representation, and Power in Modern China*. Durham: Duke University Press.

Anderson, Benedict. [1983] 1991. *Imagined Communities: Reflections on the Origin and Spread of Nationalism*. 2nd ed., revised. London: Verso.

Appadurai, Arjun. [1990] 1994. "Disjuncture and Difference in the Global Cultural Economy." In Patrick Williams and Laura Chrisman, eds., *Colonial Discourse and Post-Colonial Theory*, 324–339. New York: Columbia University Press. [Orig. in *Public Culture* 2.2: 1–24.]

———. 1991. "Global Ethnoscapes." In Richard G. Fox, ed., *Recapturing Anthropology: Working in the Present*, 190–210. Santa Fe, New Mexico: School of American Research Press.

Armijo-Hussein, Jaqueline. 1997. "Sayyid 'Ajall Shams Al-din: A Muslim from Central Asia, Serving the Mongols in China and Bringing 'Civilization' to Yunnan." Ph.D. dissertation. Harvard University.

Ashima (Ashma). 1964. Directed by Liu Qiong. Haiyan Studio.

Ateljevic, Irena, and Stephen Doorne. 2003. "Culture, Economy and Tourism Commodities: Social Relations of Production and Consumption." *Tourist Studies* 3.2: 123–141.

Atwill, David G. 2003. "Blinkered Visions: Islamic Identity, Hui Ethnicity, and the Panthay Rebellion in Southwest China, 1856–1873." *Journal of Asian Studies* 62.4: 1079–1108.

Augé, Marc. [1992] 2000. *Non-Places: Introduction to an Anthropology of Supermodernity*. Trans. John Howe. London: Verso. [Orig. *Non-Lieux: Introduction à une anthropologie de la surmodernité*. Éditions de Seuil.]

Babb, Florence E. 2004. "Recycled *Sandalistas*: From Revolution to Resorts in the New Nicaragua." *American Anthropologist* 106.3: 541–555.

———. 2005. "Post-Revolutionary Tourism: Heritage Celebrated or Forgotten?" *Anthropology News* 46.5: 11–12.

Babcock, Barbara A. 1978. "Introduction." In Barbara A. Babcock, ed., *The Reversible World: Symbolic Inversion in Art and Society*, 13–36. Ithaca: Cornell University Press.

Baber, Mr. [E. Colborne]. [1878] 1915. "Report by Mr. Baber on the Route Followed by

Mr. Grosvenor's Mission between Tali-fu and Momien (with itinerary and map of road from Yünnan-fu)." Presented to both Houses of Parliament by Command of Her Majesty. Bound in *British Parliamentary Papers: Journeys and Expeditions in China, 1869–1904*. Cleveland. [Orig. China No. 3. London: Harrison and Sons.]

Backus, Charles. 1981. *The Nan-chao Kingdom and T'ang China's Southwestern Frontier.* Cambridge: Cambridge University Press.

Bai Lian. 2001. "Tourism and Historical Memory: A Case Study of the Social Movement of Manchu Identity Reconstruction." In Tan Chee-Beng, Sidney C. H. Cheung, and Yang Hui, eds., *Tourism, Anthropology and China*, 237–255. Studies in Asian Tourism No. 1. Bangkok: White Lotus Press.

Baizu jianshi bianxie zu (A Concise History of the Bai Nationality Editorial Group), ed. 1988. *Baizu jianshi* (A Concise History of the Bai Nationality). Guojia minwei minzu wenti wuzhong congshu (Part of the National Minority Commission's Collected Series on Nationality Issues). Kunming: Yunnan renmin chubanshe.

Bakhtin, Mikhail. 1984. *Rabelais and His World.* Trans. Hélène Iswolsky. Bloomington: Indiana University Press.

Bammer, Angelika, ed. 1994. *Displacements: Cultural Identities in Question,* Bloomington: Indiana University Press.

Bao Hongfeng, ed. 1996. *Dali Zhou jiaotong lüyou tuse* (Illustrated Transportation and Travel Atlas of Dali Prefecture). Kunming: Yunnan meishu chubanshe.

Baranovitch, Nimrod. 2003. *China's New Voices: Popular Music, Ethnicity, Gender, and Politics, 1978–1997.* Berkeley: University of California Press.

Barber, Benjamin. 1995. *Jihad vs. McWorld.* New York: Times Books.

Barmé, Geremie R. 1999. *In the Red: On Contemporary Chinese Culture.* New York: Columbia University Press.

Basso, Keith H. 1979. *Portraits of "the Whiteman": Linguistic Play and Cultural Symbols among the Western Apache.* Cambridge: Cambridge University Press.

———. 1988. "'Speaking with Names': Language and Landscape among the Western Apache." *Cultural Anthropology* 3.2: 99–130.

———. 1996. "Wisdom Sits in Places: Notes on a Western Apache Landscape." In Steven Feld and Keith H. Basso, eds., *Senses of Place*, 53–90. Santa Fe: School of American Research Press.

Battaglia, Debbora. 1995. "On Practical Nostalgia: Self-Prospecting among Urban Trobrianders." In Debbora Battaglia, ed., *Rhetorics of Self-Making*, 77–96. Berkeley: University of California Press.

Baudrillard, Jean. 1983. *Simulations.* Trans. Paul Foss, Paul Patton, and Philip Beitchman. New York: Semiotext(e).

———. 1988. *Selected Writings.* Trans. and ed. Mark Poster. Stanford: Stanford University Press.

Becker, Jasper. [1996] 1998. *Hungry Ghosts: Mao's Secret Famine.* New York: Henry Holt.

Bell, Michael Mayerfeld. 1997. "The Ghosts of Place." *Theory and Society* 26.6: 813–836.

Benjamin, Walter. [1936] 1969. "The Work of Art in the Age of Mechanical Repro-
    duction." Trans. Harry Zohn. In *Illuminations,* 217–251. New York: Schocken
    Books. [Orig. in *Zeitschrift für Sozialforschung* 5.1.]
Berry, Chris. 1986. "Han and Non-Han: China's Avant-Garde and the National Mi-
    norities Genre." *China Screen* 1: 34.
———. 1992. "Race *(minzu):* Chinese Film and the Politics of Nationalism." *Cinema
    Journal* 31.2: 45–58.
Bhabha, Homi K. 1984. "Of Mimicry and Man: The Ambivalence of Colonial Dis-
    course." *October* 28: 125–133.
———. 1994. "Frontlines/Borderposts." In Angelika Bammer, ed., *Displacements: Cul-
    tural Identities in Question,* 269–272. Bloomington: Indiana University Press.
Biansai fenghuo (Beacon Fire of a Border Hamlet). 1957. Directed by Lin Nong. Chang-
    chun Film Studio.
Bigenho, Michelle. 2002. *Sounding Indigenous: Authenticity in Bolivian Music Perfor-
    mance.* New York: Palgrave Macmillan.
Bingshan shang de laike (Glacier Guests; also Visitor to Ice Mountain). 1963. Directed
    by Zhao Xinshui. Changchun Film Studio.
Bird, S. Elizabeth, ed. 1996. *Dressing in Feathers: The Construction of the Indian in
    American Popular Culture.* Boulder: Westview Press.
Bissell, William Cunningham. 2005. "Engaging Colonial Nostalgia." *Cultural Anthro-
    pology* 20.2: 215–248.
Blackmore, Michael. 1967. "The Ethnological Problems Connected with the Nan-
    chao." In F. S. Drake, ed., *Symposium on Historical, Archaeological and Linguistic
    Studies on Southern China, South East Asia and the Hong Kong Region,* 59–69.
    Hong Kong: Hong Kong University Press.
Blum, Susan D. 2001. *Portraits of "Primitives": Ordering Human Kinds in the Chinese
    Nation.* Lanham, MD: Rowman and Littlefield.
Boas, Franz. 1934. "Geographical Names of the Kwakiutl Indians." Columbia Univer-
    sity Contributions in Anthropology 20. New York.
Booz, Patrick R. [1987] 1989. *An Illustrated Guide to Yunnan.* Hong Kong: The Guide-
    book Co.
[Bourne, Mr. F. S. A]. [1888] 1915. "Report by Mr. F. S. A. Bourne of a Journey in South-
    Western China." Presented to both Houses of Parliament by Command of Her
    Majesty, June 1888. Bound in *British Parliamentary Papers: Journeys and Expedi-
    tions in China 1869–1904.* Cleveland. [Orig. London: Harrison and Sons.]
Boym, Svetlana. 1994. *Common Places: Mythologies of Everyday Life in Russia.* Cam-
    bridge, MA: Harvard University Press.
———. 2001. *The Future of Nostalgia.* New York: Basic Books.
Bradley, Neville. 1945. *The Old Burma Road.* London: William Heinemann.
Breckenridge, Carol, ed. 1995. *Consuming Modernity: Public Culture in a South Asian
    World.* Minneapolis: University of Minnesota Press.
British Parliamentary Papers. 1915. *Journeys and Expeditions in China, 1869–1904.*
    Cleveland.

Brown, Melissa, ed. 1996. *Negotiating Ethnicities in China and Taiwan*. Berkeley: Institute of East Asian Studies, University of California.

Bruner, Edward M. 1991. "Transformation of Self in Tourism." *Studies in Symbolic Interaction* 10: 109–114.

———. 1994. "Abraham Lincoln as Authentic Reproduction: A Critique of Postmodernism." *American Anthropologist* 92.2: 397–412.

———. 1996a. "Tourism in Ghana: The Representation of Slavery and the Return of the Black Diaspora." *American Anthropologist* 98.2: 290–304.

———. 1996b. "Tourism in the Balinese Borderzone." In Smadar Lavie and Ted Swedenburg, eds., *Displacement, Diaspora, and Geographics of Identity*, 157–179. Durham: Duke University Press.

———. 2001. "Ethnic Tourism: One Group, Three Contexts." In Tan Chee-Beng, Sidney C. H. Cheung, and Yang Hui, eds. *Tourism, Anthropology and China*, 55–70. Studies in Asian Tourism No. 1. Bangkok: White Lotus Press.

———. 2005. "Tourism Fieldwork." *Anthropology News* 46.5: 16, 19.

Buck, John Loessing. [1937] 1956. *Land Utilization in China*. Reprint. New York: Council on Economic and Cultural Affairs.

Bulag, Uradyn E. 2002. *The Mongols at China's Edge: History and the Politics of National Unity*. Lanham, MD: Rowman and Littlefield.

———. [2000] 2003. "Alter/native Mongolian Identity: From Nationality to Ethnic Group." In Elizabeth J. Perry and Mark Selden, eds., *Chinese Society: Change, Conflict and Resistance*, 223–246. 2nd ed. London: RoutledgeCurzon.

"Burmese Prime Minister Vacations in Yunnan." 1961. *Peking Review* 4.15 (April 14): 23.

Butler, Judith, 1993. *Bodies That Matter: On the Discursive Limits of "Sex."* New York: Routledge.

Cai, Yongshun. 2003. "Collective Ownership or Cadres' Ownership? The Nonagricultural Use of Farmland in China." *China Quarterly* 175: 662–680.

Calloway, Colin G., Gerd Gemünden, and Susanne Zantop, eds. 2002. *Germans and Indians: Fantasies, Encounters, Projections*. Lincoln: University of Nebraska Press.

Cannibal Tours. 1987. Directed by Dennis O'Rourke. CameraWork Pty Ltd.

Cao Zhengwen. 1994. "Chinese Gallant Fiction." In Wu Dingbo and Patrick D. Murphy, eds., *Handbook of Chinese Popular Culture*, 237–255. Westport, CT: Greenwood Press.

Caoyuan chenqu (Morning Song of the Grasslands). 1959. Directed by Zhu Wenshu and Zhulanqiqike. Changchun Film Studio.

Caoyuan shang de renmin (People of the Grasslands). 1953. Northeast Film Studio.

Carlson, Marta. 2002. "Germans Playing Indian." In Colin G. Calloway, Gerd Gemünden, and Susanne Zantop, eds., *Germans and Indians: Fantasies, Encounters, Projections*, 213–216. Lincoln: University of Nebraska Press.

Casey, Edward S. 1996. "How to Get from Space to Place in a Fairly Short Stretch of Time: Phenomenological Prolegomena." In Steven Feld and Keith H. Basso, eds., *Senses of Place*, 13–52. Santa Fe: School of American Research Press.

Ceng Huiyan. 1998. "Jin Yong re: fang xing wei ai" (Jin Yong Fever: Still Going Strong). *Shijie zhoukan* (World Weekly), May 31–June 6: 10–14.

Certeau, Michel de. [1974] 1988. *The Practice of Everyday Life*. Berkeley: University of California Press. [Orig. *L'Invention du quotidian: Arts de faire*. (Paris): Éditions Seuil.]

Changchun dianying zhipianchang (Changchun Film Studio), ed. 1996. *Changying wushi nian, 1945–1995* (English title: Fifty Years of Chang Chun Film Studio). Changchun: Jilin sheying chubanshe.

Changchun shi difangzhi bianzuan weiyuanhui (Changchun Municipal Gazetteer Editorial Committee), ed. 1992. *Changchun shi zhi: Dianying zhi* (Changchun Municipal Gazetteer: Film Gazetteer). Changchun: Dongbei shifan daxue chubanshe.

Chao, Emily Kay. 1995. "Depictions of Difference: History, Gender, Ritual and State Discourse among the Naxi of Southwest China." Ph.D. dissertation, University of Michigan, Ann Arbor.

Chapin, Helen B. 1972. *A Long Roll of Buddhist Images*. Revised by Alexander C. Soper. Ascona, Switzerland: Artibus Asiae.

Chaplin, Ian, Carlos M. M. Costa, and Aliana Leong Man Wai. 2001. "Conservation and Interpretation of Cultural Legacies for Ethnic Tourism in Macau." In Tan Chee-Beng, Sidney C. H. Cheung, and Yang Hui, eds., *Tourism, Anthropology and China*, 271–287. Studies in Asian Tourism No. 1. Bangkok: White Lotus Press.

Chen Fengxiang. 1998. "Ya su gong shang hua Jin Yong" (Refined and Common Together, in Praise of Jin Yong). In Shi Lizhuo and Zhang Naiguang, eds., *Jin Yong yu Dali* (Jin Yong and Dali), 178–181. Kunming: Yunnan renmin chubanshe.

Chen Lüfan. 1990. *Taizu qiyuan wenti yanjiu* (Whence Came the Thai Race—an Inquiry). [Kunming]: Guoji wenhua chubanshe.

———. 1991. "Nanzhao bushi Daizu jianli de guojia" (English title: Nanzhao Regime Is Not Established by Dai Nationality). In Yang Zhonglu, Zhang Fusan, and Zhang Nan, eds., *Nanzhao wenhua lun* (English title: The Treatises on Culture of Nanzhao Kingdom), 128–146. Kunming: Yunnan renmin chubanshe.

Chen Mo. 1998. "Duan Yu xingxiang ji qi yiyi" (Duan Yu's Image and Its Meaning). In Shi Lizhuo and Zhang Naiguang, eds., *Jin Yong yu Dali* (Jin Yong and Dali), 56–72. Kunming: Yunnan renmin chubanshe.

Chen, Nancy N., Constance D. Clark, Suzanne Z. Gottschang, and Lyn Jeffery, eds. 2001. *China Urban: Ethnographies of Contemporary Culture*. Durham: Duke University Press.

Chen, Tina. 2003. "Propagating the Propaganda Film: The Meaning of Film in Chinese Communist Party Writings, 1949–1965." *Modern Chinese Literature and Culture* 15.2: 154–193.

Cheung, Sidney C. H. 2001. "Preservation and Tourism Development in Hong Kong: An Anthropological Perspective." In Tan Chee-Beng, Sidney C. H. Cheung, and Yang Hui, eds., 257–270. *Tourism, Anthropology and China*. Studies in Asian Tourism No. 1. Bangkok: White Lotus Press.

Cheung, Siu-woo. 1996a. "Representation and Negotiation of Ge Identities in Southeast Guizhou." In Melissa J. Brown, ed., *Negotiating Ethnicities in China and Taiwan*, 240–273. Berkeley: Center for Chinese Studies, University of California.

———. 1996b. "Subject and Representation: Identity Politics in Southeast Guizhou." Ph.D. dissertation, University of Washington, Seattle.

Chien Chiao and Nicholas Tapp, eds. 1989. *Ethnicity and Ethnic Groups in China.* Hong Kong: New Asia College.

"China Population." 2005. http://www.cpirc.org.cn/en/eindex.htm (accessed August 11, 2005).

"China Tourism Statistics." 2005. China National Tourist Office. *http://www.cnto.org/chinastats.asp* (accessed July 14, 2005).

"China's Land Disputes: Turning Ploughshares into Staves." 2005. *The Economist,* June 25: 40–41.

Chow, Rey. 1994. "Where Have All the Natives Gone?" In Angelika Bammer, ed., *Displacements: Cultural Identities in Question*, 125–151. Bloomington: Indiana University Press.

Chu, Godwin C., ed. 1978. *Popular Media in China: Shaping New Cultural Patterns.* Honolulu: University Press of Hawai'i.

Chu, Godwin C., and Philip H. Cheng. 1978. "Revolutionary Opera: An Instrument for Cultural Change." In Godwin C. Chu, ed., *Popular Media in China: Shaping New Cultural Patterns,* 73–103. Honolulu: University Press of Hawai'i.

Chūgoku no toribito (English title: The Bird People). [1998] 2004. Directed by Takashi Miike. DVD. Excellent Film/Sedic International. Distributed by Arts Magic Ltd.

Ci, Jiwei. 1994. *Dialectic of the Chinese Revolution: From Utopianism to Hedonism.* Stanford: Stanford University Press.

Clark, Paul. 1987a. *Chinese Cinema: Culture and Politics since 1949.* Cambridge: Cambridge University Press.

———. 1987b. "Ethnic Minorities in Chinese Films: Cinema and the Exotic." *East-West Film Journal* 1.2: 15–31.

Clifford, James. 1997. *Routes: Travel and Translation in the Late Twentieth Century.* Cambridge, MA: Harvard University Press.

Cohen, Alvin P. 1993. "A New Deity in the People's Republic of China: Mao Zedong." *Journal of Chinese Religions* 21: 129–130.

Cohen, Erik. 1988. "Authenticity and Commodification in Tourism." *Annals of Tourism Research* 15.3: 371–386.

———. 1996. *Thai Tourism: Hill Tribes, Islands and Open-Ended Prostitution: Collected Papers.* Studies in Contemporary Thailand No. 4. Bangkok: White Lotus Press.

———. 2001. "Ethnic Tourism in Southeast Asia." In Tan Chee-Beng, Sidney C. H. Cheung, and Yang Hui, eds., *Tourism, Anthropology and China,* 27–53. Studies in Asian Tourism No. 1. Bangkok: White Lotus Press.

———. 2004. "Backpacking: Diversity and Change." In Greg Richards and Julie Wilson, eds., *The Global Nomad: Backpacker Travel in Theory and Practice*, 43–59. Clevedon, UK: Channel View Publications.

Colloredo-Mansfeld, Rudi. 1999. *The Native Leisure Class: Consumption and Cultural Creativity in the Andes*. Chicago: University of Chicago Press.

Colquhoun, Archibald. [1885] 1985. *Ethnic History of the Shans*. Delhi: Manas. [Orig. *Amongst the Shans*. London: Field and Tuer; New York: Scribner and Welford.]

Cordier, G. [1909] 1927. *Les Musulmans du Yunnan*. Hanoi: Imprimerie Tonkinoise. [Orig. "Nouveaux documents sur la révolte musulmane au Yun-Nan." *Revue Indochinoise* 12: 656–674.]

Craig, Timothy J., and Richard King, eds. 2002. *Global Goes Local: Popular Culture in Asia*. Ann Arbor: Association for Asian Studies; Honolulu: University of Hawai'i Press.

Credner, William. 1935. *Cultural and Geographic Observations Made in the Ta-li (Yunnan) Region with Special Regard to the Nan-chao Problem*. Trans. Major Erik Seidenfaden. Bangkok: Siam Society.

Crossley, Pamela Kaye. 1990. "Thinking about Ethnicity in Early Modern China." *Late Imperial China* 11.1: 1–35.

Culler, Jonathan. 1981. "Semiotics of Tourism." *American Journal of Semiotics* 1: 127–140.

Dai Yuting and Chen Lufan. 1990. "Whether Kublai Khan's Conquest of the Dali Kingdom Gave Rise to the Mass Migration of the Thai People to the South." Trans. Xie Bokui. In Chen Lufan, *Taizu qiyuan wenti yanjiu* (Whence Came the Thai Race—an Inquiry), 261–293. [Kunming]: Guoji wenhua chubanshe.

Daji he tade fuqin (Daji and Her Fathers). 1961. Directed by Wang Jiayi. Changchun Film Studio.

Dali Baizu zizhizhou difangzhi bianzuan weiyuanhui (Dali Bai Nationality Autonomous Prefecture Gazetteer Editorial Committee), ed. 1990. *Dali Baizu zizhizhou nianjian* (Almanac of Dali Prefecture). Kunming: Yunnan minzu chubanshe.

———. 1995. *Dali zhou nianjian* (Almanac of Dali Prefecture). Kunming: Yunnan minzhu chubanshe.

———. 1999. *Dali Baizu zizhizhou zhi* (Gazetteer of Dali Prefecture). Vol. 3. Kunming: Yunnan minzu chubanshe.

———. 2004. *Dali zhou nianjian* (Yearbook of Dali Prefecture). Kunming: Yunnan minzu chubanshe.

Dali Baizu zizhizhou wenhuaju (Dali Bai Nationality Autonomous Prefecture Culture Bureau), ed. 1984. *Baizu minjian gushi xuan* (A Selection of Bai Nationality Folk Tales). Shanghai: Wenyi chubanshe.

Dali shi diming weiyuanhui bangongshi (Place Names of Municipal Dali Committee Office), ed. 1990. *Dali shi diming* (Place Names of Municipal Dali). Dali.

Dali shi wenhuaju bian (Dali Municipal Culture Bureau), ed. 1988. *Baizu benzhu shenhua* (Bai Local Deity Legends). Beijing: Zhongguo minjian wenyi chubanshe.

Dali shi zhi bianzuan weiyuanhui (Annal of Dali Municipality Editorial and Compilation Committee), ed. 1998. *Dali shi zhi* (Annal of Dali Municipality). Beijing: Zhonghua shuju.

"Dali Tianlong babu yingshicheng jianjie" (A Brief Introduction to Dali Heavenly Dragons Film City). N.d. Unpublished press release courtesy of the Dali Tianlong Babu Yingshicheng management.

"Dali Tianlong babu yingshicheng fazhan qingkuang jieshao" (An Introduction to Dali Heavenly Dragons Film City's Development). N.d. Unpublished press release courtesy of the Dali Tianlong Babu Yingshicheng management.

Daniels, E. Valentine. [1984] 1987. *Fluid Signs: Being a Person the Tamil Way*. Berkeley: University of California Press.

Davis, Deborah S., ed. 2000a. *The Consumer Revolution in Urban China*. Berkeley: University of California Press.

———. 2000b. "Introduction: A Revolution in Consumption." In Deborah S. Davis, ed., *The Consumer Revolution in Urban China*, 1–22. Berkeley: University of California Press.

Davis, Deborah S., Richard Kraus, Barry Naughton, and Elizabeth J. Perry, eds. [1995] 1999. *Urban Spaces in Contemporary China*. Cambridge: Woodrow Wilson Center Press and Cambridge University Press.

Davis, Fred. 1981. "Contemporary Nostalgia and the Mass Media." In Elihu Katz and Tamás Szecskö, eds., *Mass Media and Social Change*, 219–229. London: Sage.

de Bary, Wm. Theodore, Wing-tsit Chan, and Burton Watson, eds. [1960] 1969. *Sources of Chinese Tradition*. 2 vols. New York: Columbia University Press.

Deleuze, Félix, and Gilles Guattari. 1983. *Anti-Oedipus: Capitalism and Schizophrenia*. Trans. Robert Hurley, Mark Seem, and Helen R. Lane. Minneapolis: University of Minnesota Press.

Dell, François. 1981. *La langue Bai: Phonologie et lexique*. Paris: Centre de Recherches Linguistiques sur l'Asie Orientale de l'École des Hautes Études en Sciences Sociales.

Deloria, Philip J. 1998. *Playing Indian*. New Haven: Yale University Press.

DeLyser, Dydia. 1999. "Authenticity on the Ground: Engaging the Past in a California Ghost Town." *Annals of the Association of American Geographers* 89.4: 602–632.

———. 2003. "Ramona Memories: Fiction, Tourist Practices, and Placing the Past in Southern California." *Annals of the Association of American Geographers* 93.4: 886–908.

Desforges, Luke. 1998. "Checking Out the Planet: Global Representations/Local Identities and Youth Travel." In Tracey Skelton and Gill Valentine, eds., *Cool Places: Geographies of Youth Cultures*, 175–192. London: Routledge.

Desmond, Jane C. 1999. *Staging the Body for Tourism: Bodies on Display from Waikiki to Sea World*. Chicago: University of Chicago Press.

Diamond, Norma. 1975. "Collectivization, Kinship, and the Status of Women in Rural China." In Rayna R. Reiter, ed., *Toward an Anthropology of Women*, 372–395. New York: Monthly Review Press.

———. 1983. "Model Villages and Village Realities." *Modern China* 9.2: 163–181.

———. 1988. "The Miao and Poison: Interactions on China's Southwest Frontier." *Ethnology* 27.1: 1–25.

———. 1995. "Defining the Miao: Ming, Qing, and Contemporary Views." In Stevan Harrell, ed., *Cultural Encounters on China's Ethnic Frontiers*, 92–116. Seattle: University of Washington Press.

Dickey, Sara. 1995. "Consuming Utopia: Film Watching in Tamil Nadu." In Carol Breckenridge, ed., *Consuming Modernity: Public Culture in a South Asian World*, 131–156. Minneapolis: University of Minnesota Press.

di Leonardo, Micalea. 1984. *Varieties of Ethnic Experience: Kinship, Class and Gender among California Italian-Americans*. Ithaca: Cornell University Press.

Dodd, W. C. 1923. *The Tai Race, Elder Brother of the Chinese*. Iowa: The Torch Press.

Doorne, S., I. Ateljevic, and Z. Bai. 2003. "Representing Identities through Tourism: Encounters of Ethnic Minorities in Dali, Yunnan Province, People's Republic of China." *International Journal of Tourism Research* 5: 1–11.

Drake, F. S., ed. 1967. *Symposium on Historical, Archaeological and Linguistic Studies on Southern China, South East Asia and the Hong Kong Region*. Hong Kong: Hong Kong University Press.

Dreyer, June Teufel. 1976. *China's Forty Millions: Minority Nationalities and National Integration in the People's Republic of China*. Cambridge, MA: Harvard University Press.

Du Shanshan. 2002. *"Chopsticks Only Work in Pairs": Gender Unity and Gender Equality among the Lahu of Southwest China*. New York: Columbia University Press.

Duara, Prasenjit. [1988] 1991. *Culture, Power, and the State: Rural North China, 1900–1942*. Stanford: Stanford University Press.

Dutton, Michael. [1998] 2000. *Streetlife China*. Cambridge: Cambridge University Press.

Dyer, Richard. 1985. "Entertainment and Utopia." In B. Nichols, ed., *Movies and Methods*, vol. 2, 220–232. Berkeley: University of California Press.

Ebrey, Patricia. 1996. "Surnames and Han Chinese Identity." In Melissa J. Brown, ed., *Negotiating Ethnicities in China and Taiwan*, 11–36. Berkeley: Center for Chinese Studies, University of California.

Eco, Umberto. [1967] 1987. *Travels in Hyperreality*. Trans. William Weaver. San Diego: Harcourt Brace and Co.

Ecsedy, Hilda. 1974. "Cultivators and Barbarians in Ancient China." *Acta Orientalia* 28.3: 327–349.

Editorial Department of the PRC Year Book, Beijing. 1996. *PRC Year Book 1995/96*. Vol. 15. (English edition.) Hong Kong and Beijing: N.C.N. Limited and PRC Year Book Ltd.

Elsrud, Torun. 2001. "Risk Creation in Traveling: Backpacker Adventure Narration." *Annals of Tourism Research* 28.3: 597–617.

Enloe, Cynthia. 1990. *Bananas, Beaches, and Bases: Making Feminist Sense of International Politics*. Berkeley: University of California Press.

Errington, Frederick, and Deborah Gewertz. 1989. "Tourism and Anthropology in a Post-modern World." *Oceania* 60.1: 37–54.

Fan Zhuo. [864] 1962. *Manshu jiaozhu* (Annotated Book of Barbarians). Annotated by Xiang Da (Xiang Juemin). Beijing: Zhonghua shuju.

Fang Guoyu. 1957. "Guanyu 'Wuman,' 'Baiman' de jieshi" (An Explanation Regarding the "Black Barbarians" and the "White Barbarians"). In Yang Kun et al., *Yunnan Baizu de qiyuan he xingcheng lunwen ji* (A Collection of Essays on the Origin and Formation of the Yunnan Bai Nationality), 1–11. Yunnan remin chubanshe.

———. 1984. *Yizu shigao* (A Draft History of the Yi Nationality). Chengdu: Sichuan minzu chubanshe.

Fang Guoyu and Lin Chaomin. 1994. *"Make bolo xingji" Yunnan shidi congkao* (The Travels of Marco Polo: An Examination of Yunnan's History and Geography). Beijing: Minzu chubanshe.

"Farmers in Olympics Land Protest." 2005. *The Standard*, June 17. http://www .thestandard.com.hk/ (accessed July 18, 2005).

Fawcett, Clare, and Patricia Cormack. 2001. "Guarding Authenticity at Literary Tourism Sites." *Annals of Tourism Research* 28.3: 686–704.

Featherstone, Mike. [1990] 1997a. "Global Culture: An Introduction." In Mike Featherstone, ed., *Global Culture: Nationalism, Globalization and Modernity*, 1–14. London: Sage.

———, ed. [1990] 1997b. *Global Culture: Nationalism, Globalization and Modernity*. London: Sage.

Fei Xiaotong. 1980. "Ethnic Identification in China." *Social Science in China* 1: 94–107.

Feld, Steven, and Keith H. Basso, eds. 1996. *Senses of Place*. Santa Fe: School of American Research Press.

Feng Xiaoran. 2000. "Cong Jin Yong wuxia xiaoshuo kan Zha Liangyong aiguo qinghuang de zhuanbian" (Observing the Transformation in Zha Liangyong's Patriotic Feelings Based on Jin Yong's Martial Arts Novels). In Lin Lijun, ed., *Jin Yong xiaoshuo yu ershi shiji Zhongguo wenxue* (Jin Yong's Novels and Twentieth-Century Chinese Literature), 531–550. Hong Kong: Minghe.

Fitzgerald, C. P. 1941. *The Tower of Five Glories—the Min Chia of Ta Li*. London: The Cresset Press.

Fitzgerald, John. 1996. *Awakening China: Politics, Culture, and Class in the Nationalist Revolution*. Stanford: Stanford University Press.

Fjellman, Stephen M. 1992. *Vinyl Leaves: Walt Disney World and America*. Boulder, CO: Westview Press.

Flower, John Myers. 2004. "A Road Is Made: Roads, Temples, and Historical Memory in Ya'an County, Sichuan." *Journal of Asian Studies* 63.3: 649–686.

Forêt, Philippe. 2000. *Mapping Chengde: The Qing Landscape Enterprise*. Honolulu: University of Hawai'i Press.

Foster, Robert J. 2002. *Materializing the Nation: Commodities, Consumption, and Media in Papua New Guinea*. Bloomington: Indiana University Press.

Franck, Harry A. 1925. *Roving through Southern China*. New York: The Century Co.

Frayling, Christopher. 1995. *Spaghetti Westerns: Cowboys and Europeans from Karl May to Sergio Leone*. London: Routledge and Kegan Paul.

French, Howard W. 2005. "Chinese Pressing to Keep Village Silent on Clash." Dec. 17. *http://www.nytimes.com* (accessed Jan. 13, 2006).

Friedman, Jonathan. [1990] 1997. "Being in the World: Globalization and Localization." In Mike Featherstone, ed., *Global Culture: Nationalism, Globalization and Modernity*, 311–328. London: Sage.

Friedman, Sara L. 2004. "Embodying Civility: Civilizing Processes and Symbolic Citizenship in Southeastern China." *Journal of Asian Studies* 63.3: 687–718.

Friend, Tad. 2005. "The Parachute Artist: Have Tony Wheeler's Guidebooks Travelled Too Far?" *The New Yorker*, April 18: 78–91.

Frow, John. 1991. "Tourism and the Semiotics of Nostalgia." *October* 57: 123–151.

Gates, Hill. 1991. "'Narrow Hearts' and Petty Capitalism: Small Business Women of Chengdu, China." In Alice Littlefield and Hill Gates, eds., *Marxist Approaches to Economic Anthropology*, 13–36. Monographs in Economic Anthropology No. 9. Lanham, MD: University Press of America.

Gaubatz, Piper Rae. [1995] 1999. "Urban Transformation in Post-Mao China: Impacts of the Reform Era on China's Urban Form." In Deborah S. Davis, Richard Kraus, Barry Naughton, and Elizabeth J. Perry, eds., *Urban Spaces in Contemporary China*, 28–60. Cambridge: Woodrow Wilson Center Press and Cambridge University Press.

Gewertz, Deborah B., and Frederick K. Errington. [1991] 1994. *Twisted Histories, Altered Contexts: Representing the Chambri in a World System*. Cambridge: Cambridge University Press.

Gill, Captain William, R.E. 1883. *The River of Golden Sand: Being a Narrative of a Journey through China and Eastern Tibet to Burmah*. Condensed by Edward Colborne Baber, Chinese Secretary to H.M.'s Legation at Peking. Edited by Colonel Henry Yule, C.B., R.E. London: John Murray.

Gillett, Sir Michael. 1969. "Some Walks along the China-Burma Frontier." Occasional Papers No.16. London: The China Society.

Gillette, Maris Boyd. 2000. *Between Mecca and Beijing: Modernization and Consumption among Urban Chinese Muslims*. Stanford: Stanford University Press.

Gilmartin, Christina K., Gail Hershatter, Lisa Rofel, and Tyrone White, eds. 1994. *Engendering China: Women, Culture, and the State*. Cambridge, MA: Harvard University Press.

Gladney, Dru C. 1991. *Muslim Chinese: Ethnic Nationalism in the People's Republic*. Cambridge, MA: Council on East Asian Studies, Harvard University.

———. 1994. "Representing Nationality in China: Refiguring Minority/Majority Identities." *Journal of Asian Studies* 53.1: 92–123.

———. 1995. "Tian Zhuangzhuang, the Fifth Generation, and Minorities Film in China." *Public Culture* 8.1: 161–175.

Goodman, Peter S. 2002. "China Finds Its Shangri-La in Tourism." *The Washington Post*, September 2: A1, A20.

———. 2005. "Rural Poor Aren't Sharing in Spoils of China's Changes." July 12. http:www.washingtonpost.com/ (accessed July 20, 2005).

Gold, Thomas B. 1993. "Go with Your Feelings: Hong Kong and Taiwan Popular Culture in Greater China." *China Quarterly,* special Issue: Greater China, 136: 907–925.

Graburn, Nelson H. H. 2001. "Tourism and Anthropology in East Asia Today: Some Comparisons." In Tan Chee-Beng, Sidney C. H. Cheung, and Yang Hui, eds., *Tourism, Anthropology and China,* 71–92. Studies in Asian Tourism No. 1. Bangkok: White Lotus Press.

Greenwood, Davydd J. 1993. "Culture by the Pound: An Anthropological Perspective on Tourism as Cultural Commoditization." In Valene L. Smith, ed., *Hosts and Guests: The Anthropology of Tourism,* 171–185. 2nd edition. Philadelphia: University of Pennsylvania Press.

Guides, Madrolle. 1939. *Indochine du Nord: Tonkin, Annam, Laos, Yünnan, Hongkong, Kouang-tcheou Wan.* 3rd ed. Paris: Société d'Éditions Géographiques, Maritimes et Coloniales.

Guo, Xiaolin. 2001. "Land Expropriation and Rural Conflicts in China." *China Quarterly* 166: 422–439.

Gupta, Akhil, and James Ferguson. 1992. "Beyond 'Culture': Space, Identity, and the Politics of Difference." *Cultural Anthropology* 7.1: 6–23.

———, eds. 1997a. *Anthropological Locations: Boundaries and Grounds of a Field Science.* Berkeley: University of California Press.

———. 1997b. "Culture, Power, Place: Ethnography at the End of an Era." In Akhil Gupta and James Ferguson, eds., *Culture, Power, Place: Explorations in Critical Anthropology,* 1–29. Durham: Duke University Press.

———, eds. 1997c. *Culture, Power, Place: Explorations in Critical Anthropology.* Durham: Duke University Press.

———. 1997d. "Discipline and Practice: 'The Field' as Site, Method, and Location in Anthropology." In Akil Gupta and James Ferguson, eds., *Anthropological Locations: Boundaries and Grounds of a Field Science,* 1–46. Berkeley: University of California Press.

Hall, Stuart. 1981. "Notes on Deconstructing 'the Popular.' " In Raphael Samuel, ed., *People's History and Socialist Theory,* 227–240. London: Routledge and Kegan Paul.

Hamm, John C[hristopher]. 2002. "Local Heroes—Guangdong School *Wuxia* Fiction and Hong Kong's Imagining of China." In Wu Xiaodong and Ji Birui, eds., *2000 Beijing Jin Yong xiaoshuo guoji yantaohui lunwenji* (2000 Beijing International Conference Proceedings on Jin Yong's Novels), 309–340. Beijing: Beijing daxue.

———. 2005. *Paper Swordsmen: Jin Yong and the Modern Chinese Martial Arts Novel.* Honolulu: University of Hawai'i Press.

Han Min. 2001. "The Meanings of Mao in Mao Tourism of Shaoshan." In Tan Chee-Beng, Sidney C. H. Cheung, and Yang Hui, eds., *Tourism, Anthropology and China,* 215–236. Studies in Asian Tourism No. 1. Bangkok: White Lotus Press.

Handler, Richard. 1986. "Authenticity." *Anthropology Today* 2.1: 2–4.

Handler, Richard, and William Saxton. 1988. "Dyssimulation: Reflexivity, Narrative, and the Quest of Authenticity in 'Living History.'" *Cultural Anthropology* 3.3: 242–260.

Hannerz, Ulf. 1989. *Transnational Connections: Culture, People, Places.* London: Routledge.

———. [1990] 1997. "Cosmopolitans and Locals in World Culture." In Mike Featherstone, ed., *Global Culture: Nationalism, Globalization and Modernity,* 237–251. London: Sage.

———. [1997] 2000. "Scenarios for Peripheral Cultures." In Anthony D. King, ed., *Culture, Globalization and the World-System: Contemporary Conditions for the Representation of Identity,* 107–128. Minneapolis: University of Minnesota Press.

Harkin, Michael [E.]. 1995. "Modernist Anthropology and Tourism of the Authentic." *Annals of Tourism Research* 22: 650–670.

———. 2003. "Staged Encounters: Postmodern Tourism and Aboriginal People." *Ethnohistory* 50.3: 575–585.

———. 2004. "Thirteen Ways of Looking at a Landscape." In Marie Mauzé, Michael E. Harkin, and Sergei Kan, eds., *Coming to Shore: Northwest Coast Ethnology, Traditions, and Visions,* 385–406. Lincoln: University of Nebraska Press.

Harper, Ralph. 1966. *Nostalgia: An Existential Exploration of Longing and Fulfilment in the Modern Age.* Cleveland: The Press of Western Reserve University. [First published as *The Sleeping Beauty.* Harper and Brothers and Harvill Press, 1955.]

Harrell, Stevan. 1990. "Ethnicity, Local Interests, and the State: Yi Communities in South-west China." *Comparative Studies in Society and History* 32.3: 515–548.

———, ed. 1995a. *Cultural Encounters on China's Ethnic Frontiers.* Seattle: University of Washington Press.

———. 1995b. "The History of the History of the Yi." In Stevan Harrell, ed., *Cultural Encounters on China's Ethnic Frontiers,* 63–91. Seattle: University of Washington Press.

———. 1995c. "Introduction." In Stevan Harrell, ed., *Cultural Encounters on China's Ethnic Frontiers,* 3–36. Seattle: University of Washington Press.

———. 1995d. "Jeeping against Maoism." *Positions* 3.3: 728–758.

———. 2001a. "The Anthropology of Reform and the Reform of Anthropology: Anthropological Narratives of Recovery and Progress in China." *Annual Review of Anthropology* 30: 139–161.

———. 2001b. *Ways of Being Ethnic in Southwest China.* Seattle: University of Washington Press.

Harrison, Henrietta. 2000. *The Making of the Republican Citizen: Political Ceremonies and Symbols in China, 1911–1929.* Oxford: Oxford University Press.

Harvey, David. [1989] 1990. *The Condition of Postmodernity.* Cambridge, MA: Blackwell.

———. 1993. "From Space to Place and Back Again: Reflections on the Condition of

Postmodernity." In Jon Bird, Barry Curtis, Tim Putnam, George Robertson, and Lisa Tickner, eds., *Mapping the Futures: Local Cultures, Global Change,* 3–29. London: Routledge.

He, Liyi. [1993] 2003. With Claire Ann Chik. *Mr. China's Son: A Villager's Life.* 2nd ed. Boulder: Westview Press.

Heberer, Thomas. [1984] 1989. *China and Its National Minorities: Autonomy or Assimilation?* Armonk, NY: M. E. Sharpe. [Orig. *Nationalitätenpolitik und Entwicklungspolitik in den Gebieten nationaler Minderheiten in China* (Ethnic Politics and Development Politics in National Minority Areas of China). Bremen: Universität Bremen.]

Hechter, Michael. [1975] 1999. *Internal Colonialism: The Celtic Fringe in British National Development.* Revised ed. New Brunswick, NJ: Transaction. [Orig. Berkeley: University of California Press.]

Hendry, Joy. 2000. *The Orient Strikes Back: A Global View of Cultural Display.* Oxford: Berg.

Herzfeld, Michael. 1991. *A Place in History: Social and Monumental Time in a Cretan Town.* Princeton: Princeton University Press.

Hilton, James. [1933] 1960. *Lost Horizon.* New York: Pocket Books.

Hirsch, Eric. 1995. "Landscape: Between Place and Space." In Eric Hirsch and Michael O'Hanlon, eds., *The Anthropology of Landscape: Perspectives on Place and Space,* 1–30. Oxford: Clarendon Press.

Hitchcock, Michael, Victor T. King, and Michael J. G. Parnwell, eds. 1993a. *Tourism in South-East Asia.* London and New York: Routledge.

———. 1993b. "Tourism in South-East Asia: Introduction." In Michael Hitchcock, Victor T. King and Michael J. G. Parnwell, eds., *Tourism in South-East Asia,* 1–31. London and New York: Routledge.

Ho, Peter. [2000] 2003. "Contesting Rural Spaces: Land Disputes, Customary Tenure and the State." In Elizabeth J. Perry and Mark Selden, eds., *Chinese Society: Change, Conflict and Resistance,* 93–112. 2nd ed. London: RoutledgeCurzon.

Hobsbawm, Eric. 1983. "Introduction: Inventing Traditions." In Eric Hobsbawm and Terence Ranger, eds., *The Invention of Tradition,* 1–14. Cambridge: Cambridge University Press.

hooks, bell. 1989. *Talking Back: Thinking Feminist, Thinking Black.* Boston: South End Press.

Horkheimer, Max, and Theodor W. Adorno. [1944] 1972. *Dialectic of Enlightenment.* Trans. John Cumming. New York: Continuum.

Hosie, [Alexander]. [1884] 1915. "Report by Mr. Hosie of a Journey through the Provinces of Ssu-ch'uan, Yünnan, and Kuei Chou: February 11 to June 14, 1883." Presented to both Houses of Parliament by Command of Her Majesty. Bound in *British Parliamentary Papers: Journeys and Expeditions in China, 1869–1904.* Cleveland. [Orig. China No. 2. London: Harrison and Sons.]

———. 1897. *Three Years in Western China.* 2nd ed. London: George Philip and Son.

Hostetler, Laura. 2001. *Qing Colonial Enterprise: Ethnography and Cartography in Early Modern China.* Chicago: University of Chicago Press.

Howes, David, ed. 1996a. *Cross-Cultural Consumption: Global Markets, Local Realities.* London: Routledge.

———. 1996b. "Cultural Appropriation and Resistance in the American Southwest: Decommodifying 'Indianness.' " In David Howes, ed., *Cross-Cultural Consumption: Global Markets, Local Realities,* 138–160. London: Routledge.

———. 1996c. "Introduction: Commodities and Cultural Borders." In David Howes, ed., *Cross-Cultural Consumption: Global Markets, Local Realities,* 1–18. London: Routledge.

Hsieh Shih-chung. 1995. "On the Dynamics of Tai/Dai–Lue Ethnicity: An Ethnohistorical Analysis." In Stevan Harrell, ed., *Cultural Encounters on China's Ethnic Frontiers,* 301–328. Seattle: University of Washington Press.

Hsu, Francis L. K. [1948] 1967. *Under the Ancestors' Shadow: Kinship, Personality, and Social Mobility in Village China.* Revised ed. Stanford: Stanford University Press. [Orig. New York: Columbia University Press.]

Huang Changgu, ed. 1926 (Minguo 15). *Sun Zhongshan xiansheng yanshuoji* (A Collection of Mr. Sun Yat-sen's Speeches). Shanghai: Minzhi shuju.

Huang Zonghui. 1999. "Ta bu kan ta shi, ta zai ma?" (When He Does Not See Her, Is She There?). In Wang Chougui, ed., *Jin Yong xiaoshuo—guoji xueshu yantaohui lunwenji* (Proceedings of the International Conference on Jin Yong's Novels), 181–205. Taipei: Yuanliu.

Huggins, Jackie, Rita Huggins, and Jane M. Jacobs. 1995. "Kooramindanjie: Place and the Postcolonial." *History Workshop Journal* 39: 164–181.

Hutnyk, John. 1996. *The Rumour of Calcutta: Tourism, Charity and the Poverty of Representation.* London: Zed Books.

Hyde, Sandra Teresa. 2001. "Sex Tourism Practices on the Periphery: Eroticizing Ethnicity and Pathologizing Sex on the Lancang." In Nancy N. Chen, Constance D. Clark, Suzanne Z. Gottschang, and Lyn Jeffery, eds., *China Urban: Ethnographies of Contemporary Culture,* 143–162. Durham, NC: Duke University Press.

"India Tourism 2004 Statistics, Facts and Figures." 2006. http://neoncarrot.co.uk/h_aboutindia/india_tourism_stats.html (accessed Jan. 17, 2006).

Jameson, Frederick. 1989. "Nostalgia for the Present." *South Atlantic Quarterly* 88.2: 517–537.

Jin Yong [Zha Liangyong]. 1965. *Tianlong babu.* (Heavenly Dragons). Vol. 19. Hong Kong: Wushi chubanshe.

———. [1978] (date of reprint not given). Revised ed. *Tianlong babu* (Heavenly Dragons). 5 vols. Hong Kong: Wuxia chubanshe.

———. 2000. "Xiaoshuo chuangzao de jidian sikao—Jin Yong zai bimushi shang de jianghua" (Some Thoughts on Novel Creation—Jin Yong's Closing Ceremony Speech). In Lin Lijun, ed., *Jin Yong xiaoshuo yu ershi shiji Zhongguo wenxue* (Jin

Yong's Novels and Twentieth-Century Chinese Literature), 23–28. Hong Kong: Minghe.

———— [Louis Cha]. 2004. *The Book and the Sword: A Martial Arts Novel*. Trans. Graham Earnshaw; ed. Rachel May and John Minford. Oxford: Oxford University Press.

————. 1997–2002. *The Deer and the Cauldron: A Martial Arts Novel*. Trans. and ed. John Minford. Oxford: Oxford University Press.

————. 1996. *Fox Volant of the Snowy Mountain*. Trans. Olivia Mok. Hong Kong: Chinese University Press.

Jing Dexin. 1986. *Yunnan Huimin qiyi shiliao* (Historical Materials on the Yunnan Hui People's Uprising). Kunming: Yunnan minzu chubanshe.

————, ed. 1991. *Du Wenxiu qiyi* (The Du Wenxiu Uprising). Kunming: Yunnan minzu chubanshe.

Jing, Jun. 1996. *The Temple of Memories: History, Power, and Morality in a Chinese Village*. Stanford: Stanford University Press.

Jingpo guniang (Jingpo Girl). 1965. Directed by Wang Jiayi. Changchun Film Studio.

"Jin Yong: Kungfu Novel Master." 2001. http://www.china.org.cn/english/2001/Aug/17511.htm (accessed May 14, 2005). [Orig. in *China Daily*, Aug. 15, 2001.]

Jin Yuji. 1959. Directed by Wang Jiayi. Changchun Film Studio.

Kahn, Miriam. 1990. "Stone-Faced Ancestors: The Spatial Anchoring of Myth in Wamira, Papua New Guinea." *Ethnology* 29: 51–66.

————. 1996. "Your Place and Mine: Sharing Emotional Landscapes in Wamira, Papua New Guinea." In Steven Feld and Keith H. Basso, eds., *Senses of Place*, 167–196. Santa Fe: School of American Research Press.

————. 2000. "Tahiti Intertwined: Ancestral Land, Tourist Postcard, and Nuclear Test Site." *American Anthropologist* 102.1: 7–26.

Kane, Penny. 1988. *Famine in China, 1959–61: Demographic and Social Implications*. London: Macmillan.

Kapferer, Jean-Noël. [1987] 1990. *Rumors: Uses, Interpretations, and Images*. Trans. Bruce Fink. New Brunswick: Transaction Publishers. [Orig. *Rumeurs: Le plus vieux média du monde*. Paris: Éditions du Seuil.]

Keane, Michael. 2002. "Television Drama in China: Engineering Souls for the Market." In Timothy J. Craig and Richard King, eds., *Global Goes Local: Popular Culture in Asia*, 120–137. Ann Arbor: Association for Asian Studies; Honolulu: University of Hawai'i Press.

Kennedy, Laurel B., and Mary Rose Wiliams. 2001. "The Past without the Pain: The Manufacture of Nostalgia in Vietnam's Tourism Industry." In Hue-Tam Ho Tai, ed., *The Country of Memory: Remaking the Past in Late Socialist Vietnam*, 135–163. Berkeley: University of California Press.

Keyes, Charles. 2002. "Presidential Address: 'The Peoples of Asia'—Science and Politics in the Classification of Ethnic Groups in Thailand, China, and Vietnam." *Journal of Asian Studies* 61.4: 1163–1203.

Khan, Almaz. 1996. "Who Are the Mongols? State, Ethnicity, and the Politics of Representation in the PRC." In Melissa J. Brown, ed., *Negotiating Ethnicities in China and Taiwan*, 125–159. Berkeley: Institute of East Asian Studies, University of California.

Kim, Hyounggon, and Sarah L. Richardson. 2003. "Motion Picture Impacts on Destination Images." *Annals of Tourism Research* 1: 216–237.

Kincaid, Jamaica. 1988. *A Small Place*. London: Virago.

Kipnis, Andrew B. 1997. *Producing Guanxi: Sentiments, Self and Subculture in a North China Village*. Durham: Duke University Press.

Kirshenblatt-Gimblett, Barbara. 1998. *Destination Culture: Tourism, Museums and Heritage*. Berkeley: University of California Press.

Komroff, Manuel, ed. 1926. *The Travels of Marco Polo*. New York: The Modern Library.

Lacouperie, Terrien de. [1885] 1985. "Introduction: The Cradle of the Shan Race." In Archibald R. Colquhoun, *Ethnic History of the Shans*, xxi–lv. Delhi: Manas. [Orig. *Amongst the Shans*. London: Field and Tuer; New York: Scribner and Welford.]

"Land Administration Law of the People's Republic of China (2004 Revision)." 2004. *Amendments to the Constitution of the People's Republic of China*. http://www.lawinfochina.com/ (accessed July 21, 2005).

"Land Management Law." 2004. http://english.sohu.com/2004/07/04/80/article 220848073.shtml (accessed July 21, 2005).

Larsen, Neil. 2000. "Imperialism, Colonialism, Postcolonialism." In Henry Schwarz and Sangeeta Ray, eds., *A Companion to Postcolonial Studies*, 23–52. Malden, MA: Blackwell.

Lash, Scott, and John Urry. [1994] 1996. *Economies of Signs and Space*. London: Sage.

Lass, Andrew. 1994. "From Memory to History: The Events of November 17 Dis/membered." In Rubie Watson, ed., *Memory, History and Opposition under State Socialism*, 87–104. Santa Fe: School of American Research Press.

Lavie, Smadar. 1990. *The Poetics of Military Occupation*. Berkeley: University of California Press.

Lefebvre, Henri. [1974] 1996. *The Production of Space*. Trans. Donald Nicholson-Smith. Oxford: Blackwell. [Orig. *La production de l'espace*. Éditions Anthropos.]

Leng Xia. 1995. *Jin Yong zhuan* (Biography of Jin Yong). Taipei: Yuanjin chuban shiye gongsi.

Lew, Alan A. 1995. "Overseas Chinese and Compatriots in China's Tourism Development." In Alan A. Lew and Lawrence Yu, eds., *Tourism in China: Geographic, Political, and Economic Perspectives*, 155–175. Boulder: Westview.

Lew, Alan A., and Lawrence Yu, eds. 1995. *Tourism in China: Geographic, Political, and Economic Perspectives*. Boulder: Westview.

Leyda, Jay. 1972. *Dianying: An Account of Films and the Film Audience in China*. Cambridge, MA: MIT Press.

Li Hongwen. 1998. "Wuxia xiaoshuo *Tianlong babu* de renxing mei" (The Beauty of Humanity in the Martial Arts Novel *Heavenly Dragons*). In Shi Lizhuo and Zhang Naiguang, eds., *Jin Yong yu Dali* (Jin Yong and Dali), 119–124. Kunming: Yunnan renmin chubanshe.

Li Hsiao-t'i. 2001. "Making a Name and a Culture for the Masses in Modern China." *Positions,* special issue: *Chinese Popular Culture and the State,* Jing Wang, guest editor, 9.1: 29–68.

Li Kunwu. 1999. *Li Xiaowu: Yunnan youmo fengqing you* (Li Xiaowu: Humorous, Flirtatious Travels in Yunnan). Kunming: Chenguang chubanshe.

Li Lin-ts'an. 1982. *Nanzhao Dali guo xin ziliao de zonghe yanjiu* (English title: A Study of the Nan-chao and Ta-Li Kingdoms in the Light of Art Materials Found in Various Museums). Taipei: National Palace Museum.

Lighte, Peter Rupert. 1981. "The Mongols and Mu Ying in Yunnan—at the Empire's Edge." Ph.D. dissertation, Princeton University.

Lin Lijun, ed. 2000. *Jin Yong xiaoshuo yu ershi shiji Zhongguo wenxue* (Jin Yong's Novels and Twentieth-Century Chinese Literature). Hong Kong: Minghe.

Link, Perry, Richard Madsen, and Paul Pickowicz, eds. 1989. *Unofficial China: Popular Culture and Thought in the People's Republic.* Boulder, CO: Westview Press.

———, eds. 2002. *Popular China: Unofficial Culture in a Globalizing Society.* Lanham, MD: Rowman and Littlefield.

Litzinger, Ralph A. 1995. "Making Histories: Contending Conceptions of the Yao Past." In Stevan Harrell, ed., *Cultural Encounters on China's Ethnic Frontiers,* 117–139. Seattle: University of Washington Press.

———. 1998. "Memory Work: Reconstituting the Ethnic in Post-Mao China." *Cultural Anthropology* 13.2: 224–255.

———. 2000a. *Other Chinas: The Yao and the Politics of National Belonging.* Durham: Duke University Press.

———. 2000b. "Questions of Gender: Ethnic Minority Representation in Post-Mao China." *Bulletin of Concerned Asian Scholars* 32.4: 3–14.

———. 2001. "Government from Below: The State, the Popular, and the Illusion of Autonomy." *Positions,* special issue: *Chinese Popular Culture and the State.* Jing Wang, guest editor, 9.1: 253–266.

Liu, Lydia H. 1995. *Translingual Practice: Literature, National Culture, and Translated Modernity—China, 1900–1937.* Stanford: Stanford University Press.

Liu Ts'un-yan [Cunren]. 2002. "Jin Yong xiaoshuo de shiye: *Tianlong babu*" (Jin Yong's Field of Vision: *Heavenly Dragons*). In Wu Xiaodong and Ji Birui, eds., *2000 Beijing Jin Yong xiaoshuo guoji yantaohui lunwenji* (2000 Beijing International Conference Proceedings on Jin Yong's Novels), 559–570. Beijing: Beijing Daxue.

Liu Zaifu. 2000. Xu (Preface). In Lin Lijun, ed., *Jin Yong xiaoshuo yu ershi shiji Zhongguo wenxue* (Jin Yong's Novels and Twentieth-Century Chinese Literature), 1–5. Hong Kong: Minghe.

Liu Sanjie (Third Sister Liu). 1960. Directed by Su Li. Changchun Film Studio.

Loh, Wai-fong. 1984. "From Romantic Love to Class Struggle: Some Reflections on the Film *Liu Sanjie.*" In Bonnie S. McDougall, ed., *Popular Chinese Literature and Performing Arts in the People's Republic of China, 1949–1979,* 165–176. Berkeley: University of California Press.

Loker-Murphy, L., and P. Pearce. 1995. "Young Budget Travelers: Backpackers in Australia." *Annals of Tourism Research* 22: 819–843.

Lopez, Donald S., Jr. 1998. *Prisoners of Shangri-La: Tibetan Buddhism and the West.* Chicago: University of Chicago Press.

"Louis Cha's *Kung Fu* Tale Retold." n.d. http://www.china.org.cn/english/culture/52910.htm (accessed May 14, 2005). [Orig. in *China Daily,* Jan. 7, 2002.]

Lowenthal, David. 1975. "Past Time, Present Place: Landscape and Memory." *Geographical Review* 65.1: 1–36.

———. 1985. *The Past Is a Foreign Country.* Cambridge: Cambridge University Press.

Luo Zhufeng, ed. 1986. *Hanyu da cidian* (Great Chinese Dictionary). N.p.: Hanyu da cidian chubanshe.

Lu sheng liange (Love Song of the Calabash Pipes). 1957. Directed by Yu Yanfu. Changchun Film Studio.

Lutz, Hartmut. 2002. "German Indianthusiasm: A Socially Constructed German National(ist) Myth." In Colin G. Calloway, Gerd Gemünden, and Susanne Zantop, eds., *Germans and Indians: Fantasies, Encounters, Projections,* 167–184. Lincoln: University of Nebraska Press.

Lyotard, Jean-François. [1989] 1998. "The Tensor." Trans. Sean Hand. In Andrew Benjamin, ed., *The Lyotard Reader,* 1–18. Oxford: Blackwell, 1998 [1989]. [Orig. in *Économie libidinale,* Paris: 57–115. Éditions de Minuit, 1974.]

Ma, Y. W. and Joseph S. M. Lau, eds. 1978. *Traditional Chinese Stories: Themes and Variations.* New York: Columbia University Press.

Ma Yin, ed. 1989. *China's Minority Nationalities.* Beijing: Foreign Languages Press.

MacCannell, Dean. 1976. *The Tourist: A New Theory of the Leisure Class.* New York: Schocken Books.

———. 1992. *Empty Meeting Grounds: The Tourist Papers,* London: Routledge.

Mackerras, Colin. 1988. "Aspects of Bai Culture: Change and Continuity in a Yunnan Nationality." *Modern China* 14.1: 51–84.

———. 1994. *China's Minorities: Integration and Modernization in the Twentieth Century.* Hong Kong: Oxford University Press.

Makley, Charlene. 1999. "Embodying the Sacred: Gender and Monastic Revitalization in China's Tibet." Ph.D. dissertation, University of Michigan, Ann Arbor.

———. 2003. "Gendered Bodies in Motion: Space and Identity on the Sino-Tibetan Frontier." *American Ethnologist* 30.4: 597–619.

Margary, Augustus Raymond. 1876. *The Journey of Augustus Raymond Margary, from Shanghae to Bhamo, and Back to Manwyne.* 2nd ed., concluding chapter by Sir Rutherford Alcock. London: Macmillan.

Marion, Donald J. 1997. *The Chinese Filmography.* Jefferson, NC: McFarland and Co.

"Mark Twain House and Museum, The." 2005. http://www.marktwainhouse.org/ (accessed July 14, 2005).

Marquand, Robert. 2005. "In China, Stresses Spill Over into Riots." *Christian Science Monitor*. http://www.csm.com/ (accessed July 20, 2005).

Massey, Doreen. 1993. "Power-Geometry and a Progressive Sense of Place." In Jon Bird, Barry Curtis, Tim Putnam, George Robertson, and Lisa Tickner, eds., *Mapping the Futures: Local Cultures, Global Change*, 59–69. London: Routledge.

———. 1995. "Places and Their Pasts." *History Workshop Journal* 39: 182–191.

May, Jon. 1996. "In Search of Authenticity Off and On the Beaten Track." *Environment and Planning D: Society and Space* 14: 709–736.

McDougall, Bonnie S. ed. 1984. *Popular Chinese Literature and Performing Arts in the People's Republic of China, 1949–1979*. Berkeley: University of California Press.

McKhann, Charles F. 1995. "The Naxi and the Nationalities Question." In Stevan Harrell, ed., *Cultural Encounters on China's Ethnic Frontiers*, 39–62. Seattle: University of Washington Press.

———. 2001. "Reflections on Tourism Development in Lijiang, China." In Tan Chee-Beng, Sidney C. H. Cheung, and Yang Hui, eds., *Tourism, Anthropology and China*, 147–166. Studies in Asian Tourism No. 1. Bangkok: White Lotus Press.

Meethan, Kevin. 2001. *Tourism in Global Society: Place, Culture, Consumption*. New York: Palgrave.

Meisch, Lynn A. 2002. *Andean Entrepreneurs: Otavalo Merchants and Musicians in the Global Arena*. Austin: University of Texas Press.

Meisner, Mitch. 1978. "Dazhai: The Mass Line in Practice." *Modern China* 4.1: 27–62.

Melton, Jeffrey Alan. 2002. *Mark Twain, Travel Books, and Tourism: The Tide of a Great Popular Movement*. Tuscaloosa and London: University of Alabama Press.

Michaud, Jean. 1993. "Tourism as Catalyst of Economic and Political Change. The Case of Highland Minorities in Ladakh (India) and Northern Thailand." *Internationales Asienforum* 24.1: 21–43.

Miller, Daniel. 1995a. "Consumption and Commodities." *Annual Review of Anthropology* 24: 141–161.

———, ed. 1995b. *Worlds Apart: Modernity through the Prism of the Local*. London: Routledge.

Miller, Lucien, ed. 1994. *South of the Clouds: Tales from Yunnan*. Seattle: University of Washington Press.

"Minzu wenti wuzhong congshu" Yunnan sheng bianji weiyuanhui (Yunnan Province Editorial Committee of the "Five Types of Collected Books on Nationality Problems"), ed. 1981. *Baizu shehui lishi diaocha* (Investigations into Bai Nationality Social History), 1. Kunming: Yunnan renmin chubanshe.

Mitchell, Joni. 1971. "All I Want." Song lyrics. In *Joni Mitchell Anthology*. Miami: Warner Bros. Publishing.

Morgan, Louis Henry. [1877] 1974. *Ancient Society, or Researches in the Lines of Human Progress from Savagery through Barbarism to Civilization*. Ed. Eleanor Burke Leacock. Gloucester, MA: Peter Smith.

Morrison, G. E. 1902. *An Australian in China: Being the Narrative of a Quiet Journey across China to Burma.* 3rd ed. London: Horace Cox.

Muren zhi zi (Son of the Herdsman). 1957. Directed by Zhu Wenshun and Guang-budao'erji (Gombodorji). Changchun Film Studio.

Mueggler, Erik. 1991. "Money, the Mountain, and State Power in a Naxi Village." *Modern China* 17.2: 188–226.

———. 1996. "Filth and Power: Administrative, Economic, and Corporeal Geographies in Yi Healing Ritual." Paper presented at the Center for Chinese Studies, University of Michigan, October 28.

———. 1998. "A Carceral Regime: Violence and Social Memory in Southwest China." *Cultural Anthropology* 13.2: 167–192.

———. 2001. *The Age of Wild Ghosts: Memory, Violence, and Place in Southwest China.* Berkeley: University of California Press.

Mukerji, Chandra, and Michael Schudson. 1991. "Introduction: Rethinking Popular Culture." In Chandra Mukerji and Michael Schudson, eds., *Rethinking Popular Culture: Contemporary Perspectives in Cultural Studies,* 1–61. Berkeley: University of California Press.

Nadel-Klein, Jane. 2003. *Fishing for Heritage: Modernity and Loss along the Scottish Coast.* Oxford: Berg.

Nash, Dennison. 1993. "Tourism as a Form of Imperialism." In Valene L. Smith, ed., *Hosts and Guests: The Anthropology of Tourism,* 37–52. 2nd ed. Philadelphia: University of Pennsylvania Press.

Neimeng renmin de shengli (Victory for the People of Inner Mongolia). 1950. Directed by Gan Xuewei. Northeast Film Studio.

Nilsson, John, and Tan Ying. 2001. "Advocacy Work on Conservation and Tourism Development in the Old City of Quanzhou, Fukian [sic], China." In Tan Chee-Beng, Sidney C. H. Cheung, and Yang Hui, eds., *Tourism, Anthropology and China,* 289–312. Studies in Asian Tourism No. 1. Bangkok: White Lotus Press.

"No Sign of a Landing: China's Economy Continues to Grow at Breakneck Speed." 2005. *The Economist,* Jan. 29: 39–40.

Notar, Beth E. 1992. "Contested History: Re-reading the *Book of Barbarians.*" M.A. thesis, University of Michigan, Ann Arbor.

———. 1994. "Of Labor and Liberation: Images of Women in Current Chinese Television Advertising." *Visual Anthropology Review* 10.2: 29–44.

———. 1996. "From Class Cash to Multicultural Money: Socialist Imperialism and Nationality Fetishism in the PRC." Paper presented at the American Anthropological Association, San Francisco, Nov. 21.

———. 1999. "Wild Histories: Popular Culture, Place and the Past in Southwest China." Ph.D. dissertation, University of Michigan, Ann Arbor.

———. 2001a. "Blood Money: Women's Desire and Consumption in *Ermo.*" *Asian Cinema,* Fall/Winter: 132–153.

———. 2001b. "Du Wenxiu and the Politics of the Muslim Past." *Twentieth-Century China* 26.2: 63–94.

————. 2002. "Viewing Currency 'Chaos': Money for Advertising, Ideology and Resistance in Republican China." In Terry Bodenhorn, ed., *Defining Modernity: Guomindang Rhetorics of a New China, 1920–1970,* 123–149. Ann Arbor: University of Michigan Press.

————. 2004. "Ties that Dissolve and Bind: Competing Currencies, Prestige, and Politics in Early Twentieth-Century China." In Cynthia Werner and Duran Bell, eds., *Value and Valuables: From the Sacred to the Symbolic,* 128–157. Walnut Creek, CA: Alta Mira Press.

————. 2006. "Authenticity Anxiety and Counterfeit Confidence: Outsourcing Souvenirs, Changing Money and Narrating Value in Reform-Era China." *Modern China* 32.1: 64–98.

————. n.d.a "Dangerous Daughters of Dali: Gender and Ethnicity in Jin Yong's *Tianlong babu* (Heavenly Dragons)." Article manuscript.

————. n.d.b "From Red to Black: The Tragic Tale of Yang Likun." Article manuscript.

"Nu, U." 2001–2005. *http://bartelby.com/65/nu/Nu-U.html* (accessed Dec. 19, 2003).

"Number of Visitors." 2006. The Official Site of the Eiffel Tower. http://www.tour-eiffel .fr/teiffel/uk/documentation/chiffres/page/frequentation.html (accessed Jan. 17, 2006).

Oakes, Tim[othy S.] 1995. "Tourism in Guizhou: The Legacy of Internal Colonialism." In Alan A. Lew and Lawrence Yu, eds., *Tourism in China: Geographic, Political, and Economic Perspectives,* 203–222. Boulder: Westview.

————. 1997. "Ethnic Tourism in Rural Guizhou: Sense of Place and the Commerce of Authenticity." In Michel Picard and Robert E. Wood, eds., *Tourism, Ethnicity, and the State in Asian and Pacific Societies,* 35–70. Honolulu: University of Hawai'i Press.

————. 1998. *Tourism and Modernity in China.* London: Routledge.

————. 1999. "Bathing in the Far Village: Globalization, Transnational Capital, and the Cultural Politics of Modernity in China." *Positions* 7.2: 307–342.

————. 2006. "The Village as Theme Park: Authenticity and Mimesis in Chinese Tourism." In T. Oakes and L. Schein, eds., *Translocal China: Linkages, Identities, and the Reimagining of Space,* 166–192. London and New York: Routledge.

Olson, Martha Stevenson. 2004. "In Frodo's Footsteps: Fans are Drawn to the Places Where Hobbits Quested, Harry Potter Worked Magic and the Samurai Battled." *New York Times,* Jan. 25: 6–7, 14.

Ong, Aihwa. 1997. "Chinese Modernities: Narratives of Nation and of Capitalism." In Aihwa Ong and Donald Nonini, eds., *Ungrounded Empires: The Cultural Politics of Modern Chinese Transnationalism,* 171–202. London: Routledge.

Ou Yansheng, Zhang Nan, and Bai Man. 1990. *Dali.* Kunming: Yunnan Minzu chubanshe.

Pang, Keng-Fong. 1992. "The Dynamics of Gender, Ethnicity and State Among the Austronesian-Speaking Muslims (Hui/Utsat) of Hainan Island, People's Republic of China." Ph.D. Dissertation, University of California, Los Angeles.

Parker, E. H. 1890. "The Old Thai or Shan Empire of Western Yunnan." *China Review* 20: 337–346.

———. 1891. "The Early Laos and China." *China Review* 19: 67–106.

Pelliot, Paul. 1904. "Deux itinéraires de Chine en Inde à la fin du VIIIe siècle." *Bulletin de l'École Française d'Extrême-Orient* 4: 131–413.

Pemberton, John. 1994. *On the Subject of "Java."* Ithaca and London: Cornell University Press.

Peters, Heather A. 2001. "Making Tourism Work for Heritage Preservation: Lijiang—a Case Study." In Tan Chee-Beng, Sidney C. H. Cheung, and Yang Hui, eds., *Tourism, Anthropology and China,* 313–332. Studies in Asian Tourism No. 1. Bangkok: White Lotus Press.

Picard, Michel, and Robert E. Wood, eds. 1997. *Tourism, Ethnicity, and the State in Asian and Pacific Societies.* Honolulu: University of Hawai'i Press.

Pipan ducao dianying ji (A Collection of Criticisms of Poisonous Weed Films). 1971. Vol. 2. Shanghai: Renmin chubanshe.

Pi-Sunyer, Oriol. 1993. "Changing Perceptions of Tourism and Tourists in a Catalan Resort Town." In Valene L. Smith, ed., *Hosts and Guests: The Anthropology of Tourism,* 187–199. 2nd ed. Philadelphia: University of Pennsylvania Press.

Planet Talk. 1996. 28: 12–14.

Pleasant Hawaii Magazine. 2003. 8: 7–9.

"Police detained, injured 5 farmers." 2005. *South China Morning Post,* May 5: A7.

Potter, Sulamith Heins, and Jack M. Potter. 1990. *China's Peasants: The Anthropology of a Revolution.* Cambridge: Cambridge University Press.

Prasertkul, Chiranan. 1989. *Yunnan Trade in the Nineteenth Century: Southwest China's Cross-Bounderies [sic] Functional System.* Asian Studies Monograph No. 044. Bangkok: Institute of Asian Studies, Chulalongkorn University.

Pratt, Mary Louise. 1992. *Imperial Eyes: Travel Writing and Transculturation.* London: Routledge.

Prusek, Jaroslav. 1971. *Chinese Statelets and the Northern Barbarians in the Period 1400–300 B.C.* New York: Humanities Press. Copublished by D. Reidel, Dordrect, Holland.

Pun Ngai. 2005. *Made in China: Women Factory Workers in a Global Workplace.* Durham: Duke University Press and Hong Kong: Hong Kong University Press.

Qiang disong (A Song for the Qiang's Whistle). 1960. Directed by Zhang Xinshi. Changchun Film Studio.

Ramirez, Luis. 2005. "China Hands Stiff Sentences to Twenty-Seven Farmers over Land Seizure Protest." Voice of America, Jan. 24. http://www.voanews.com/english/2005-01-24-voa22.cfm (accessed July 18, 2005).

Ramsey, Robert S. 1987. *The Languages of China.* Princeton: Princeton University Press.

Ramusack, Barbara N. 1995. "The Indian Princes as Fantasy: Palace Hotels, Palace Museums, and Palace on Wheels." In Carol Breckenridge, ed., *Consuming Modernity: Public Culture in a South Asian World,* 66–89. Minneapolis: University of Minnesota Press.

Rees, Martha W., and Josephine Smart. 2001. "Plural Globalities in Multiple Localities: Introductory Thoughts." In Martha W. Rees and Josephine Smart, eds., *Plural Globalities in Multiple Localities: New World Borders,* 1–18. Monographs in Economic Anthropology No. 17. Lanham, MD: University Press of America.

Relph, Edward. 1976. *Place and Placelessness.* London: Pion.

———. 1991. "Post-modern Geography." *Canadian Geographer* 35.1: 98–105.

"Revising Draft Property Law." 2005. *http://www.chinadaily.com.cn/english/doc/2005-7/11/content-459093.htm* (accessed July 21, 2005).

Richards, Greg, and Julie Wilson, eds. 2004a. *The Global Nomad: Backpacker Travel in Theory and Practice.* Clevedon, UK: Channel View Publications.

———. 2004b. "The Global Nomad: Motivations and Behaviour of Independent Travellers Worldwide." In Greg Richards and Julie Wilson, eds., *The Global Nomad: Backpacker Travel in Theory and Practice,* 14–39. Clevedon, UK: Channel View Publications.

———. 2004c. "Widening Perspectives on Backpacker Research." In Greg Richards and Julie Wilson, eds., *The Global Nomad: Backpacker Travel in Theory and Practice,* 253–279. Clevedon, UK: Channel View Publications.

Riley, P. 1988. "Road Culture of International Long-Term Budget Travelers." *Annals of Tourism Research* 15: 337–352.

Riley, Roger, Dwayne Baker, and Carlton S. Van Doren. 1998. "Movie Induced Tourism." *Annals of Tourism Research* 25.4: 919–935.

Ritzer, George, and Allan Liska. 1997. " 'McDisneyization and 'Post-Tourism': Complementary Perspectives on Contemporary Tourism." In Chris Rojek and John Urry, eds., *Touring Cultures: Transformations of Travel and Theory,* 96–109. London: Routledge.

Robertson, Jennifer. 1991. *Native and Newcomer: Making and Remaking a Japanese City.* Berkeley: University of California Press.

———. 1995. "Mon Japan: The Revue Theater as a Technology of Japanese Imperialism." *American Ethnologist* 22.4: 970–996.

———. 1998. *Takarazuka: Sexual Politics and Popular Culture in Modern Japan.* Berkeley: University of California Press.

Rocher, Émile. 1879. *La Province chinoise du Yün-nan.* Part 1. Paris: Ernest Leroux, ed., Libraire de la Société Asiatique de L'École des Langues Orientales Vivantes.

———. 1880. *La Province chinoise du Yün-nan.* Part 2. Paris: Ernest Leroux, ed., Libraire de la Société Asiatique de L'École des Langues Orientales Vivantes.

Rodman, Margaret C. 1987. *Masters of Tradition: Consequences of Customary Land Tenure in Longana, Vanuatu.* Vancouver: University of British Columbia Press.

———. 1992. "Empowering Place: Multilocality and Multivocality." *American Anthropologist* 94.3: 640–656.

Rofel, Lisa. 1999. *Other Modernities: Gendered Yearnings in China after Socialism.* Berkeley: University of California Press.

Rojas, Carlos (Luo Peng). 2000. "*Tianlong babu* yu Jin Yong tupu de biaoxiang shijie" (*Heavenly Dragons* and Jin Yong's expressive world of illustrations). In Lin Lijun, ed., *Jin Yong xiaoshuo yu ershi shiji Zhongguo wenxue* (Jin Yong's Novels and Twentieth-Century Chinese Literature), 479–486. Hong Kong: Minghe.

Rojek, Chris. 1997. "Indexing, Dragging, and the Social Construction of Tourist Sights." In Chris Rojek and John Urry, eds., *Touring Cultures: Transformations of Travel and Theory*, 52–74. London: Routledge.

Rojek, Chris, and John Urry, eds. 1997a. *Touring Cultures: Transformations of Travel and Theory*. London: Routledge.

———. 1997b. "Transformations of Travel and Theory." In Chris Rojek and John Urry, eds., *Touring Cultures: Transformations of Travel and Theory*, 1–22. London: Routledge.

Roosevelt, Theodore, and Kermit Roosevelt. 1929. *Trailing the Giant Panda*. New York: Charles Scribner's Sons.

Root, Deborah. 1996. *Cannibal Culture: Art, Appropriation, and the Commodification of Difference*. Boulder: Westview.

Rosaldo, Renato. 1980. *Ilongot Headhunting, 1883–1974: A Study in Society and History*. Stanford: Stanford University Press.

———. 1989. *Culture and Truth: The Remaking of Social Analysis*. Boston: Beacon Press.

Rosenblatt, Roger. 1973. "Look Back in Sentiment." *The New York Times*, (July 28): 23.

Roth, Joshua Hotaka. 2002. *Brokered Homeland: Japanese Brazilian Migrants in Japan*. Ithaca: Cornell University Press.

Rydell, Robert W. 1984. *All the World's a Fair: Visions of Empire at American International Expositions, 1876–1916*. Chicago: University of Chicago Press.

Said, Edward W. [1978] 1979. *Orientalism*. New York: Vintage Books.

Samagalski, Alan. 1984. *China—a Travel Survival Kit*. South Yarra, Victoria, and Berkeley, CA: Lonely Planet Publications.

Santos-Granero, Fernando. 1998. "Writing History into the Landscape: Space, Myth, and Ritual in Contemporary Amazonia." *American Ethnologist* 25.2: 128–148.

Schafer, Edward. [1963] 1985. *The Golden Peaches of Samarkand: A Study in T'ang Exotics*. Berkeley: University of California Press.

———. 1967. *The Vermilion Bird: T'ang Images of the South*. Berkeley: University of California Press.

Schama, Simon. 1995. *Landscape and Memory*. New York: A. A. Knopf.

Schein, Louisa. 1994. "The Consumption of Color and the Politics of White Skin in Post-Mao China." *Social Text* 41: 141–164.

———. 1997. "Gender and Internal Orientalism in China." *Modern China* 23.1: 69–98.

———. 2002. *Minority Rules: The Miao and the Feminine in China's Cultural Politics*. Durham: Duke University Press.

Schensul, Jill. 2005. "Making Peace with Vietnam." *The Record*, April 17: T01.

Schwartz, Vanessa R. 1998. *Spectacular Realities: Early Mass Culture in Fin-de-Siècle Paris*. Berkeley: University of California Press.

Schwarz, Sherry. 2001. "Travels with Tony: Lonely Planet Co-Founder Shares Story." *Abroad View* 3.1: 69.

Scott, James C. 1985. *Weapons of the Weak: Everyday Forms of Peasant Resistance.* New Haven: Yale University Press.

————. 1990. *Domination and the Arts of Resistance: Hidden Transcripts.* New Haven: Yale University Press.

Selden, Mark. 1993. *The Political Economy of Chinese Development.* Armonk, NY: M. E. Sharpe.

Selwyn, Tom. 1993. "Peter Pan in South-East Asia: Views from Brochures." In Michael Hitchcock, Victor T. King, and Michael J. G. Parnwell, eds., *Tourism in South-East Asia,* 117–137. London and New York: Routledge.

Shapiro, Judith. 2001. *Mao's War against Nature: Politics and Environment in Revolutionary China.* Cambridge: Cambridge University Press.

Shao Xianshu. 1990. *Nanzhao he Daliguo* (The Nanzhao and Dali Kingdoms). Zhongguo shaoshu minzu wenku. Jilin: Jilin chubanshe.

Shenon, Philip. 1996. "The End of the World on 10 Tugriks a Day." *The New York Times Magazine,* June 30: 35.

Shi Lizhuo. 1998. "Jin Yong bixia yishu shijie de lishi zhenshi—Dali guo shulüe" (The Historical Truth beneath Jin Yong's Artistic World—an Account of the Dali Kingdom). In Shi Lizhuo and Zhang Naiguang, eds., *Jin Yong yu Dali* (Jin Yong and Dali), 214–224. Kunming: Yunnan renmin chubanshe.

Shi Lizhuo and Zhang Naiguang, eds. 1998. *Jin Yong yu Dali* (Jin Yong and Dali). Kunming: Yunnan renmin chubanshe.

Shields, Rob. 1991. *Places on the Margin: Alternative Geographies of Modernity.* London: Routledge.

Shoudu chubanjie geming zaofan zongbu (Capital Publishing World Revolutionary Rebel Headquarters), ed. 1967. "Guanyu dianying wenti de tanhua 'Mao zhuxi de geming wenyi luxian de weida shengli—Jiang Qing tongzhi zhongyao jianghua' "(Discussions Regarding Problems in Film, Important Speeches by Comrade Jiang Qing—a Great Victory for Chairman Mao's Revolutionary Line in Literature and the Arts). Beijing: Shoudu chubanjie geming zaofan zongbu.

Sieg, Katrin. 2002. "Indian Impersonation as Historical Surrogation." In Colin G. Calloway, Gerd Gemünden, and Susanne Zantop, eds., *Germans and Indians: Fantasies, Encounters, Projections,* 217–242. Lincoln: University of Nebraska Press.

Sima Qian. [c. 91 B.C.] 1978. "The Biography of Yü Jang." Trans. William H. Nienhauser, Jr. In Y. W. Ma and Joseph S. M. Lau, eds., *Traditional Chinese Stories: Themes and Variations,* 41–42. New York: Columbia University Press.

Siu, Helen F. 1989. *Agents and Victims in South China: Accomplices in Rural Revolution.* New Haven: Yale University Press.

Smart, Alan. 1998. "Economic Transformation in China: Property Regimes and Social Relations." In John Pickles and Adrian Smith, eds., *Theorising Transition: The Political Economy of Post-Communist Transformations,* 428–449. London and New York: Routledge.

"Smash the Old World: Jiang Qing Critiques Feature Films." 2003. *Morning Sun: A Film and Website about [the] Cultural Revolution.* http://www.morningsun.org/smash/jq_films.html (accessed Jan. 17, 2006). [Orig. in Shoudu chubanjie geming zaofan zongbu 1967, 33–37.]

Smith, Nicol. 1940. *Burma Road.* Indianapolis: Bobbs-Merrill Co.

Smith, Valene L., ed. 1993. *Hosts and Guests: The Anthropology of Tourism.* 2nd ed. Philadelphia: University of Pennsylvania Press.

Sofield, Trevor H. B., and Fung Mei Sarah Li. 1998. "Tourism Development and Cultural Policies in China." *Annals of Tourism Research* 25.2: 362–392.

Solinger, Dorothy J. [1995] 1999. "The Floating Population in the Cities: Chances for Assimilation?" In Deborah S. Davis, Richard Kraus, Barry Naughton, and Elizabeth J. Perry, eds., *Urban Spaces in Contemporary China: The Potential for Autonomy and Community in Post-Mao China,* 113–139. Cambridge: Cambridge University Press.

Song Weijie. 2000. "Lun Jin Yong xiaoshuo de 'jiaguo xiangxiang' " (Discussing the "National Imagination" in Jin Yong's Novels). In Lin Lijun, ed., *Jin Yong xiaoshuo yu ershi shiji Zhongguo wenxue* (Jin Yong's Novels and Twentieth-Century Chinese Literature), 325–341. Hong Kong: Minghe.

Soothill, William Edward. [1937] 1977. *A Dictionary of Chinese Buddhist Terms.* Compiled with Lewis Hodous. Delhi: Motilal Banarsidass. [Orig. London: K. Paul.]

Spivak, Gayatri. 1988. "Can the Subaltern Speak?" In C. Nelson and L. Grossberg, eds., *Marxism and the Interpretation of Culture,* 271–313. Basingstoke: Macmillan Education.

Stalin, Joseph. 1934. *Marxism and the National and Colonial Question.* New York: International Publishers.

Stallybrass, P., and White, A. 1986. *The Poetics and Politics of Transgression.* London: Methuen.

Stewart, Kathleen [C.] 1988. "Nostalgia—a Polemic." *Cultural Anthropology* 3.3: 227–241.

———. 1996. "An Occupied Place." In Steven Feld and Keith H. Basso, eds., *Senses of Place,* 137–166. Santa Fe: School of American Research Press.

Stewart, Susan. 1984. *On Longing: Narratives of the Miniature, the Gigantic, the Souvenir, the Collection.* Durham: Duke University Press.

Storey, Robert, Nicko Goncharoff, Damian Harpter, Marie Cambon, Thomas Huhti, Caroline Liou, and Alexander English. 1998. *China—a Travel Survival Kit.* 6th ed. Hawthorn, Victoria, Australia: Lonely Planet Publications.

Storey, Robert, Chris Taylor, and Clem Lindenmayer. [1984] 1994. *China—a Travel Survival Kit.* 4th ed. Hawthorn, Victoria, Australia: Lonely Planet Publications.

Su Qun and Xu Shijie. 1959. "Quanmian Dayaojin, wugu da fengshou" (All Out Great Leap Forward, Great Harvest of the Five Grains). *YNRB,* Jan. 1: 1.

Su Yun. 1985. "Changchun dianying zhipian chang de fazhan licheng" (The Historical

Development of the Changchun Film Studio). In Zhongguo dianyingjia xiehui (Chinese Filmmakers Association) and Dianyingshi yanjiubu (Film History Research Bureau), eds., *Zhonghua renmin gongheguo dianying siye sanshiwu nian, 1949–1984* (Thirty-Five Years of the Film Industry in the People's Republic of China, 1949–1984), 23–55. N.p.: Zhongguo dianying chubanshe.

Sun Yat-sen (Zhongshan). [1921] 1926 (Minguo 15). "Sanmin zhuyi—dui Zhongguo Guomindang teshe banshichu jiangyan" (The Three Principles of the People—a Speech for a Specially Established Nationalist Party [KMT] Branch Office). In Huang Changgu, ed., *Sun Zhongshan xiansheng yanshuoji* (A Collection of Mr. Sun Yat-sen's Speeches), 1–18. Shanghai: Minzhi shuju.

Swain, Margaret Byrne. 1990. "Commoditizing Ethnicity in Southwest China." *Cultural Survival* 14.1: 26–32.

———. 1994. "Ashima: A Tale of Sani Identity and the Chinese Civilizing Project." Paper presented at the Association for Asian Studies Annual Meeting, Boston, March 24–27.

———. 1995a. "Gender in Tourism." *Annals of Tourism Research* 22.2: 247–266.

———. 1995b. "Père Vial and the Gni-p'a: Orientalist Scholarship and the Christian Project." In Stevan Harrell, ed., *Cultural Encounters on China's Ethnic Frontiers*, 140–185. Seattle: University of Washington Press.

———. 2001. "Cosmopolitan Tourism and Minority Politics in the Stone Forest." In Tan Chee-Beng, Sidney C. H. Cheung, and Yang Hui, eds., *Tourism, Anthropology and China*. Studies in Asian Tourism No. 1, 125–146. Bangkok: White Lotus Press.

———. 2005. "Desiring Ashima: Sexing Landscape in China's Stone Forest." In Carolyn Cartier and Alan Lew, eds., *Seductions of Place: Geographical Perspectives on Globalization and Touristed Landscapes*, 245–259. London and New York: Routledge.

Tai, Hue-Tam Ho. 2001. "Introduction: Situating Memory." In Hue-Tam Ho Tai, ed., *The Country of Memory: Remaking the Past in Late Socialist Vietnam*, 1–17. Berkeley: University of California Press.

Tan Chee-Beng. 2001. "Tourism and the Anthropology of China." In Tan Chee-Beng, Sidney C. H. Cheung, and Yang Hui, eds., *Tourism, Anthropology and China*, 1–26. Studies in Asian Tourism No. 1. Bangkok: White Lotus Press.

Tan Chee-Beng, Sidney C. H. Cheung, and Yang Hui, eds. 2001. *Tourism, Anthropology and China*. Studies in Asian Tourism No. 1. Bangkok: White Lotus Press.

Tan Qixiang, ed. 1989. *Zhongguo lishi ditu ji* (The Historical Atlas of China). Vol. 5. 2nd ed. Shanghai: Zhonguo ditu chubanshe.

Tang Shijie. 1998. "Shilun *Tianlong babu* de diyu wenhua miaoxie" (Discussing the Description of Local Culture in *Heavenly Dragons*). In Shi Lizhuo and Zhang Naiguang, eds., *Jin Yong yu Dali* (Jin Yong and Dali), 182–192. Kunming: Yunnan renmin chubanshe.

Taussig, Michael. 1993. *Mimesis and Alterity: A Particular History of the Senses*. New York: Routledge.

Taylor, Nora A., and Hjorleifur Jonsson. 2002. "Other Attractions in Vietnam." *Asian Ethnicity* 3.2: 233–248.

Thomas, Philip. 2002. "The River, the Road and the Rural-Urban Divide: A Postcolonial Moral Geography from Southeast Madagascar." *American Ethnologist* 29.2: 366–391.

Thompson, Ginger. 2002. "Mexico Drops Planned Airport after Protests from Peasants." *The New York Times*, Aug. 3: A3.

Thornton, Thomas F. 1997. "Know Your Place: The Organization of Tlingit Geographic Knowledge." *Ethnology* 36.4 (Fall): 295–307.

———. 2004. "The Geography of Tlingit Character." In Marie Mauzé, Michael E. Harkin, and Sergei Kan, eds., *Coming to Shore: Northwest Coast Ethnology, Traditions, and Visions*, 363–384. Lincoln: University of Nebraska Press.

"Thousands of Chinese Farmers Protest Government-Backed Land Grab." 2005. July 3. http://news.yahoo.com/ (accessed July 18, 2005).

Tianlong babu (Heavenly Dragons). 2003. DVD set. Directed by Zhou Xiaowen. Jiangsu sheng guangbo dianshi zongtai; Jiuzhou yinxiang chuban gongsi. Distributed by Weijia yinxiang zhipin youxian gongsi.

T'ien Ju-k'ang. 1981. "Moslem Rebellion in China: A Yunnan Controversy." The Forty-Second George Ernest Morrison Lecture in Ethnology. Canberra: Australian National University.

———. 1982. "New Light on the Yün-nan Rebellion and the Panthay Mission." *The Memoirs of the Toyo Bunko* 40: 19–54.

Tuan, Yi-Fu. [1977] 1997. *Space and Place: The Perspective of Experience*. Minneapolis: University of Minnesota Press.

———. 1991. "Language and the Making of Place: A Narrative-Descriptive Approach." *Annals of the Association of American Geographers* 81.4: 684–696.

Twain, Mark. [1869, 1872] 1984. *Innocents Abroad* and *Roughing It*. New York: The Library of America.

———. 1883. *Life on the Mississippi*. Boston: James R. Osgood and Co.

Urry, John. [1990] 1994. *The Tourist Gaze: Leisure and Travel in Contemporary Societies*. London: Sage.

———. [1995] 1997. *Consuming Places*. London: Routledge.

van den Berghe, Pierre L. 1994. *The Quest for the Other: Ethnic Tourism in San Cristobal, Mexico*. Seattle and London: University of Washington Press.

van den Berghe, Pierre L., and Charles F. Keyes. 1984. "Introduction, Tourism and Re-Created Ethnicity." *Annals of Tourism Research*, special issue: *Tourism and Ethnicity*, 11.3: 343–351.

Veijola, S., and E. Jokinen. 1994. "The Body in Tourism." *Theory, Culture and Society* 11: 125–151.

Verdery, Katherine. 1996. *What Was Socialism and What Comes Next?* Princeton: Princeton University Press.

———. 2003. *The Vanishing Hectare: Property and Value in Postsocialist Transylvania*. Ithaca: Cornell University Press.

Volkman, Toby. 1989. "Visions and Revisions: Toraja Culture and the Tourist Gaze." *American Ethnologist* 17.1: 91–110.

Walsh, Eileen R[ose]. 2001. "Living with the Myth of Matriarchy: The Mosuo and Tourism." In Tan Chee-Beng, Sidney C. H. Cheung, and Yang Hui, eds., *Tourism, Anthropology and China*, 93–124. Studies in Asian Tourism No. 1. Bangkok: White Lotus Press.

———. 2005. "From Nü Guo to Nü'er Guo: Negotiating Desire in the Land of the Mosuo." *Modern China* 31.4: 448–486.

Wang Dulu. 2001. *Wohu canglong* (Crouching Tiger, Hidden Dragon). Taipei: Yuanjing.

Wang Fu. 2003. *Luchuan zhigao* (Draft Gazetteer of Luchuan). Dali: Dali Baizu zizhizhou Nanzhao shi yanjiuhui.

Wang Jianping. 1996. *Concord and Conflict: The Hui Communities of Yunnan Society in a Historical Perspective*. Lund Studies in African and Asian Religions 11. Lund, Sweden: Studentlitteratur.

Wang, Jing. 2001a. "Culture as Leisure and Culture as Capital." *Positions,* special issue: *Chinese Popular Culture and the State,* Jing Wang, guest editor, 9.1: 69–104.

———. 2001b. "Guest Editor's Introduction." *Positions,* special issue: *Chinese Popular Culture and the State,* Jing Wang, guest editor, 9.1: 1–27.

Wang, Ning. 1999. "Rethinking Authenticity in Tourism Experience." *Annals of Tourism Research* 26.2: 349–370.

Wang Qiugui, ed. 1999. *Jin Yong xiaoshuo—guoji xueshu yantaohui lunwenji* (Proceedings of the International Conference on Jin Yong's Novels). Taipei: Yuanliu.

Wang Shucun. 1992. *Zhongguo gudai minsu banhua* (China's Ancient Folk Prints). Beijing: Xin shijie chubanshe.

Wang Shuwu. 1988. "Baizu yuanyu Dian Bo, Sou, Cuan kaoshu" (An Examination of Bai Nationality Origins among the Dian Bo, Sou, and Cuan). *Yunnan shehui kexue* (Yunnan Social Sciences), 3: 54–63.

Wang Xiaoming. 2000. "Tianshan tonglao de shengli—du Jin Yong de *Tianlong babu*" (Tianshan Tonglao's Victory—Reading *Heavenly Dragons*). In Lin Lijun, ed., *Jin Yong xiaoshuo yu ershi shiji Zhongguo wenxue* (Jin Yong's Novels and Twentieth-Century Chinese Literature), 487–495. Hong Kong: Minghe.

Wang Zhusheng. 1991. "Road of Change: A Jingpo Village on China's Border." Ph.D. dissertation, State University of New York, Stony Brook.

Wank, David L. 2000. "Cigarettes and Domination in Chinese Business Networks: Institutional Change during the Market Transition." In Deborah S. Davis, ed., *The Consumer Revolution in Urban China*, 268–286. Berkeley: University of California Press.

Wasserstrom, Jeffrey N. 2004. "Traveling with Twain in an Age of Simulations: Rereading and Reliving the Innocents Abroad." *Common-Place* 4.3. http://www.common-place.org/vol-04/no-03/wasserstrom/ (accessed May 14, 2004).

Watson, James L. ed. 1997a. *Golden Arches East: McDonald's in East Asia*. Stanford: Stanford University Press.

———. 1997b. "Introduction: Transnationalism, Localization, and Fast Foods in East Asia." In James L. Watson, ed., *Golden Arches East: McDonald's in East Asia*, 1–38. Stanford: Stanford University Press.

———. 1997c. "McDonald's in Hong Kong: Consumerism, Dietary Change, and the Rise of Children's Culture." In James L. Watson, ed., *Golden Arches East: McDonald's in East Asia*, 77–109. Stanford: Stanford University Press.

Watson, Rubie S. 1994a. "Making Secret Histories: Memory and Mourning in Post-Mao China." In Rubie S. Watson, ed., *Memory, History, and Opposition under State Socialism*, 65–86. Santa Fe: School of American Research Press.

———, ed. 1994b. *Memory, History, and Opposition under State Socialism.* Santa Fe: School of American Research Press.

———. 1994c. "Memory, History, and Opposition under State Socialism: An Introduction." In Rubie S. Watson, ed., *Memory, History, and Opposition under State Socialism*, 1–20. Santa Fe: School of American Research Press.

Wei, Alice Bihyun Gan. 1974. "The Moslem Rebellion in Yunnan, 1855–1873." Ph.D. dissertation, University of Chicago.

"Welcome to the Mark Twain Boyhood Home and Museum." 2001–2005. *http://www.marktwainmuseum.org/* (accessed Jan. 17, 2006).

Welk, Peter. 2004. "The Beaten Track: Anti-Tourism as an Element of Backpacker Identity Construction." In Greg Richards and Julie Wilson, eds, 77–91. *The Global Nomad: Backpacker Travel in Theory and Practice.* Clevedon, UK: Channel View Publications.

Wheeler, Tony. 1996. "The Lonely Planet Story." *Planet Talk* 28: 15.

White, Sydney D. 1997. "Fame and Sacrifice: The Gendered Construction of Naxi Identities." *Modern China* 23.3: 298–327.

Wiersma, Grace. 1990. "A Study of the Bai (Minchia) Language along Historical Lines." Ph.D. dissertation, University of California, Berkeley.

———. 2003. "Yunnan Bai." In Graham Thurgood and Randy LaPolla, eds., *The Sino-Tibetan Languages*, 651–673. Routledge Language Family Series. London: Taylor and Francis.

Wigen, Karen. 1999. "Culture, Power, Place: The New Landscapes of East Asian Regionalism." *The American Historical Review* 104.4: 1183–1201.

Wilk, Richard R. 1993. "Beauty and the Feast: Official and Visceral Nationalism in Belize." *Ethnos* 294–316.

———. 1995. "Learning to Be Local in Belize: Global Systems of Common Difference." In Daniel Miller, ed., *Worlds Apart: Modernity through the Prism of the Local*, 110–133. London: Routledge.

———. 1999. " 'Real Belizean Food': Building Local Identity in the Transnational Caribbean." *American Anthropologist* 101.2: 244–255.

Williams, C. A. S. [Charles Alfred Speed]. [1941] 1975. *Outlines of Chinese Symbolism and Art Motives.* 3rd ed. Rutland, VT: Charles E. Tuttle. [Orig. Shanghai: Kelly and Walsh.]

Wizard of Oz. 1939. Directed by Victor Fleming. MGM.

Wohu canglong (Crouching Tiger, Hidden Dragon). 2000. DVD. Directed by Ang Lee (Li An). Columbia/Tristar.

Wolf, Arthur. 1974a. "Gods, Ghosts and Ancestors." In Arthur Wolf, ed., *Religion and Ritual in Chinese Society,* 131–182. Stanford: Stanford University Press.

———, ed. 1974b. *Religion and Ritual in Chinese Society.* Stanford: Stanford University Press.

Wolf, Eric R. 1982. *Europe and the People without History.* Berkeley: University of California Press.

Wood, William Alfred Rae. 1926. *A History of Siam.* London: T. F. Unwin.

Wu, David Y. H. 1989. "Culture Change and Ethnic Identity among Minorities in China." In Chien Chiao and Nicholas Tapp, eds., *Ethnicity and Ethnic Groups in China,* 11–22. Hong Kong: New Asia College.

———. 1990. "Chinese Minority Policy and the Meaning of Minority Cultures: The Example of Bai in Yünnan, China." *Human Organization* 49.1: 1–13.

———. 1997. "McDonald's in Taipei: Hamburgers, Betel Nuts, and National Identity." In James L. Watson, ed., *Golden Arches East: McDonald's in East Asia,* 110–135. Stanford: Stanford University Press.

Wu Dingbo and Patrick D. Murphy, eds. *Handbook of Chinese Popular Culture.* Westport, CT: Greenwood Press.

Wu Xiaodong and Ji Birui, eds. 2002. *2000 Beijing Jin Yong xiaoshuo guoji yantaohui lunwenji* (2000 Beijing International Conference Proceedings on Jin Yong's Novels). Beijing: Beijing daxue.

Wuduo Jinhua (Five Golden Flowers). 1959. Directed by Wang Jiayi. Changchun Film Studio. Released on video compact disk by Hubei yinxiang yishu chubanshe.

Xu Lin and Zhao Yansun. 1984. *Baiyu jianzhi* (A Concise Gazetteer of the Bai Language). Beijing: Renmin chubanshe.

Xu Xinjian. 2001. "Developing China: Formation and Influence of 'Ethnic Tourism' and 'Ethnic Tourees.' " In Tan Chee-Beng, Sidney C. H. Cheung, and Yang Hui, eds. 2001. *Tourism, Anthropology and China,* 193–214. Studies in Asian Tourism No. 1. Bangkok: White Lotus Press.

Yan Hairong. 2003. "Spectralization of the Rural: Reinterpreting the Labor Mobility of Rural Young Women in Post-Mao China." *American Ethnologist* 30.4: 578–596.

Yan Liyun. 1959. "Cangshan Erhai de xinfu gesheng" (The Auspicious Songs of Mount Cang and Lake Er). *YNRB,* Sept. 21: 3.

Yan Yun-xiang. 1996. *The Flow of Gifts: Reciprocity and Social Networks in a Chinese Village.* Stanford: Stanford University Press.

———. 1997. "McDonald's in Beijing: The Localization of Americana." In James L. Watson, ed., *Golden Arches East: McDonald's in East Asia,* 39–76. Stanford: Stanford University Press.

Yang, Dali L. 1996. *Calamity and Reform in China: State, Rural Society, and Institutional Change since the Great Leap Famine.* Stanford: Stanford Univesity Press.

Yang Guangfu. 1998. "Jin Yong wuxia xiaoshuo yu Dali de bu jie zhi yuan" (The Indivisible Destiny between Jin Yong's Novel and Dali). In Shi Lizhuo and Zhang Naiguang, eds., *Jin Yong yu Dali* (Jin Yong and Dali), 200–204. Kunming: Yunnan renmin chubanshe.

Yang, Guobin. 2003. "China's *Zhiqing* Generation: Nostalgia, Identity, and Cultural Resistance in the 1990s." *Modern China* 29.1: 267–296.

Yang Guocai. 1995. *Yunnan minzu nüxing wenhua congshu—Baizu: qingxi Cangshan, hunbo Erhai* (English title: Daughters of Mount Cangshan and Erhai Lake—The Bais). Kunming: Yunnan jiaoyu chubanshe.

Yang Guoqiong. 1998. "*Tianlong babu* yu feng hua xue yue" (Heavenly Dragons and Wind, Flowers, Snow, Moon [i.e., gaiety and romance]). In Shi Lizhuo and Zhang Naiguang, eds., *Jin Yong yu Dali* (Jin Yong and Dali), 193–199. Kunming: Yunnan renmin chubanshe.

Yang Hong and Xiaohe Zhang. 2003. "Economy and Trade." In Xiao-bin Ji, ed., *Facts about China*, 257–298. New York: H. W. Wilson.

Yang Hui, Liu Chun, Liu Yongqing, and Duan Ying. 2001. "Man-chun-man Village at the Crossroads: Conservation and Vicissitudes of Ethnic Cultures during the Development of Tourism." In Tan Chee-Beng, Sidney C. H. Cheung, and Yang Hui, eds., *Tourism, Anthropology and China*, 167–178. Studies in Asian Tourism No. 1. Bangkok: White Lotus Press.

Yang Kuinie. 1998. "Jin Yong yu jingshang" (Jin Yong and Commerce). In Shi Lizhuo and Zhang Naiguang, eds., *Jin Yong yu Dali* (Jin Yong and Dali), 209–213. Kunming: Yunnan renmin chubanshe.

Yang Kun. 1957. "Shilun Yunnan Baizu de xingcheng he fazhan guocheng" (Discussion of the Formation and Developmental Process of the Yunnan Bai Nationality). In Yunnan renmin chubanshe (Yunnan People's Publishing House), ed., *Yunnan Baizu de qiyuan he xingcheng lunwen ji* (A Collection of Essays on the Origin and Formation of the Yunnan Bai Nationality), 1–11. Kunming: Yunnan renmin chubanshe.

Yang Li. 2005. "Wuxia xiaoshuo *Tianlong babu* ji *Wolong zanghu* ruxuan gaozhong keben" (Martial Arts Novels *Heavenly Dragons* and *Crouching Tiger, Hidden Dragon* Enter High School Textbooks). http://gb.chinabroadcast.cn/3821/2005/03/01/1 42@464060.htm (broadcast date March 1; accessed March 7, 2005). [Orig. in *Chongqing wanbao*.]

Yang, Mayfair Mei-hui. 1994. *Gifts, Favors, and Banquets: The Art of Social Relationships in China*. Ithaca: Cornell University Press.

———. 1997. "Mass Media and Transnational Subjectivity in Shanghai: Notes on (Re) Cosmopolitanism in a Chinese Metropolis." In Aihwa Ong and Daniel Nonini, eds., *Ungrounded Empires: The Cultural Politics of Modern Chinese Transnationalism*, 287–319. New York: Routledge.

———. 2004. "Spatial Struggles: Postcolonial Complex, State Disenchantment, and Popular Reappropriation of Space in Rural Southeast China." *Journal of Asian Studies* 63.3: 719–755.

Yang Yingxin. 1992. "Baiwen fangkuaizi wenxian, wenwu ziliao shulun" (A Discussion of Documentary and Artifactual Data on Bai Square Character Writing). In Yunnan minzu guji congshu bianxuan weiyuanhui (Committee for Compilation of the Series on Yunnan Nationalities Ancient Books), ed., *Yunnan minzu guji luncong* (Discussion Series on Yunnan Nationalities Ancient Books), vol. 1, 33–47. Kunming: Yunnan minzu chubanshe.

Yang Yuan Jun, ed. n.d. *Dali shengji lüyou dujiaqu touzi zhinan* (Dali Provincial Travel and Vacation Region Investment Guide). Dali: Dali shengji lüyou dujiaqu guanli weiyuanhui (Management Committee of Dali Provincial Travel and Vacation Region) (distributed in 1995).

Yang Zhengye. 1994. *Baizu benzhu wenhua* (Bai Nationality Local Deity Culture). Kunming: Yunnan renmin chubanshe.

Yardley, James. 2004. "Farmers Being Moved Aside by China's Real Estate Boom." Dec. 8. http://www.nytimes.org/ (accessed July 19, 2005).

Yau, Esther. 1989. "Is China the End of Hermeneutics? Or, Political and Cultural Usage of Non-Han Women in Mainland Chinese Films." *Discourse* 11.2: 115–136.

Yeh, Emily T. 2000. "Forest Claims, Conflicts and Commodification: The Political Ecology of Tibetan Mushroom-Harvesting Villages in Yunnan Province, China." *China Quarterly* 161: 264–278.

Yin Mingzhu, Shi Lizhuo, Zhang Nan, and Zhang Shiqing, eds. 1981. *Dali fengqing lu* (Scenery of Dali). Kunming: Yunnan renmin chubanshe.

Yokoyama, Hiroko. 1987. "Dairi bonchi no minzoku shudan" (Nationality Groups of the Dali Basin). *Tōyō Eiwa jogakuin tanki daigaku kenkyū kiyō* (Research Bulletin of the Tōyō Eiwa Women's Institute Short-Term College), 26.

———. 1991. "Haku zoku no honshu shinkō" (Local Deity Beliefs of the Bai Nationality). Osaka: Koku ritsu minzokugaku hakubutsukan kenkyū hōkoku bessatsu (National Ethnology Museum Research Report Papers), 14.

———. 1994. "Uxorilocal Marriage among the Bai of the Dali Basin, Yunnan." In Suenari Michio, J. S. Eades, and Christian Daniels, eds., *Perspectives on Chinese Society: Anthropological Views from Japan,* 182–190. Tokyo: Institute for the Study of Languages and Cultures of Asia and Africa.

You Zhong. 1980. *Zhongguo xi'nan de gudai minzu* (Ancient Nationalities of China's Southwest). Kunming: Yunnan renmin chubanshe.

Yuan Langhua. n.d. *Dali sanyue jie* (Dali Third Month Fair). Dali: Dali zhou minzu wenhua yanjiushi and Dali zhou shici yinglian xuehui.

Yule, Sir Henry, trans. and ed. 1929. *The Book of Ser Marco Polo.* 3rd ed. New York: Charles Scribner's Sons.

Yunnan sheng bianjizu (Yunnan Province Editorial Group). 1983. *Baizu shehui lishi diaocha* (Investigations of Bai Nationality Social History). Vol. 1. Kunming: Yunnan renmin chubanshe.

———, ed. 1985. *Yunnan Huizu shehui lishi diaocha* (Investigations of Yunnan Hui Nationality Social History). Kunming: Yunnan renmin chubanshe.

Yunnan sheng Dali shi linyeju (Yunnan Province, Dali Municipal Forestry Bureau), ed. 1993. *Dali shi linyezhi* (Gazetteer of Dali Municipal Forestry). Dali: Dali Baizu zhizhizhou wenhuaju.

Yunnan sheng ditu yuan, ed. 2004–2005. *Dali—Lijiang daoyou tu* (The tourist map of Dali *[sic]*). Hunan ditu chubanshe.

Yunnan sheng minjian wenxue jicheng bangongshi (Yunnan Province Folk Literature Collection Office), ed. 1986. *Baizu shenhua chuanshuo jicheng* (Collection of Bai Nationality Myths and Legends). Beijing: Zhongguo minjian wenyi chubanshe.

Yunnan sheng renkou pucha bangongshi (Population Census of Yunnan Office), ed. 2002. *Yunnan Sheng 2000 nian renkou pucha ziliao* (English title: The Reference of Population Census of Yunnan in 2000). 4 vols. Kunming: Yunnan keji chubanshe (Yunnan Science and Technology Press).

Yunnan sheng shaoshu minzu yuwen zhidao gongzuo weiyuanhui (Committee for the Guidance Work of Yunnan Province's Minority Nationality Languages). 1992. "Baizu wenzi fang'an (caogao)" (Orthographic Scheme for the Bai Nationality, Draft).

Yunnan sheng tongji ju renkou ban (Yunnan Province statistical bureau, population office). 1990. *Yunnan sheng renkou tongji ziliao huibian, 1949–1988* (English title: Compiled Material on Population Statistics of Yunnan Province, 1949–1988). Kunming: Yunnan renmin chubanshe.

Zantop, Susanne. 2002. "Close Encounters: Deutsche and Indianer." In Colin G. Calloway, Gerd Gemünden, and Susanne Zantop, eds., *Germans and Indians: Fantasies, Encounters, Projections*, 3–14. Lincoln: University of Nebraska Press.

Zhang, Li. 2001. *Strangers in the City: Reconfigurations of Space, Power, and Social Networks within China's Floating Population*. Stanford: Stanford University Press.

Zhang Nan. 1994. "Kaifa *Tianlong babu* zhong you guan Dali lishi minsu miaoxie de lüyou jingdian jianyi" (Suggestions for Developing Tourist Sites Based on Depictions of Dali's History and Folk Customs in *Heavenly Dragons*). *Baizu xue yanjiu* (Research in Bai Nationality Studies), 4: 141–146.

Zhang Xilu. 1999. *Dali Baizu fojiao mizong* (The Esoteric Buddhism of the Dali Bai People). Kunming: Yunnan minzu chubanshe.

Zhang Yaya. 2002. "Shenmei jiazhi xiangyu wuixia xiaoshuo duzhe" (Aesthetic Value Trends among Martial Arts Novel Readers). In Wu Xiaodong and Ji Birui, eds., *2000 Beijing Jin Yong xiaoshuo guoji yantaohui lunwenji* (2000 Beijing International Conference Proceedings on Jin Yong's Novels), 672–683. Beijing: Beijing daxue.

Zhang, Yingjing. 2002. *Screening China: Critical Interventions, Cinematic Reconfigurations, and the Transnational Imaginary in Contemporary Chinese Cinema*. Ann Arbor, MI: Center for Chinese Studies, University of Michigan.

Zhang, Yingjing, and Xiao Zhiwei. 1998. *Encyclopedia of Chinese Film*. London and New York: Routledge.

Zhao Yansun and Xu Lin, eds. 1996. *Bai-Han cidian* (Bai-Han Dictionary). Chengdu: Sichuan minzu chubanshe.

Zhong Xiu. 1983. "Where the 'Golden Flowers' Blossom." In *Yunnan Travelogue—100 Days in Southwest China*, 60–65. Beijing: New World Press.

Zhong gong Shenzhen shiwei xuanchuanbu (Propaganda Department of the Shenzhen Municipal Committee of the Chinese Communist [Party]), ed. 1992. *Deng Xiaoping yu Shenzhen* (Deng Xiaoping and Shenzhen). Shenzhen: Haitian chubanshe.

"Zhongguo changpian, 1959 di yi qi xin pian" (China's Songs: The First New Songs of 1959). 1959. *YNRB*, Jan. 3: 3.

Zhongguo dianyingjia xiehui (Chinese Filmmakers Association) and Dianyingshi yanjiubu (Film History Research Bureau), eds. 1985. *Zhonghua renmin gongheguo dianying shiye sanshiwu nian, 1949–1984.* (Thirty-Five Years of the Film Industry in the People's Republic of China, 1949–1984). Beijing: Zhongguo dianying chubanshe.

Zhongguo nianjian bianjibu (China Yearbook Editorial Board), ed. 1995. *Zhongguo nianjian* (China Yearbook). Beijing: Zhongguo nianjian she.

Zhonghua renmin gongheguo guojia tongjiju (National Bureau of Statistics of China). 2001. *Zhongguo tongji nianjian* (China Statistical Yearbook). Beijing: Zhongguo tongji chubanshe.

Zhou Yang. 1958. "Xin minge kaituo le shige de xin daolu" (New People's Songs Have Opened a New Road for Songs and Poetry). *Hongqi* (Red Flag), 1: 33–38.

Zizek, Slavoj. 1989. *The Sublime Object of Ideology.* New York: Verso.

Zukin, Sharon. 1991. *Landscapes of Power: From Detroit to Disney World.* Berkeley: University of California Press.

Index

Page numbers in **boldface** refer to figures.

accidents. *See* transportation
actors, 4, 7, 47, 51, 60, 61, **62**, 63, 68, 92, 97, 146n. 14. *See also* performance
adventure: narratives of, 25, 29, 30
agriculture, 12, 60, 70–72, 116, 120, 123. *See also* collectivization; decollectivization; land
alienation, 21, 35, 109. *See also* modernity
American, 17, 18, 25, 26, 27, 30, 35, 36
amusement park, 2, 81, 85, 123. *See also* Daliwood; *Heavenly Dragons*; theme park
Anagnost, Ann, 7, 72, 101, 102
Anderson, Benedict, 52, 53
anthropologist, 4, 5, 7, 8, 13, 46, 49, 53–54, 93, 113, 124, 126, 139, 141n. 4, 142n. 13
anthropology, 4, 7, 8, 49
Appadurai, Arjun, 5, 21
Ashima, 51
assimilation, 64, 144n. 12
Augé, Marc, 102, 113, 136, 149n. 3
Australian, 25, 27, 29, 32, 34, 36
authenticity, 21–22, 31, 35–36, 45–46, 48, 60–61, 65, 95, 99, 109, 144n. 12

Babb, Florence, E., 2, 141n.1
backpacker: 1, 20–29, 31–33, 36, 40–46, 139–140, 142n. 2, 143n. 6. *See also* café; Foreigner Street; lonely planeteer; tourist; transnational; traveler
backwardness, perceptions of, 29, 31, 104, 109–110, 114, 115, 138
Bai: classification of, 9; as consumers, 64, 139; culture, 39, 48, 79; dress, 29, 50, 55–56, 60–61, 64, 92, 139; food, 16, 18, 115–118, 127; host families, 15, 18, 37, 113–114; language, xii–xiii, 15, 17, 25, 37, 126; Minjia, 13; officials, 48, 73, 82, 100, 104–106, 111–112, 116–117, 119–126, 130, 132–136, 137; older, 48, 69–75, 78–79, 127, 136–140; origins of, 9; population, 9; representations of, 13, **49**, 49–54, 56–57, 92–93, 103–104, 106–109; younger, 54–57, 60–61, 64, 78, 136–140. *See also* Dali; *Five Golden Flowers*; folk; household; minority; *minzu*; townspeople; villagers; women

baochan daohu. *See* decollectivization; household
barbarians, 52
Barmé, Geremie, 59
Baudrillard, Jean, 81, 109–110
beggars, 15, 44, 90, 99
Beijing, 13, 14, 21, 24, 42, 74, 81, 87, 100, 105, 114, 133
Benjamin, Walter, 51
Bingshan shang de laike. *See Glacier Guests*
body, 25, 52, 55, 127, 131, 137, 149n. 8
borderlands, 1, 3–7, 14, 49–53, 69, 93–103, 106–110, 114, 138, 140
Boym, Svetlana, 47, 58–59, 146n. 18
British, 22–23, 26, 29, 33–35
Buddhist, 3, 12, 25, 80–81, 84, 88–89, 92, 103, 107, 127
Bulag, Uradyn, 7, 106, 144–145n. 3; 148n. 23
Burma 9, 13, 22, 23, 26, 34, 143n. 3; road, 12, 13, 18. *See also* Myanmar
Butterfly Spring, **11**, **49**, 56–57, **62**, 62–65, 68–69, 71, 75, **76**–77, 78, 82, 93, 110, 111, 135

café, 1, 14, 16, 20, 21, **28**, 28–33, 37–46, 139, 142n. 18, 143nn. 5, 10, 11, 144n. 21
Cai, Yongshun, 122, 126, 133
Canadian, 31–33, 40
Cang, Mount, **11**, 12, 26, 54, 70, 71, 83
Cangshan. *See* Cang, Mount
Cannibal Tours, 30, 144n. 13
Canton. *See* Guangzhou
capital, 2, 38, 100, 140, 148n. 21
Certeau, Michel de, 8
Cha Liangyong. *See* Jin Yong
Cha, Louis. *See* Jin Yong
Changchun Film Studio, 50, 66–67
China: map, **10**
Chinese. *See* Han Chinese; Overseas Chinese; tourist
Chinese Communist Party, 51, 73, 100, 133, 140. *See also* officials; state
cigarettes, 15, 17, 74, 114, 116, 117, 127
civilizing projects, 7, 53
Clemens, Samuel. *See* Twain, Mark
Cohen, Erik, 31, 45, 144nn. 18–19
collective, 58, 78, 122–123, 133, 134, 136, 149n. 10. *See also* collectivization; land; nostalgia

collectivization, 2, 47, 48, 49, 74. *See also* collective; decollectivization; land

colonial, 22, 25–27, 30, 33, 45–46, 48, 50–53, 63, 109, 139

commodification, 27, 30, 31, 46, 100, 105, 135

competition, 2, 39, 54, 59, 82

Confucian, civilizing influence, 138; commerce, 108

connections, 38, 39, 126. See also *guanxi*

construction, 2, 16, 55, 69, 71, 83–85, 91–92, 100–102, 113–118, **118**, 120–126, 133–140

consumer: culture 2, 7; desire, 2, 3, 86; status, 82, 104, 109

consumption, 2, 7, 8, 17, 22, 27, 64, 104, 109, 139, 144nn. 14, 16

corruption, 39, 59, 125–126, 135, 149n. 5

cosmopolitanism, 1, 20, 22, 29

cross-dress, **62**, 63–64, 95, 96, 97

cross-ethnick, 34, 61, **62**, 63, **97**

Crouching Tiger, Hidden Dragon, 86, 91

cultural geography, 4, 8

Cultural Revolution, 38, 47, 51, 57, 59, 66, 69–70, 145n. 9

culture, 1, 3, 7, 21–22, 28, 30–31, 35, 39, 41, 45–46, 48, 51–52, 107–108, 114, 139. *See also* Bai; minority; popular culture

currency, exchange rates, xiv; Mexican dollars, 35; shells as, 25; *See also* money; yuan

cynicism, 48, 54, 109

Dai, 103. *See also* minority; *minzu*; Tai.

Dali: basin, 9, 36, 82, 100, 119, 131; as crossroads, 9, 12; dialect, xii; history of, 9–13, 106–108, 143n. 7; map, **11**; marketing of, 46, 48, 64, 80–81, 91, 108, 112, 135, 137–140; "opening" to outside, 22–23; population of, 9, 121, 142n. 16; prefecture, 9, 73, 120; representations of, 13, 22–26, 36, 47–50, 54, 56–57, 88–91, 141n. 4; as site of desire, 5; town of, 1–3, 9, 12, 33, 44, 54–55, 73, 83, 91, 101, 129, 143n. 7. *See also* Bai; Dali Kingdom; Daliwood; Foreigner Street; Muslim; Nanzhao Kingdom; Tibetan; townspeople; villagers; Yi

Dali Kingdom, 9, 12, 25, 81, 89–90, 93–95, 97–99, 101–102, 107, 148–149nn. 26, 28

Daliwood, 3, **11**, 19, 81, 91–94, **95**, 95–98, **97–98**, 99–102, 135, 138, 147–148nn. 3,

14, 16. *See also* amusement park; *Heavenly Dragons*; theme park

Daoist, 25, 118–119, 128–130, **130**

Davis, Fred, 58, 146n. 17

decollectivization, 2, 119–120. *See also* collectivization; household; land

deforestation, 69–70, 72, 73, 137

Deng Xiaoping, 14, 15

desire, 2, 3, 5, 69, 86. *See also* consumer; consumption

destruction, 1–2, 69–74, 79, 101–102, 116–118, **118**, 136–140. *See also* construction

deterritorialization. *See* displacement

developers, 2, 18, 80, 82, 100, 124, 138

development, 2, 32, 43, 70, 85, 104, 107, 108, 111–112, 121, 125, 133, 135–136, 138

Disney: cartoons, 90; World, 65, 93–94, 99, 110. *See also* amusement park; theme park

displacement, 2, 16, 111, 119, 125, 126, 131, 135

drugs, 1, 33, 35, 83

eminent domain, 120. *See also* land; officials; property; state

Erhai. *See* Er, Lake

Er, Lake, **11**, 12, 14, 55, 69, 71, 81, 83, 121, 125, 131, 137

Errington, Frederick, 29, 31, 33

ethnicity, 142nn. 10, 14, 148n. 25. *See also* minority; *minzu*

ethnomusicologist, 36, 54

European, 25, 27, 29, 30, 32, 35

exoticism, 1, 3, 5, 21, 31, 92, 109. *See also* representation

expositions, 82, 104. *See also* folk; theme park; world fair

fake, 57, 65, 67, 99

famine, 48, 73–74

fans, 3, 6, 109, 142n. 13. *See also* martial arts; popular culture; tourist

fantasy, 3, 5–6, 48, 59, 61–65, 78, 82, 89, 93, 97–100, 105 109–110

film: audience, 51–52, 54; city, 3, **11**, 67–68, 93; Japanese, 143n. 11; and memory, 57; and minorities, 3, 4, 39, 46, 50–51, 66, 144nn. 2–3; Palace, 66–67; projectionists, 51; as propaganda, 48, 51; and tourism, 6, 48, 54, 56–58, 60–68, 135, 137, 140; Westerns, 58. *See also* Daliwood; *Five Golden Flowers*; *Heavenly Dragons*; movie musical

fishing, 14, 55, 60, 137–138
Fitzgerald, Charles Patrick, 12–13, 70, 142n. 15
Five Golden Flowers, 3, 4, 7, 16, 39, 46–49, 49, 56–57, 61–69, 74, 79, 81, 91–92, 109–110, 135–140. *See also* film
Fjellman, Stephen, 65, 90, 93–94, 99–101, 105, 110
folk, 51, 54–57, 100, 103–105, 111–112, 149n. 2. See also minority; *minzu*
food, 14–16, 18, 20–21, 25, 33–36, 42, 115–118, 127, 139, 144nn. 14, 16. *See also* café
Foreigner Street, 1, 20–23, 27–28, **28**, 29–30, 35–43, **43**, 44–46, 49, 101, 135, 139–140. *See also* backpacker; café; globalization; tourist; transnational; traveler
Foster, Robert, 50
future, 20–21, 31–32, 47, 71, 80, 113, 130, 133, 135–136, 140, 149n. 11

Gang of Four, 38
gender, 48, 61, 142n. 10, 148n. 25. *See* cross-dress; women
Gewertz, Deborah, 29, 31, 33
ghost, 112, 131, 136, 149n. 9
Glacier Guests, 50, 66, 68
global, 5, 46, 108
globalization, 2, 20–22, 32–33, 44–46, 64, 139
Great Leap Forward, 47–48, 51, 54, 59, 69–74, 78, 131
Guangzhou, 68, 81, 94, 133
guanxi, 39, 119. *See also* connections
guesthouses, 1, 14, 27, 28, 39, 44, 82
Guizhou, 24, 104, 107

Han Chinese, 3–4, 12, 14, 18, 37–45, 51–53, 61, 64, 86, 90–91, 97–99, 103, 106, 145n. 8. *See also* Overseas Chinese; tourism; tourist
Han dynasty, 57
Harper, Ralph, 48, 57
Harrell, Stevan, 7, 52, 53, 106, 142nn.10–12, 145n. 10
Harvey, David, 4, 113, 138
Heavenly Dragons: Amusement Palace, 81; Cave, 80, 84, 111–112; Film (Movie) City, **11**, 81, 91–95, **95**, 96, **97**, **98**, 98–102, 147–148nn. 14, 16; novel, 3, 7, 46, 80–81, 87–91, 99, 106–107, 109, 135, 138, 140, 148n. 25; popularity of, 86–88; television series, 19, 81, **89**, 91, 99. *See*

also Daliwood; Jin Yong; martial arts; theme park; *Tianlong babu*
hill tribes, 32, 45
Hilton, James, 43
Hong Kong, 3, 21, 24, 47, 80, 81, 86, 87, 101, 102, 105
hooks, bell, 8. *See also* talking back
hotels, 1, 83, 113, 114, 140
Houli Kingdom, 12
household, 17, 38, 115–118, 119–120, 123, 126. *See also* construction; decollectivization; destruction; land; property
Hsu, Francis L.K., 13, 141n. 4, 142n. 15
Hudie chuan. See Butterfly Spring
Hui; Huizu. *See* Muslim
hyperreal, 109

identity, 6, 8, 18, 90, 91, 102, 104, 112, 114, 130, 136, 144n. 16
income gap, 2, 93, 134, 136, 140
India, 26, 40, 108, 148n. 21
indigenous, 33. See borderlands; minority; *minzu*
Indochina, 26, 143n. 8. *See also* Southeast Asia; Vietnam
Indonesia, 45, 102
infrastructure, 2, 31, 114, 115
Internet, 40, 134
Israeli, 36

Jameson, Frederick, 33
Japanese, 6, 18, 29, 32, 35, 37, 84, 104, 143nn. 4, 5, 11
Jianchuan, xii, 73
Jiang Qing, 38, 48
Jin Yong, 3, 7, 80–82, 84–92, 100, 105–106, 108–110, 111–112, 115, 138, 140, 147nn. 7–10, 13
Journey to the West, 35, 100–101

Keyes, Charles F., 31, 54
Khitan, 90, 99
Kublai Khan, 9, 12, 25, 107
Kunming, 12, 13, 15, 24–26, 30, 56, 59, 71, 82, 83, 103–104, 113, 143n. 7

land: allocation, 116–117, 119; and compensation, 116–117, 119, 124–127, 131, 132–134, 149n. 4; disputes, 132–134; expropriation, 116–120, 123–126, 132–136, 149n. 4; farm-, 116–117, 119–126, 132–136, 138; management law, 122–125; and memory, 74;

land: *continued*
  ownership, 122–124; reclamation,
  70–72, 120; rights, 123, 126; terms for,
  141n. 8; use, 17, 91, 116, 120–124. *See
  also* landscape; place; property
landlords, 1–2, 17, 38, 50, 119
landscape, 69, 71, 74, 78–79, 90, 102–103,
  109–110, 141n. 8, 146n. 21. *See also* land;
  place
Laos, 9, **10**, 42
Lash, Scott, 113, 114
law. *See* land management law
Lee, Ang (Li An), 86. *See also Crouching
  Tiger, Hidden Dragon*; martial arts
leisure, 2, 3, 136, 139. *See also* tourism
Liao, 92, 102
Lijiang, 39, 43–44, 101
Litzinger, Ralph, 9, 106, 108, 142nn. 10–12,
  145n. 10
Liu Sanjie. See Third Sister Liu
localization, 21, 46, 139. *See also*
  globalization
Lonely Planet guides, 1, 3, 7, 13, 21, 23–25,
  27, 29, 45–46, 48, 81, 109, 135, 139–140,
  143nn. 5–6
lonely planeteer, 1, 14, 16, 18, 25, 27, 29,
  35, 41, 42, 45
longing, 47, 69, 71, 146n. 23. *See also* memory; nostalgia
Lost Horizon, 43, 46
Lyotard, Jean-François, 5, 25

MacCannell, Dean, 21–22, 31, 35, 144n. 13
malls, 1, 44
Manchu, 53, 103, 145n. 8
Mao Zedong, 14, 23, 59, 66; as symbol, 59;
  theme park, 102
Margary, Augustus Raymond, 22–23, 34,
  142–143n. 2
marginality, 3, 5, 38, 108, 140
market, 1, 5, 16, 29, 31–32, 95, 129
marriage, 18, 39, 60, 94
martial arts, 1, 3, 46–47, 80–81, 85–91, 99,
  105–109, 138, 140
mass: culture, 7; tourism, 45; tourists, 31,
  45, 139
material after-effects, 49, 81, 135, 140;
  definition of, 3
May, Karl, 6, 91
memory, 57, 59, 74–75, 141–142n. 9. *See
  also* longing; nostalgia
mimesis, 46, 63, 65, 67–68, 78, 104
Min-chia; Minjia. *See* Bai
Ming dynasty, xii, 9
minority: café owners, 1, 14, 16, 20, 21,

29, 37–45, 139; classification of, 53–54,
  145n. 9; consumption, 64, 139; culture,
  1, 3, 39, 114–115; dress, 14, 24, 29, 31,
  50, 55–56, 61–64, 68, 92, 139; equality,
  39, 106; film genre, 50–51, 144nn. 2–3,
  145nn. 4–5; identity, 51; men, 14, 16–18,
  20, 30, 37–45, 50, 54–57, 60–65, 69, 72,
  92, 106–109, 111–119, 127–132, 138;
  and modernity, 29, 64, 109, 113–115;
  nationalities, 1, 3, 6, 9, 39, 52, 100,
  103–105, 140; officials, 3, 18, 48, 73,
  82, 100, 104–106, 111–112, 116–117,
  119–126, 130, 132–136, 137; performers,
  46–47, 51, 54–57, 60, 92; population, 3,
  12, 38; readers, 106; representations of,
  1, 3, 6, 24, **49**, 49–54, 56–57, 61, 92–93,
  103–104, 106; tourists, 114; women,
  1, 14–16, 17, 29, 35, 37–44, 47–48, 50,
  54–57, 60–64, 66, 69, 92, 111–114, 116,
  127–132, 137; *See also* Bai; borderlands;
  Dai; Manchu; *minzu*; Mongolian; Muslim; Naxi; Tajik; Tibetan; townspeople;
  villagers; Wa; Yi
minzu, classification of, 53; *duo-* 53; origins
  of term, 52; *shaoshu*, 6, 9, 100; translations of, 142n.14; *wenhua*, 114–115. *See
  also* minority
modernity, 21, 29, 50, 63–64, 93, 102, 104,
  109, 113–115, 130, 134–135, 149n. 9
modernization, 47, 49, 74, 78, 113
money, 1, 15, 38, 116, 117, 118, 119, 126,
  130, 131, 137. *See also* currency; income
  gap; *yuan*
Mongolian, 12, 53, 107, 145n. 8. *See also*
  Kublai Khan
Mount Cang. *See* Cang, Mount
movie musical, 1, 3, 7, 46, 47, 54, 91, 137.
  See also film; *Five Golden Flowers*
Mueggler, Erik, 4, 51, 72, 73, 136, 146n. 26
music, 33, 40, 55–57, 119, 127, 128
Muslim, 1, 12, 14, 16, 18, 20, 22, 25, 29,
  38–42, 53, 90, 139, 145n. 8. *See also* minority; *minzu*
Myanmar, 3, 9, **10**, 42, 107. *See also* Burma

Nadel-Klein, Jane, 6, 58, 71
Nanzhao Kingdom, 9, 12, 13, 107, 148–
  149nn. 27–28
narrative: of past, 82, 106–109, 148–149n.
  28; of place, 4, 43, 49, 136; popular, 5,
  49, 82, 93; and tourist sites, 5–8, 56–57,
  64, 93–94, 98–99, 109; travel, 25, 29–30,
  33–34
nation, 50, 52–53, 63, 100–105
nationality. *See* minority; *minzu*

Native American Indians, representations of, 5, 91, 103–104
Naxi, 12, 13, 101, 148n. 22. *See also* Lijiang; minority; *minzu*
Nepal, 32, 40, 45, 108, 140
nonplaces (*non-lieux*), 113, 115, 136–139. *See also* Augé, Marc; place
nostalgia: collective, 58, 78; colonial, 27, 30, 46, 48, 109, 139; commodification of, 27; as critique, 57–59; and desire, 69; and fantasy, 5, 59, 82, 109; and film, 57–58, 68; imperial, 30; and memory, 59; and performance, 68, 141–142n. 9; and present, 33, 58; private, 146nn. 17–18; terms for, 57–58; totalitarian, 59; tourist, 48, 54, 57–59, 65, 69, 78, 82, 98, 137; traveler, 27, 30, 46, 48; utopian, 4, 47–48, 57–59, 68, 78, 82, 109, 146n. 18. *See also* longing; memory

Oakes, Tim(othy), 7, 100–102, 104–106, 112, 141n. 3
objectification, 46, 105
off the beaten track, 1, 3, 24, 26, 31, 43, 45, 48, 139
officials, 3, 18, 48, 73, 82, 100, 104–106, 111–112, 116–117, 119–126, 130–140, 149n. 5
old society, 50, 71
Orientalism, 7
Overseas Chinese, 44, 46, 81, 84, 91, 109, 138

Panthay Rebellion, 12, 22
performance: and fantasy, 97; of nostalgia, 68, 82, 97; and popular narrative, 56; by tourists, 62–63, 68, 82, 94, 97–98, 109, 141n. 9; for tourists, 55–57, 60, 67–68, 93–99, 139, 146n.14; trans-, 62, 63, 68, 97; travel as, 5, 141n. 9. *See also* actors; play
pesticides, 71, 137, 146n. 24
photographs, 29, 31, 36, 42, 60, **62**, 67, **84**, **95**, 97, **98**, 102, 114
Pingnan Kingdom, 12, 139
place: and authenticity, 46, 48; contested meanings of, 4, 111–113, 130–132; 135–140; cultural constructions of, 4–5; and fantasy, 3, 5–6, 65, 89, 109–110; future of, 8, 20, 31–33, 44, 113; globalized, 37, 48; haunted, 65, 74, 112, 115, 131, 135–136, 138; interconnected, 8; and longing, 69–71, 74, 78–79; as mimetic, 48, 65, 78, 104, 137; and memory, 74; narratives of, 4, 43, 49, 136; non-, 113,

115, 136–138; politics of, 138; power of, 112; and praxis, 49; representations of, 3–5, 25–26, 32–33, 49–50, 69, 93–103, 106; struggles over, 4, 132–134, 138; terms for, 141n. 8; theories of, 4, 8, 138; transformations of 1–4, 44, 49, 64–65, 69–79, 80–82, 91–92, 101–102; 111–112, 109–110, 111–118, **118**, 120–121, 125–126, 134–140, 149n. 3. *See also* land; landscape; property
planetary conciousness, 24
play, 61–63, 78, 82, 93, 97–98, 105, 109–110
Polo, Marco, 25–26, 46
popular culture: 3, 5–7, 48–49, 86–91, 93, 105–110, 136–140, 141n. 3. *See also* representation
population: of China, 4; of Dali, 9, 12; of minorities, 3; pressure, 4, 138
postrevolutionary, 1, 141n. 1
postsocialist, 124, 141n. 1
poverty, 30, 136
preservation, 30, 102
propaganda, 48, 51, 125, 133, 135
property, 124, 133. *See also* land; household; place

Qing dynasty, 9, 12, 52, 101, 102–103, 145n. 8, 147n. 1

race, 104, 142n. 14. See also ethnicity; minority; *minzu*
real estate, 120, 134. *See also* construction; development; land
reembodiment, 61, **62**, 63, 68, 78. *See also* body; play; performance
reform era, 1–3, 13–15, 20, 42, 48, 57, 64, 69, 74, 86, 100, 119, 130, 132, 136–140
Relph, Edward, 111, 149n. 3
representation, 3–8, 25–26, 32–33, 48–54, 69, 81, 93–109, 135, 140. *See also* popular culture
Republic of China, 52–53, 145n. 8
research: assistant, 15, 17, 60, 64–65, 115–121, 126–130; visa, 15
resistance, 112, 134, 136, 138. *See also* subversion
retourism, 25, 26, 45. *See also* backpacker; tourism; tourist; traveler
revolutionary: era, 1–2, 38, 48, 51, 69–74; realism, 54, 146n. 12; romanticism, **49**, 54, 146n.12
ritual, 18, 118, 127–130, **130**, 149nn. 6–7
Robertson, Jennifer, 7, 8, 34, 63, 97
Rodman, Margaret C., 4, 49, 126

rumors, 18, 111–112, 136, 138

Said, Edward, 7
Schein, Louisa, 7, 106, 142n. 10
serpents, 25, 111, 136
Shanghai, 13, 22, 55, 81
Shangri-La, 10, 43–44. *See also* Zhongdian
shaoshu minzu. See minority; *minzu*
Shenzhen, 102, 103
Sichuan province, 10, 40, 55, 80, 100, 107, 114, 144n. 20
simulacrum, 81, 85, 136, 138. *See also* mimesis; simulation
simulation, 68, 99, 109. *See also* mimesis; simulacrum
Sino-Tibetan, xii, 9
socialism: celluloid, 52; collective dream of, 57
Song dynasty, 57–58, 92, 95, 101, 107, 148–149n. 28
Southeast Asia, 12, 24, 44, 45, 53, 81, 84. *See also* Thailand; Vietnam
souvenir, 1, 16, 37, 44, 75, 95, 101, 105
Soviet Union, 14, 47, 58–59
space, 4, 21, 37, 45. *See also* place
spirits, 47, 72–73, 112, 118–119, 128–131, 138. *See also* ghost; place, haunted
Spivak, Gayatri, 135
Splendid China, 102–103. *See also* theme park
state, 50–53, 73, 120, 122–125, 149n. 4. *See also* officials
status, 82, 109, 114, 119
Stewart, Kathleen, 58
struggle: class, 2, 50; over place, 4, 132–134, 138
student: demonstrations, 14; travelers, 29, 36
subversion, 136, 138. *See also* resistance
surveys: household, 17, 117, 120; traveler, 32, 143nn. 5, 11
Swain, Margaret, 5, 7, 105, 106, 142nn. 10–12, 145n. 10

Tai, 9, 103. *See also* Dai
Taiwan, 21, 82–84, 86, 87
Tajik, 50, 68. *See also* minority; *minzu*
talking back, 8, 106, 110, 138 142n.13
Tang dynasty, 63, 101, 107, 148–149n. 28
television, 47, 81, 92–93, 111. See also *Heavenly Dragons*
Thailand, 6, 31, 45, 46, 53, 114, 140, 144nn. 18–19, 148n. 21

theme park, 7, 19, 59, 65, 80, 82, 91–105, 110, 135, 138. *See also* amusement park; Daliwood; *Heavenly Dragons*; world fair
Third Month Fair, 13, 39, 50, 56, 93
Third Sister Liu, 50, 66
Three Pagodas, 11, 68, 80, 89, 93
Tianlong babu, 3, 141n. 5, 147nn. 10, 14. See also *Heavenly Dragons*
Tibet, 3, 9, 31, 40, 108
Tibetan, 1, 12–14, 16, 38–39, 41–43, 53, 55–56, 102, 103, 114, 145n. 8. *See also* minority; *minzu*
time-space compression, 113–114, 115, 130
tour guides, 29, 30, 42, 55, 60, 66, 83, 94, 99, 139
tourism: backpacker, 45; and borderlands, 5–6; experience, 5, 112; and film, 6, 48, 54, 56–58, 60–68, 81, 135, 137, 140; growth of, 2, 5; and identity, 112; literary, 6–7, 80, 91; and minorities, 6; and performance, 55–57, 60, 62–63, 67–68, 82, 93–99, 109, 139, 141n. 9; profits from, 27, 43; of the return, 25; sex, 105; and transformations of place, 31–32, 49, 75, 79, 80–82, 100–103, 109–110, 111–118, **118**, 120–121, 125–126, 134–140, 141n. 3; virtual, 5. See also backpacker; tourist; travel
tourist, 16, 18, 114, 131, 135–140; Buddhist, 84; Chinese, 2–4, 27, 42–46, 48–49, 54–61, **62**, 62–64, 66–68, 74–79, 80–81, 91, 93–96, **97**, 97–100, 103–105, 108–110, 135–140; difficulties, 40; dollars, 44; Euro-American, 30, 143n. 4; expectations, 29, 64; gaze, 5, 8, 22, 30, 42–43, 54, 60–61, 103–104; from Hong Kong, 27, 44, 143n. 4; Japanese, 6, 143n. 4; from Macao, 27, 143n. 4; map, **11**; mass, 31, 45, 139; middle-class, 93, 109; minority, 113–114; national, 2–4, 27, 44, 48–49, 54–61, **62**, 62–64, 66–68, 74–79, 80–81, 91, 93–96, **97**, 97–105, 108–110, 135–140; numbers, 27, 43, 54, 81, 143n. 4, 147n. 3; Overseas Chinese, 44, 46, 80–81, 91, 109, 138; from Taiwan, 27, 44, 82–83, 143n. 4; temples, 80–81, **84**, 135; transnational 2, 20, 22, 81, 143n. 4; women, 29–32, 113–114. *See also* backpacker; lonely planeteer; nostalgia; tourism; traveler
townspeople, 1, 3, 16, 28, 37, 45, 73, 82, 92, 110, 113–115, 130–132, 134–140
tradition, 50, 56, 104

transnational, 3, 16, 18, 20–23, **28**, 28–29, 35–46, 54, 81, 84, 86, 100, 109, 130, 138
transperformance, **62**, 63, 68, **97**, 146n. 20. *See also* performance; play; reembodiment
transportation: accidents, 83, 127–132, 134, 136, 138; airport, 2, 82–84, 113, 116, 135–136, 138; bicycle, 29, 38, 55, 132, 134; boat, 55, 137; bus, 13, 14, 55, 61, 83, 93, 113, 125, 128, 130, 136; car, 15, 130, 136; drivers, 55, 83, 127, 131–132, 134; highway, 2, 4, 16, 71, 83–84, 113, 116–117, 127–132, 135–136, 138; minivan, 130; railway, 2, 26, 84, 113, 116, 135–136, 138; road, 70, 84, 115–117, 119, 127–132, 136–137, 140; ship, 55, 60–61, 137; sports utility vehicle, 128, 134; taxi, 83, 131–132; tractor, 127, 132; train, 13, 14, 113, 136; truck, 83, 127, 130, 131
travel, 5, 24–25, 33, 35, 54–55, 113–114. *See also* tourism; tourist; transportation; traveler
traveler: colonial, 22–23, 26–27, 34–35, 45; dignitaries, 23; Euro-American, 26, 29–32, 31–35, 40, 143n. 5; Israeli, 36; Japanese, 32, 35, 143n. 5; low-budget, 44, 46; nostalgia, 27, 30, 46, 48; student, 1, 29, 36; survey, 32–33, 143nn. 5, 11; transnational, 3, 16, 18, 20, 21, 22, 23, **28**, 31, 35–46, 109, 139; views of tourists; 31; women, 23, 29–33. *See also* backpacker; lonely planeteer; tourist
Twain, Mark, 6–7

United States, 19, 20, 22, 88, 116
Urry, John, 22, 30, 113, 114
utopia, 3, 47–48, 59, 74, 78. *See also* nostalgia

van den Berghe, Pierre L., 31
Vietnam, 9, **10**, 26, 31, 42, 46, 51, 53, 107
villagers: 4, 82, 111–114; and accidents, 127–132, 134; and consumption 3, 64, 139; and corruption, 39, 59, 125–126, 135; and famine, 73–74; and film, 47–48, 69, 79, 92; and food, 16, 18, 115–118, 127; and household, 17, 38, 115–118, 119–120, 123, 126; and income, 93, 134; older, 17, 18, 48, 69–75, 78–79, 113, 135–140; and poverty, 29–30, 126, 136; and ritual, 18, 118, 127–130, **130**, 149nn.

6–7; and voice, 104, 110, 126, 136, 137; and work, 16, 54, 60–61, 63–65, 70–72, 78, 120, 138–139; Yi, 25, 136; younger, 54–57, 60–61, 64, 113, 135–140. *See also* agriculture; Bai; collectivization; decollectivization; Great Leap Forward; land; women

Wa, 103. *See also* minority; *minzu*
Walt Disney World. *See* Disney; Fjellman, Stephen; theme park
Wheeler, Tony and Maureen, 23–24
wildlife, disappearance of, 69–74
Wilk, Richard, 20, 46, 144n. 14
Wolf, Eric, 8
women: backpackers, 25, 31; Bai, 1, 15–16, 17, 29, 35, 37–39, 42, 47–48, 54, 55, 60–64, 92, 111–114, 116, 127–132; café owners, 29, 40–42; and dress, 14, 15, 25, 29, 37, 44, 64, 92; Euro-American, 1, 15–17, 29–33, 36–37; Han Chinese, 37–42, 55; liberation of, 47; managers, 27; market, 1, 16, 35; and marriage, 18, 35, 38; minority, 1, 6, 14–17, 25, 29, 35, 37–44, 50, 54–56, 60–64, 66, 92, 103, 111–114, 116, 127–132; social sphere of, 17, 60; souvenir sellers, 1, 16, 35, 44, 61; in town of Dali, 29, 35, 113–114; tourists, 29–32, 113–114; travelers, 23, 27, 29–32; village, 16–17, 63–64, 111–112, 116, 127–132
world fair, 104. *See also* amusement park; exposition; theme park
Wuduo Jinhua. See *Five Golden Flowers*

Xiaguan, **11**, 12, 55, 107, 121

Yang Likun, 47, 51, 66, 146n. 22
Yi, 1, 9, 12, 13, 16, 25, 40–41, 47, 50, 51, 66, 136. *See also* minority; *minzu*
yuan, xiv, 2, 27, 28, 41, 64, 66–67, 92, 93, 96, 97, 116, 126, 127, 134, 143n. 10. *See also* currency; money
Yunnan Nationalities Institute, 15, 56
Yunnan province, 3, 9, **10**, 26–27, 30–31, 33–35, 42, 50–51, 82–83, 105, 114, 142n. 14, 149n. 2

Zhongdian, **10**, 43–44, 46. *See also* Shangri-La
Zhou Xiaowen, 92
Zizek, Slavoj, symbolic identification, 63

About the Author

Beth E. Notar did her undergraduate work in Chinese studies at Wellesley College. After receiving her B.A. there, she spent three years studying at Beijing University, Nanjing University, and Taiwan Normal University. She returned to the United States to receive her M.A. in Chinese Studies and M.A. and Ph.D. in anthropology from the University of Michigan. Currently she is assistant professor of anthropology at Trinity College in Hartford, Connecticut, where her recent research focuses on the changing meanings of money in China.